Diversity in **Coaching**

Working with gender, culture, race and age

Edited by
Jonathan Passmore

ASSOCIATION
FORCOACHING

**KOGAN
PAGE**

London and Philadelphia

First published in Great Britain and the United States in 2009 by Kogan Page Limited
Reprinted 2009

120 Pentonville Road
London N1 9JN
United Kingdom
www.koganpage.com

525 South 4th Street, #241
Philadelphia PA 19147
USA

© Association for Coaching, 2009

The right of the Association for Coaching to be identified as the author of this work has been asserted by them in accordance with the Copyright, Designs and Patents Act 1988.

ISBN 978 0 7494 5079 3

British Library Cataloguing-in-Publication Data

A CIP record for this book is available from the British Library.

Library of Congress Cataloging-in-Publication Data

Passmore, Jonathan.
    Diversity in coaching / Jonathan Passmore.
        p. cm.
    Includes index.
    ISBN 978-0-7494-5079-3
    1. Employes--Coaching of. 2. Diversity in the workplace. 3. Corporate culture. 4. Multiculturalism.   I. Title.
    HF5549.5.C53P374 2008
    658.3'12408--dc22

                                            2008031243

Typeset by Saxon Graphics Ltd, Derby
Printed and bound in India by Replika Press Pvt Ltd

Dr Val J Arnold

Val Arnold has consulted with boards of directors, CEOs and executive management on critical issues related to executive talent. He has worked extensively with executives and their teams in North and South America, Europe, the Pacific Rim, the Middle East and Africa. Val is also a respected authority on international executive assessment and coaching, and led the development of PDI's individual assessment and coaching businesses. Val can be contacted via the PDI website: www.personneldecisions.com.

Frank Bresser

Frank is head of *Bresser Consulting – Creating Coaching Cultures*, a global provider of coaching and coaching culture services. He is a nominee of the AC Award 2008 for 'Influencing the Coaching Profession' and is commonly regarded as a significant pioneer of today's coaching industry. The Bresser Consulting head office is based in Cologne, Germany. Frank can be contacted at: www.bresser-consulting.com.

Dr Mary Wayne Bush

Mary Wayne serves as Director of Research for The Foundation of Coaching and is Program Manager of Organization Effectiveness for a large aerospace company. She holds a doctorate in Organizational Change from Pepperdine University. Mary Wayne is a global traveller, with experience in organizational diversity work, and has lived in several countries outside the United States, including Canada and in Europe and Southeast Asia. She is internationally known as a speaker, author and conference presenter and has served on the Research and Development Committee of the International Coach Federation, as well as on the Editorial Boards of two journals: the *International Journal of Coaching in Organizations* (IJCO) and *Coaching: An International Journal of Theory, Research and Practice*.

Silvio Celestino

Sílvio is an executive, coaching in Latin America, Europe and Africa. He is the vice-president of Chapter São Paulo for the International Coach Federation (ICF) and director of Enlevo – training for leaders. He is a senior lecturer at Sescon, a Corporate University in São Paulo. His main work as a coach is with individuals and teams, to help them manage a wide range of transitions in a variety of industrial settings. Silvio is the author of the book *Conversa de Elevador – Uma fórmula de sucesso para sua carreira*. He can be contacted via his website: www.enlevo.com.br.

About the contributors

THE EDITOR

Dr Jonathan Passmore

Jonathan Passmore is one of the United Kingdom's leading coaches. He is a chartered occupational psychologist, an accredited AC coach, a coaching supervisor and a fellow of the CIPD. He has wide business consulting experience, having worked for PricewaterhouseCoopers, IBM Business Consulting and OPM, and as a chief executive and company chairman in the sports and leisure sector. He is based at the School of Psychology, University of East London. He is the author of several books including two previous books in this series, *Excellence in Coaching* and *Psychometrics in Coaching*. He can be contacted at: jonathancpassmore@yahoo.co.uk.

ABOUT THE CONTRIBUTORS

Jodie Anagnos

Jodie has worked in a variety of vocational and clinical settings and is currently practising as a private chartered psychologist providing coaching and clinical services in Sydney, Australia. She practises with a cognitive behavioural approach and is actively involved in research projects on the effectiveness of coaching in business settings. Jodie is contactable at: anagnos1@gmail.com.

Contents

Indrani Choudhury

Indrani is a chartered psychologist working in the areas of Educational Psychology, Paediatric Neuropsychology and Occupational Psychology. Her coaching model integrates frameworks from all these fields of applied psychology. She currently works as an independent coaching psychologist in both the public and private sectors, having previously been a senior manager in the public sector. She promotes coaching psychology by her activities in professional organizations, and her lectures and workshops on using psychological frameworks in coaching. She can be contacted at: Indrani@btinternet.com.

Julia Choukhno

Julia Choukhno is a founder of Change4Best.ru, a business coach with a background in linguistics and experience in personal and professional development. Her coaching style integrates a systemic approach with cognitive, transformational and body–mind techniques. Working with Russian and international companies as well as individuals, she trains in coaching skills creating a culture for performance. Julia can be contacted at: Julia@change4best.ru.

Tinu Cornish

Tinu is a Chartered Occupational Psychologist with thirty years' experience of developing black and other minority leaders. Tinu specializes in evidence-based solutions to complex organizational issues, often where diversity is a factor. As a coach she uses the principles of positive psychology and cognitive behavioural coaching to help individuals achieve their career, performance and development goals. Tinu can be contacted at:tinu@coachforchange.co.uk.

Dr Eddie Erlandson

Eddie is an executive coach who specializes in transforming entrenched leadership habits, especially leaders who need to make their style more inspiring or more trustworthy. As a physician, Eddie draws on his knowledge of the physiological aspects of change, and he's also developed strategies from competing in endurance sports that he applies to leadership. Eddie has written a number of books including *Radical Change, Radical Results* and *Alpha Male Syndrome* (the last two books were co-authored with Kate Ludeman). He can be contacted via Eddie@WorthEthic.com.

Janine Everson

Janine is a certified Professional Integral Coach and Academic Director of the Centre for Coaching, a centre for excellence situated at the UCT Graduate School of Business. She also holds the position of Senior Lecturer at the GSB. She lectures at the GSB in Coaching and Leadership Development to MBA and Executive Education students, and is currently doing her research and PhD in coaching. She has delivered and published research papers at several academic peer-reviewed conferences, presented at academic research seminars, and has co-authored a book chapter on the topic of coaching in leadership development. Janine can be contacted at: Janine@centreforcoaching.co.za.

Ingrid Faro

Ingrid is a Brazilian psychologist with experience in organizational and social settings, and currently works in the United Kingdom. She has previously worked for the Municipal Board for Social Assistance and Citizens, specializing in offering psychosocial support and counselling to socially vulnerable families. Her background in psychology, counselling and training led her to develop a personal interest in coaching psychology. Ingrid can be contacted at: ingrid_faro@hotmail.com.

Professor Bob Garvey

Bob is Professor of Mentoring and Coaching at the Coaching and Mentoring Research Unit, Sheffield Hallam University, United Kingdom. Bob has researched and written about coaching and mentoring extensively. His current research is focused on tracking the historical discourses surrounding coaching and mentoring in order to explain the current understanding of one-to-one developmental dialogue. Bob is an experienced coach and mentor and has worked across most business sectors. He is the current editor of *The International Journal of Mentoring and Coaching*, which is the online journal of the European Mentoring and Coaching Council. He can be contacted at: r.garvey@shu.ac.uk.

Dr Ho Law

Ho is the Founder Director of Empsy Ltd. He is a Chartered Occupational Psychologist, Chartered Scientist, and an international practitioner in psychology, coaching, mentoring and psychotherapy. He has had over 20 years' experience in consultancy in the public and private sectors. He is a founder member of the Society for Coaching Psychology. He can be contacted at: ho.law@empsy.com.

Dr Kate Ludeman

Kate is an executive coach, speaker, author and founder of Worth Ethic. She has a BS in engineering and a PhD in psychology. Kate has worked with over 1,500 senior executives in a wide range of industries, located in the United States, Europe, Asia and South America. Kate has written several books including *The Worth Ethic*, *Earn What You're Worth*, *The Corporate Mystic*, *Radical Change, Radical Results* and *Alpha Male Syndrome* (the last two books were co-authored with Eddie Erlandson). She can be contacted via www.WorthEthic.com or e-mail her at: Kate@WorthEthic.com.

Catherine Ng

Catherine is one of the founders of Enrichment Coaching Institute and Chinese Coaching Federation. She is a pioneer in bringing coaching concepts to Asia since 1995 and is passionate about Human Capital Development through coaching. She can be contacted at: catherineng@enrichment.org.cn or www.enrichment.org.cn.

Craig O'Flaherty

Craig is a highly experienced Integral Coach who has worked to coach senior executives in leading South African organizations and to train prospective business and life coaches. He is the Director of a centre of excellence – The Centre for Coaching – at the Graduate School of Business, University of Cape Town, as well as Director of Weathervane, an executive coaching practice. Craig can be contacted at: craig@centreforcoaching.co.za.

Tom Palmer

Tom works for PDI as an occupational psychologist. He has a deep under-standing of selection, development and succession planning. He presents on the topic of measuring potential and leads the assessment business for PDI's London office. He has worked with organizations such as Shell, Saudi Aramco, Abu Dhabi Investment Authority and Hanson PLC to help them identify and develop their talent. Tom can be contacted at: Tom.Palmer@personneldecisions.com.

Dr Gregory Pennington

Greg Pennington, PhD has more than 25 years of experience in organizational and leadership development. In the area of diversity and inclusion he has served as a resource in strategic design, organizational assessment, trainer and executive coach. He has presented extensively at professional associations and at corporations on personal and organizational issues related to diversity and inclusion. Dr Pennington holds a PhD in Clinical Psychology from the University of North Carolina, Chapel Hill, and a BA degree cum laude in Psychology and Social Relations from Harvard University. He is a member of the American Psychological Association and President-Elect for the Society of Consulting Psychology in 2008. He can be contacted at: drgpenn@yahoo.com.

Yogesh Sood

Yogesh is Founding President of the South East Asian and Indian Chapter of ICF. He has more than 28 years of corporate experience and works with senior leadership teams in areas such as managing change, coaching and developing leadership. Yogesh has worked with more than 25,000 participants and is active in integrating and managing large learning/OD projects and developing in-house consultants/trainers/coaches. He can be contacted at: yogesood@gmail.com.

Takashi Tanaka

Takashi Tanaka is a Business Coach specializing in the areas of leadership and succession management for many multinational companies in Japan. His professional consultancy includes 15 years coaching executives and business leaders who needed to boost their performance and business results in managing global responsibilities and transitioning to new roles. He is Managing Director of Assessment Initiative Partners. Takashi can be contacted at: takashi.tanaka@aip-llp.co.jp.

Katherine Tulpa

Katherine is Co-CEO of Wisdom8, a firm that specializes in CEO/top team development and cross-cultural coaching, and Chair and Co-Founder of the Association for Coaching. In 2004 and 2006 she was the recipient of the AC Award for Influencing and Impacting the Coaching Profession, and in 2008 was cited as Coaching Mentoring/Person of the Year by Coaching at Work. Katherine is also a sought after board-level global coach, author, keynote speaker and coach supervisor, as well as a visiting lecturer at the Coaching Psychology Unit, University of East London. She can be contacted via www.wisdom8.com.

TECHNICAL ADVISORS

Helen Baron

Helen is a Chartered Psychologist with over 20 years' experience in the design and implementation of effective and fair employee selection and assessment systems. She has researched and published widely on equal opportunities topics as well as psychometrics and selection issues. She has a strong belief that fairness is fundamental to all employment policies and procedures.

Foreword

The concept of coaching for leaders is spreading like wildfire around the world. Countless studies have shown how coaching can make a positive difference: for leaders, the people they lead and their organizations.

The time for a book like *Diversity in Coaching* is now! The field needs a comprehensive view of coaching from various countries around the world. Organizations need to understand how coaching is the same – and how it may differ – from country to country.

It's likely that you, the reader, are a coach, a leader who might hire a coach or a company representative that may employ coaching. This book will be of value to all three groups. Coaches can learn new approaches, views and processes that they may be able to apply with their own clients. They may also pick up some clear 'what not to do' ideas from around the world. Leaders can review coaching case studies from around the world – and get ideas on approaches that may fit their specific needs. Organizations can learn how a diverse variety of coaches can serve a diverse variety of leaders in a diverse variety of countries.

Whether you are a coach, a leader or the representative of an organization, please don't read this book, use it! *Diversity in Coaching* can make a positive difference for your organization, your co-workers and yourself.

Marshall Goldsmith

Introduction

Dr Jonathan Passmore

This is the third book in the original plan for the series, and it is time to review what comes next. In the past three years, since 2005, coaching has continued to develop as an organizational intervention and has developed as an intervention in health and well-being, as well as in life choices.

For those who claimed it would be a five-year fad, coaching has proved more resilient, and I would suggest that coaching is beginning to find its place alongside other organizational and personal interventions. While coaching is not a silver bullet or cure-all, it is an important intervention, which complements training, action learning and leadership development in organizations, and can support personal and well-being change.

In the first of the books, we set out to provide an overview of coaching for those familiar with coaching and for those who were less familiar with the variety of tools and techniques. *Excellence in Coaching* has truly become an industry guide, and is now a common text for many coaching courses at postgraduate level. For our publishers, it has become one of their best selling coaching titles in the United States and in the United Kingdom.

In the second book in the series, *Psychometrics in Coaching*, we wanted to explore difference. On that occasion the focus was on personality differences as assessed through a variety of psychological instruments and models. This was the first book to try to review a wide variety of psychological tools, and to explore their practical application. We were delighted with how the book was received and with how it has sold around the world.

This third book, *Diversity in Coaching*, continues that journey of exploring difference. On this occasion we have taken a gender, generational, cultural, national and race perspective.

For *Excellence in Coaching* and *Psychometrics in Coaching*, we gave very clear instructions to contributors about what we wanted and exactly how each chapter was to be laid out. In this book we have offered greater flexibility to our contributors. Readers will see that we have retained the guiding template for each of the chapters; however, we recognized that cultural differences needed to be expressed on the page as much as in the ideas. So for this book, as editor, I have adopted a lighter touch.

As a reader you will see this expressed in a stronger diversity of writing styles, more use of personal headings, and ideas that are a reflection of the individual, their approach and what happens in their culture, rather than what I, you or we in the United Kingdom, United States or elsewhere in the world may do in our own coaching practice. We see this diversity as a strength, as coaching practitioners and contributors adapt coaching styles, techniques, and the way they describe these, to meet individual needs, local demands and cultural preferences.

A number of the contributors are also not English speakers or writers, and they wrote the chapters in their own language. They subsequently worked with a translator to produce the English version that is contained here. This comes through in a number of the chapters, but we hope the chapter contents outweigh the issue of writing style.

The book is divided into three parts. In the first chapter, Ho Law and I set the scene for working with diversity in coaching practice. This chapter is followed by a series of chapters on Europe, North America and Australia/New Zealand, by practitioners working in these regions. We see this section as being of use to researchers and practitioners interested in the global development of coaching, and those who are working across national boundaries to provide coaching. Such chapters are however a snapshot in time, and reflect the perspectives of the authors in how they view the development within their network and through their eyes at a moment in time.

In the second part we have a series of chapters from practitioners across the world reflecting on their coaching practice in their countries. One feature we were keen to include was chapters from BRIC nations (Brazil, Russia, India and China). BRIC economies are the fastest growing in the world (Goldman Sach, 2008), and the potential for coaching to make a contribution to economic growth and well-being in these states is significant. However, coaching is still in its infancy among the four BRIC nations and we faced the challenge of identifying contributors and of working with the contributors and in some cases with a translator to produce the chapters. In addition to these four areas we have included chapters by contributors in Japan, the Middle East and South Africa, where coaching is further developed. Our aim was to offer a flavour of coaching practices across the globe. We see this section as being of relevance to those who are working with senior executives and boards with a global presence, as well as to those interested in the development and practice of coaching outside of their geographical sphere of practice.

In the third section we have focused on diversity in the United States and United Kingdom and invited contributors to write on ethnicity, gender and age. We have chapters on coaching those with black and Asian heritage in the United Kingdom, and of coaching black Americans. We have included two chapters on working with men and women and the issues that arise in working with gender, and also a chapter on age.

As with all of the previous AC books, the contributors have not received royalties or payments, and have taken on the project as their contribution to sharing knowledge within the developing coaching profession. All the royalties from the title goes to the Association for Coaching. As well as the good work undertaken by the contributors, we have benefited from the guidance and advice of Helen Baron, an expert in diversity issues, who has helped to ensure we stay on track.

We are currently working on two new titles, recognizing that coaching is an emerging domain of knowledge. While in 10 years' time many of these ideas will sound outdated, we hope that this book will stimulate reflection on personal practice, encourage a global conversation about coaching and stimulate others to conduct good quality research that will further inform what we do as coaching practitioners.

References

Goldman Sachs (2008) *BRICs and beyond*, Goldman Sachs, London
Passmore, J (2006) *Excellence in Coaching: The industry guide*, Kogan Page, London
Passmore, J (2008) *Psychometrics in Coaching*, Kogan Page, London

1

Cross-cultural and diversity coaching

Dr Jonathan Passmore and Ho Law

INTRODUCTION

The primary aim of this chapter is to provide readers with an understanding and knowledge of models that may be useful to their business and coaching practice when working with diversity. We do this by first making a business case to show why we need such knowledge and then providing an in-depth review of the relevant literature and cross-cultural models that may be applicable to coaching. Finally, we outline a universal integrative framework that incorporates various cross-cultural and coaching dimensions as a framework for future coaching applications.

WHY DO WE NEED A CROSS-CULTURAL MODEL?

With the developments of mobile communication and transportation, there are increasing movements and exchange between people and businesses around the globe. The world is shrinking. Migration is increasing. For anyone in business, be it coaching or any job, we need to interact with others who are different to us. For example, there has been an increased influx of people from Eastern Europe into the United Kingdom, which follows inward migration from India, the West Indies and parts of Africa. The United States too has seen significant inward migration over its history, and most recently continues to benefit from inward migration from Mexico and Central America.

In response to these changes, professional cultures, identified through traditional functionality, have been forced to merge and disseminate their skill sets in order to compete effectively and add value for money. It is increasingly important for today's business managers, especially senior executives in global companies, to raise their awareness of cultural competence through coaching. The cultural differences between individuals increases the complexity of the leadership role, and adds to the individual differences between us all, which leaders need to consider. To unpack such complexity, it is therefore important for international coaches to formulate a cross-cultural model as part of their coaching framework, as well as consider issues of gender and generational differences. Traditional coaching and training models are no longer effective if they do not consider diversity as a theme. Thus, there is a growing requirement for coaches in an international arena to integrate cross-cultural awareness into their practice.

Rosinski (2003) highlighted this point: 'By integrating the cultural dimension, coaching will unleash more human potential to achieve meaningful objectives' and thus 'enriched with coaching, intercultural professionals will be better equipped to fulfil their commitment to extend people's world views, bridge cultural gaps, and enable successful work across cultures'.

Rosinski's work (2003 and 2006) is a significant force in our understanding of developing a cross-cultural perspective in coaching. This work, however, builds on the thinking and research of other practitioners over the past three decades, particularly Hall (1976), Hofstede (1980, 1991), Trompenaars (1993) and Trompenaars and Hampden-Turner (1997). Others have explored these issues from within the bounds of one-to-one relationships, such as supervision and counselling (Sue and Sue, 1990; Ryde, 2000).

A REVIEW OF MULTIPLE DIMENSIONS OF CULTURE

Given the pretext from the above introduction, there is clearly a high level of recognition of the importance of cross-cultural issues amongst businesses, consultants and coaching organizations. However, when it comes to the question of the potential benefits of specific methods of addressing cultural dilemmas, there is a diversity of opinion about cross-cultural coaching and training methods, and there is an even greater diversity of opinion about the benefits of specific cross-cultural training solutions (St. Claire, 2005). It is therefore important to critically examine the cross-cultural models in the existing literature and find a new, effective way to incorporate culture into coaching methods. But first, we need to examine the multiplicity of culture and its meanings.

Hofstede (1991) suggests there are three levels in human mental programming. The first is personality, which is specific to the individual and which is both inherited and arises from learned experience. The second is culture, which is specific to a group and is learned. The third is human nature, which Hofstede suggests is universal and is inherited. Hofstede suggests 'culture' is a 'product of the collective programming of the mind'. In this sense, culture is a system of meanings, values and beliefs, expecta- tions and goals. These beliefs are acquired from and shared by members of a particular group of people, and it is these beliefs, Hofstede argues, which distinguish them from members of other groups.

Geertz (1986) suggests that culture is like 'the icing on the cake', and in that sense while not deep, it both changes how the individual is perceived and experienced and, in essence, makes us who we are. Many researchers have proposed that 'culture' is multi-layered, like an onion – a system that can be peeled, layer by layer, to reveal its content (Hofstede, 1991). At the core of this model of culture is the notion of values. These values are often hidden, both to outsiders and also to those within the culture, as they are unspoken rules and norms of behaviour. But it is this hidden layer that strongly influences individual behaviour.

Hofstede's cultural dimensions model of work-related values consists of five dimensions:

1. Power Distance – the degree of equality / inequality due to different indi- vidual positions in a society.
2. Individualism / Collectivism – the degree to which a society values individual or collective achievement (which governs interpersonal relationships).
3. Masculinity / Femininity – the degree to which a society reinforces the traditional masculine work role model.
4. Uncertainty Avoidance – the level of tolerance for uncertainty and ambi- guity.
5. Long-term Orientation – the degree to which a society embraces, or does not embrace, long-term devotion to traditional, forward-thinking values.

Indeed, most models of culture are multi-layered. For example, the Cultural model by Trompenaars and Hampden-Turner (1997) has seven dimensions:

1. Universalism v Particularism – rules v relationships.
2. Individualism v Communitarianism – self v society centred.
3. Specific v Diffuse cultures.
4. Affective v Neutral cultures – emotion v cognition.
5. Achievement v Ascription – active v passive status seeking.
6. Sequential v Synchronic cultures – single v multi-tasking.
7. Internal v External control – self-determinant v cooperation.

Hall (1976) simply divides culture into high-context and low-context. He argues that the concepts relate to the way in which information is communicated and hence links to language, which is located in the outer layer of the 'onion' model. The assumption is that within the low-context, the listener would know very little about the context and meaning of the communication, while in high-context, the listener already knows a lot about the subject matter (is 'contextualized'). The implication in coaching is that coachees should be given more information (a directive approach) in the low-context communication, while in the high-context situation the coach should use a more facilitative style with the coachees.

Within a wider socio-anthropological perspective, culture is seen as a complex property that is interwoven across all layers of one's personal, professional and organizational as well as national identity, and that governs one's belief systems, languages and social relationships (Hall, 1963; Levi-Strauss, 1966; Hofstede, 1980; Kondo, 1990; Schwartz, 1994; Law, Ireland, and Hussein, 2007;).

As most of the cultural models are rooted in anthropological and ethnographical studies, very little empirical research has been done to test their validity. For instance, how does the coach identify the high or low context in the first coaching session? Making a wrong assumption could be costly, as the first interaction is the most crucial in establishing the coach–coachee relationship. It also raises the question of their usefulness to coaching practice. There are considerable differences of opinion amongst businesses, consultants and coaching organizations on the 'rules v circumstances' and Individualism v Communitarianism (St Claire, 2005). Businesses tend to place a greater importance on 'rules' and 'the public and collective good'. This implies that there is an organizational culture, which may be different from the national culture, especially for multinational companies. Thus it is important to incorporate the professional dimension in parallel to the cultural dimension in a coaching model.

A REVIEW OF CROSS-CULTURAL COACHING MODELS

Most cross-cultural models such as Rosinski (2003 and 2006) and Trompenaars and Hampden-Turner (1997) are based on the works of socio-cultural anthropologists Hofstede (1980) and Schwartz (1994). On the other hand, there is a danger that the use of a simplistic model may lead to the reader making stereotypical assumptions, which might not be accurate when working with coachees from varying cultures, for example a Nigerian doctor and a Somali health-care worker. Both may be from Africa, but while one is Christian, the other may have grown up in a Muslim culture. One may have benefited from a privileged family and educational opportunities, the other may have had fewer economic and educational opportunities. Africans can be very different. This is true within countries as well as within continents, as cultures can vary between West and East, North and South, as well as across tribal, caste and class groups.

Rosinski (1999) proposed the following steps to deal with cultural differences:

1. Recognize and accept differences – acknowledge, appreciate and under-stand that acceptance does not mean agreement or surrender.
2. Adapt to differences – move outside one's comfort zone, empathize (temporary shift in perspective) and understand that adaptation does not mean adoption or assimilation.
3. Integrate differences – hold different frames of reference in mind, analyse and evaluate situations from various cultural perspectives, and remain grounded in reality; it is essential to avoid becoming dazzled by too many possibilities.
4. Leverage differences – make the most of differences, strive for synergy, proactively look for gems in different cultures, and achieve unity through diversity.

From the above work, Rosinski (2003) further developed a Cultural Orientations Framework, which consists of the following categories:

1. Sense of Power and Responsibility – *Control* (people have a determinant power and responsibility to forge the life they want). *Harmony* (strive for balance and harmony with nature). *Humility* (accept inevitable natural limitations).
2. Time Management Approaches – *Scarce* (time is a scarce resource. Manage it carefully!). *Plentiful* (time is abundant. Relax!). *Monochronic* (concentrate on one activity and/or relationship at a time). *Polychronic* (concentrate simultaneously on multiple tasks and/or relationships).

Past (learn from the past). *Present* (focus on the 'here and now' and short-term benefits). *Future* (have a bias towards long-term benefits. Promote a far-reaching vision).

3. Definitions of Identity and Purpose – *Being* (stress living itself and the development of talents and relationships). *Doing* (focus on accomplishments and visible achievements). *Individualistic* (emphasize individual attributes and projects). *Collectivistic* (emphasize affiliation with a group).

4. Organizational Arrangements – *Hierarchy* (society and organizations must be socially stratified to function properly). *Equality* (people are equals who often happen to play different roles). *Universalist* (all cases should be treated in the same universal manner). *Particularist* (emphasize particular circumstances; favour decentralization and tailored solutions). *Stability* (value a static and orderly environment). *Change* (value a dynamic and flexible environment). *Competitive* (promote success and progress through competitive stimulation). *Collaborative* (promote success and progress through mutual support, sharing of best practices and solidarity).

5. Notions of Territory and Boundaries – *Protective* (protect yourself by keeping personal life and feelings private: mental boundaries; and by minimizing intrusions into your physical space: physical boundaries). *Sharing* (build closer relationships by sharing your psychological and physical domains).

6. Communication Patterns – *High Context* (rely on implicit communication). *Low Context* (rely on explicit communication). *Direct* (in a conflict or with a tough message to deliver, get your point across clearly at the risk of offending or hurting). *Indirect* (in a conflict or with a tough message to deliver, favour maintaining a cordial relationship at the risk of misunderstanding). *Affective* (display emotions and warmth when communicating). *Neutral* (stress conciseness, precision and detachment when communicating). *Formal* (observe strict protocols and rituals). *Informal* (favour familiarity and spontaneity).

7. Modes of Thinking – *Deductive* (emphasize concepts, theories and general principles, logical reasoning, derive practical applications and solutions). *Inductive* (start with experiences, concrete situations and cases, using intuition, formulate general models and theories).

Although Rosinski's model provides fairly comprehensive indicators to address cultural differences, we propose alternative framework in the section that follows.

DESCRIPTION OF THE UNIVERSAL INTEGRATED FRAMEWORK

From a critical review of a wide range of coaching models, a cross-cultural coaching model known as Universal Integrated Framework (UIF) was developed by Law, Ireland and Hussain (2007). The framework emerged from their coaching practice in Health and Social Care in the United Kingdom and multinational programmes involving African, Asian, Chinese and European businesses. As the coachees may come from diverse nationalities and are required to deal with an international context, they focus on the cross-cultural competence that is applicable to their business. Thus UIF is a pragmatic implementation model. It embeds the following aspects:

▌ Continuous professional development (CPD) including learning and supervision.
▌ Appreciation of a cultural environment.
▌ Coach/coachee fluidity/integrative continuum.
▌ Cross-cultural Emotional Intelligence.
▌ Communication methods and feedback mechanisms.

Continuous professional development (CPD)

Continuous professional development and supervision offers the chance for coachees to review the coaching process and optimize their learning. Integrating CPD and supervision enables practitioners to achieve excellence, develop talent and ensure the quality of performance, moving from 'I-learning' (as in self-reflection) to 'we-learning' (as in peer review).

Although the coach could be either an external consultant or an internal manager within the organization, in cross-cultural coaching there are benefits in using a coach who comes from another culture (usually from the international customer's culture) to offer cross-cultural perspectives. This is particularly beneficial for international executives who are in challenging and demanding positions. In the situation where the local coaches are supervised by international coaches, it also offers an opportunity to reflect on personal practice.

Appreciation of cultural environment

One of the key themes of the coaching framework is that it aims to address the significance of culture. Understanding a culture is a general problem about understanding the life experience of others. The issues of learning, relationships and ritualistic behaviours are illusory because they are located on the boundary between the 'internal life' of an individual and the 'external world' of relationships, customs and organizations. As Krause notes, cultural themes are consciously and unconsciously reproduced in conformity with the previous pattern (Krause, 1998).

The UIF accepts that culture is multi-layered and is a feature of all coaching relationships. As a result, one solution does not fit all situations or relationships and the person who knows most about their environment is the person who experiences it. The role of the coach is to support and most of all to challenge the coachee to bring these beliefs, values and cultural elements to the forefront, recognizing their potential as both a lever for change and a barrier, when the coachee seeks to work against these ways of doing things.

A common diversity coaching journey may contain four stages. The first stage is *Assimilation*. At this stage the coach assimilates the coachee's personal experience and validates theses, which helps to establish the coaching partnership (Passmore, 2007). The second stage is *Consolidation*. This involves the coach and coachee consolidating their relationship on trust and mutual respect. The third stage is *Exploration*. During this stage the coach seeks to open up new insights from the coachee's assimilated experience, bringing hidden aspects into conscious awareness. In the fourth stage of *Maturation*, the coach uses multiple methods and media to work with these challenges and help the coachee to find culturally appropriate solutions or courses of action.

Coach/coachee fluidity/integrative continuum

In the UIF, the coachees are also trained as coaches and mentors so that they are more able to drive the process from having the knowledge of the whole process and the elements that need to be optimized if the benefits are to be realized. Individuals are encouraged to be both coachees and coaches so that they recognize the learning opportunities in both roles and identify them as transitory roles to aid learning rather than set and 'boxed-in' positions. It is key to learning that leaders experience both roles. This is also consistent with the so-called 'double loop learning' in organizations (Argyris, 1977). The Framework presents coaching and mentoring as an integrative continuum. From our practice, we have observed that there is a link between coaching and mentoring underpinned by the same skill set, which includes the common features of using questions, active listening, summarizing and paraphrasing, as well as using emotional intelligence and appropriate leadership and business models to aid learning.

Cross-cultural Emotional Intelligence

Although the idea of Emotional Intelligence (EI) was made popular by Goleman (1995), its cultural competence dimension was underdeveloped. The UIF has two extra dimensions: *Cultural Competence* and *Coaching Professional Competence* with 360-degree feedback. This was built into an online system called Cultural Social Intelligence (CSI) (Law, Ireland and Hussein, 2008). CSI consists of the following four dimensions (see Figure 1.1):

1. (Self) Personal Competence;
2. Social Competence;
3. Cultural Competence;
4. Professional Competence.

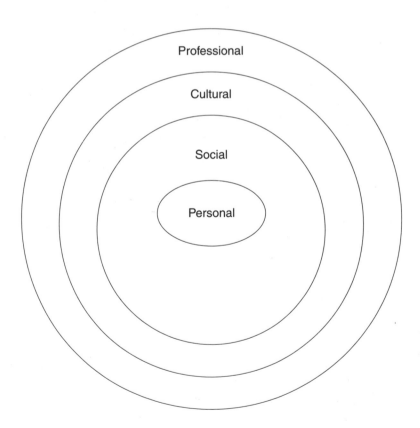

Figure 1.1 Universal Integrated Framework - a pragmatic model

Dimension I: Personal Competence

These competencies reflect how we manage ourselves. They consist of two parts:

1. Awareness of oneself (Self-awareness).
2. Management of oneself (Self-regulation / Self-management).

▮ Self-awareness – Measures whether you accept and value yourself. Awareness of one's own internal states, feelings, emotion, cognition, preferences, resources and intuitions.
▮ Self-management – The ability to manage one's emotion and motivation, and to control it productively. It measures whether you invite the trust of others by being principled, reliable and consistent (*trustworthiness*).

Dimension II: Social Competence

These competencies reflect how we manage relationships. Social competence is a didactic process as individuals gain insight through social interaction and awareness of others. This social process simply could not exist individually (Senge, 1990). It consists of Empathy (awareness of others) and Social skills (management of others):

▮ Empathy – Awareness of others' feelings, needs and concerns. It measures whether you empathize with others.
▮ Social skills – Ability to influence others, collaborate, cooperate with others by identifying a common ground and shared objectives, taking a leadership role, managing team spirit, resolving any conflicts and communicating clearly with a display of interpersonal sensitivity.

Dimension III: Cultural Competence

These competencies reflect how we manage organizational change. They consist of the following elements:

▮ Awareness of other cultures (Enlightenment).
▮ Management of organizational cultures (Champion).

Cultural competence measures the extent to which coachees inquire into or respond openly to others' cultures, ideas and values, and their willingness to challenge and question their own assumptions as well as those of others.

Coaches ought to have the ability to mediate boundaries between cultures, and connect to their own and others' cultures. In doing so, they experience themselves as part of a larger, collective consciousness, culturally and spiritually. One recognizes that collective awareness and morality transform the organization and society as a whole.

Dimension IV: Professional Competence

The final section reviews some coach knowledge and approaches, which have an impact on coaching outcomes. These require the coach to adopt professional approaches, giving and seeking authentic feedback to and from others.

Communication methods and feedback mechanism

The UIF also has a 360-degree feedback mechanism that provides performance data on an individual or group derived from a number of stakeholders in their performance. It tests the perspectives of participants in a coaching programme against those of their peers and line managers. This provides coaches/coachees with opportunities to gain further insight and self-awareness of their competence.

The four CSI dimensions are summarized in Table 1.1. The UIF provides both coaches and coachees with a handy tool to quantify their level of competence. It enables them to understand themselves as well as the complex relationship between personal, social, cultural and coaching competences.

The initial research has shown some significant differences in cultural coaching competences between participants in terms of different ethnicities, rooted from different cultural origins (Law, Ireland and Hussain, 2007). The result of the evaluation indicates that the UIF is a promising coaching framework to adopt, although further work is underway to explore the full potential of the tool for guiding coaching practice.

Table 1.1 Dimensions of UIF pragmatic model

Competence	Personal	Social	Cultural	Professional
Awareness	Self-awareness	Empathy	Enlightenment	Reflective practice
Management	Self-management	Social skills	Champion	Continued professional development

SUMMARY

In this chapter we have offered some initial thoughts on the development of cross-cultural thinking within society, organizations, counselling and coaching. We have briefly reviewed several of these models, which have become cornerstones in understanding cultural differences, and explored in more detail one model that has been developed within the UK for use by coaches and coachees, to help them reflect on their cultural awareness and sensitivity.

References

Argyris, C (1977) Double loop learning in organizations, *Harvard Business Review*, **55**(5), pp 115–25

Geertz, C (1986) Anti-anti-Relativism, *American Anthropologist*, **86**, pp 263–78

Goleman, D (1995) *Emotional Intelligence: Why it matters more than IQ*, Bloomsbury, London

Hall, E T (1963) *The Silent Language*, Fawcett Publications Inc, Greenwich, Connecticut

Hall, E T (1976) *Beyond Culture*, Anchor Press, Garden City, NY

Hofstede, G H (1980) *Culture's Consequences – International Differences in Work-Related Values*, Sage, Beverly Hills

Hofstede, G H (1991) *Cultures and Organizations – Software of the Mind*, McGraw-Hill UK, London, (1997) Third Millennium Edition, McGraw-Hill USA, New York, and (2004) McGraw-Hill USA, New York

Krause, I (1998) *Therapy Across Cultures*, Sage, London

Kondo, D (1990) *Crafting Selves: Power, gender and discourses of identity in a Japanese workplace*, University of Chicago Press, Chicago

Law, H C, Ireland, S and Hussain, Z (2007) *Psychology of Coaching, Mentoring & Learning*, Wiley, Chichester

Law, H C, Ireland, S and Hussain, Z (2008) The online Coaching/Mentoring Cultural Social Intelligence inventory [online], http://www.morphgroup.net/csi/

Levi-Strauss, C (1966) *The Savage Mind*, Weidenfeld and Nicolson, London

Passmore, J (2007) Integrative coaching: a model for executive coaching, *Consulting Psychology Journal: Practice and Research*, America Psychology Association, **59**(1), pp 68–78

Rosinski, P (1999) *Coaching Across Cultures*, Nicholas Brealey, London

Rosinski, P (2003) *Coaching Across Cultures*, 2nd ed, Nicholas Brealey, London

Rosinski, P (2006) Cross cultural coaching, in *Excellence in Coaching*, ed J Passmore, pp 153–69, Kogan Page, London

Ryde, J (2000) Supervising across difference, *International Journal of Psychotherapy*, **5**(1), pp 37–48

Schwartz, S H (1994) Beyond Individualism/Collectivism – New Dimensions of Values, in *Individualism and Collectivism: Theory Application and Methods*, ed U Kim *et al*, pp 85–119, Sage, Newbury Park, CA

Schwartz, S (1994) Theory of cultural values and some implications for work, *Applied Psychology*, **48**(1), pp 23–47

Senge, P (1990) *The Fifth Discipline. The art and practice of learning organisations*, Doubleday, London

St Claire, B A (2005) *Carrying Cultural Baggage: The Contribution of Socio-Cultural Anthropology to Cross-Cultural Coaching*, MA dissertation, Oxford Brookes University

Sue, D W and Sue, D (1990) *Counselling the cultural difference*, Wiley, New York

Trompenaars, F (1993) *Riding the Waves of Culture*, Nicholas Breadley, London

Trompenaars, F and Hampden-Turner, C (1997) *Riding the Waves of Culture: Understanding cultural diversity in business*, 2nd ed, Nicholas Breadley, London

Part 1

International perspectives

2

Coaching in Europe

Katherine Tulpa and Frank Bresser

INTRODUCTION

This chapter sets out to describe the development of coaching in Europe and its practical implications for working as a coach in this region. Geographically speaking, it covers all EU and EU-candidate countries as well as a selection of non-EU countries.

The European coaching market, given its huge size, is definitely a great opportunity and a fascinating and vibrant coaching area to work in. However, it is a great challenge at the same time: it is far from being homogeneous and holds a number of pitfalls to cope with and avoid.

International coaches and coaching provider organizations, as well as directors and managers responsible for coaching in their organizations in Europe, will benefit greatly from reading this chapter. It covers the nature and the current state of coaching in Europe, its implications for working across a multicultural Europe, and the future prospects of coaching in this region.

CURRENT STATE OF COACHING IN EUROPE

At the time of writing (2008), the state of coaching in Europe varies widely, especially as a result of the diverse economies, systems and cultures, at different stages of growth, which make up the dynamic and expanding European Union. Other than at a philosophical or purpose level, at present it would be inappropriate to identify a common platform for coaching in Europe; however, we can identify key characteristics as defined below (see also Figure 2.1).

1. Variety of existing coaching approaches

Depending on what countries and regions you are looking at in Europe, you find a vast variety of different coaching approaches, practices and development cycles. For instance, you find countries where professional one-to-one coaching is very widely accepted as a business tool today (eg Sweden, France, Germany and the United Kingdom) as well as countries where coaching is not accepted yet at all (eg Malta, Macedonia).

In some areas, coaching has not yet entered the introduction phase (eg Estonia, Latvia), whereas elsewhere in Europe you already find first signals of maturity of the coaching market (Netherlands, Norway). The coaching approach mostly taken in each European country may range from directive (eg Greece, Portugal and Slovakia) to non-directive (eg Iceland, Belgium, Denmark and the United Kingdom).

Figure 2.1 Key characteristics of coaching in Europe

In some areas, coaching is already far advanced on its way to becoming a real profession in terms of accreditation, code of ethics, supervision and professional coaching bodies (eg France, Sweden, Switzerland, Germany and the United Kingdom). Other regions within Europe are very far behind on this (eg Hungary, Russia and Ukraine).

Coaching industries in some countries have already gone far beyond one-to-one coaching and are familiar with and use, for example, the coaching culture concept (eg Netherlands, Luxembourg and Sweden), whereas in other countries you find that many coaches haven't ever heard of this term (eg Switzerland, Macedonia and Poland).

Last, but not least, depending on the country, you may observe very different originalities and preferences in the way coaching is provided. In some countries, coaching may for example be more relationship and emotion-based (eg Russia, Sweden) or be less open to phone coaching (eg Turkey, Italy and Ireland). Or it may require very good knowledge of the national culture and values and be less accessible to coaches from abroad (eg Portugal, Norway). Even within particular regions within Europe (eg Scandinavia or Baltic states) where the practice of coaching has similar patterns to an extent, you still find great differences at the same time.

Therefore, in the current state, diversity is definitely a key part of the nature of coaching in Europe. Herein lies an enormous source and potential for mutual inspiration and learning for the whole coaching community in Europe and beyond.

2. Internationalization and convergence

Given this great diversity of different coaching approaches, another element of coaching in Europe is the high degree of internationalization and continuous convergence in the field.

Coaching – in its modern form – came to Western Europe from the United States in the 1980s, where it had grown out of the sports coaching movement. However, within Western Europe, coaching underwent very different local changes and adjustments in the different European countries in the following 20 years. This resulted in coaching being increasingly defined for each country by national coaching associations autonomously. Nevertheless, there has always remained a substantial international dimension to it through international coaching associations, multinational companies promoting coaching and international coaching conferences.

After the fall of the Berlin Wall in 1989, coaching also reached the East European countries. These countries are now in the process of adopting inter-national coaching (often supported by international coaching associations at the beginning) or have already started to develop their own local approaches to coaching.

Today, we observe a clear trend across Europe in differences in practice and increased collaboration. There is a desire for openness, a desire to work together, to share experiences, to value and use the diversity of existing approaches and to establish best practices (eg code of ethics, necessity of good contracting, universal coaching principles, supervision, defining the nature and boundaries of coaching, etc).

International coaching associations like the Association for Coaching, International Coaching Federation and European Mentoring and Coaching Council are increasingly forming national branches or chapters in Europe. At the same time, they also collaborate more and more with each other to build common agreed standards of practice.

However, Europe is far from having its own official European umbrella coaching association. It remains difficult to talk about *the* European coaching approach, but such diversity reflects the healthiness of a growing profession and the diversity among the 35 nations.

3. In between the US and Asian style of coaching

When comparing the existing European coaching approaches with the ones in the United States and Asia, however, it is possible to make some observations and statements about what may be typical for coaching in Europe overall. In the United States, traditionally we have found a highly individualistic coaching approach that primarily focuses on the power of the individual to determine their own success. In Asia, a more collective attitude in coaching predominates, where the individual defines themselves through the group they belong to. The European coaching style seems to be an approach midway between the two: there is a focus on the individual power, but the high integration of social and systemic thinking ensures that the collective interests are adequately taken into consideration at any time.

Also, the US coaching style is seen as very direct in terms of communication and openness, whereas it is considered to be highly indirect in Asia due to the cultural principle of saving face. Europe is somewhere halfway between these poles: the coaching style is moderately direct.

Last, but not least, coaching is branded very positively in the United States. Having a coach is often seen as a status symbol. In contrast, in Asia, the coaching approach is rather perceived in a remedial way and a more directive coaching is prevailing. In Europe there is strong evidence of coaching being used both as a reward for high performers and to address underperformance.

So, on the basis of these observations, it may be fair to say that in comparison with the US and Asian styles of coaching, the 'European coaching approach' seems to be somewhere in between the two.

4. Existing research on coaching in Europe

Our own research (Bresser Consulting, 2008) has shown that there has been minimal research into coaching in Europe. The Bresser research has attempted to fill some of this gap in understanding by examining the situation of the European coaching market as a whole, as well as the commonalities and differences between the national coaching markets within Europe. Other existing research projects that touch the European coaching market or parts of it include the *ICF Global Study* (2007), the *Coaching Research Project 2005* (Bresser, 2005 and 2006c; Bresser Consulting, 2006), and other smaller studies from coaches or providers in the market.

It is therefore important to keep in mind that reliable knowledge on coaching in Europe is still very limited, and the market is emerging and changing.

a) Overall state of the market

Based on the results of the Bresser Consulting European Coaching Survey (2008), we may assume that there are about 16,000–18,000 business coaches operating in the European Union. This seems to be rather compatible with the suggested number of about 50,000 coaches operating worldwide.

The figures in Table 2.1 clearly illustrate the existing European diversity as well as the fact that coaching in the EU, while progressing steadily, is still a work in progress. At the same time, the research results also show that coaching is on the rise across Europe. In none of the 35 European countries covered by the European Coaching Survey is coaching in decline (see Figure 2.2).

b) Different regions and countries

Let us now have a closer look at various geographical areas within Europe and see what more can be said about these.

Comparison: United Kingdom and Germany
Both coaching industries are highly developed, and coaching is far advanced on its way to becoming a real profession (in terms of coaching bodies, code of ethics, accreditation, supervision). Regarding a comparison of the coaching approaches in the United Kingdom and Germany, the

Table 2.1 Key facts of coaching in Europe

∎ United Kingdom and Germany only – with nearly 30% of the EU population – seem to accommodate over 70% of all EU business coaches.

∎ In contrast, only about 3–4% of all EU coaches are based in the area of the former communist EU countries (representing about 20% of the EU population).

∎ In the UK, the given estimate of 7,500 business coaches would mean an average of 1 business coach per 8,000 inhabitants, which would be the highest density in the whole EU.

∎ In terms of the number of business coaches, Germany comes second (5,000), France third (over 1,000) and Italy fourth (700–1,000).

∎ Only in 12 of the 27 EU countries (all Western/Northern Europe) is coaching widely accepted and used as a business tool today.

∎ Overall, there is a clear west–east and a slight north–south divide in the development of coaching. Within each European region, however, the situation may also differ enormously (depending on each country).

∎ In just 11 EU countries, coaching is already far advanced on its way to becoming a real profession (in terms of accreditation, professional coaching bodies, code of ethics, etc). The use of supervision is widespread in only seven EU countries.

∎ In five EU countries a directive coaching approach is prevailing. In nine EU countries a non-directive approach predominates (13 undecided).

∎ The concept of coaching cultures is quite well known and widely used in 10 EU countries already – in 12 EU countries it is still hardly known or not known at all (five in between).

∎ Depending on each country, there are highly different local characteristics and preferences in the way that coaching is understood and delivered.

(Source: European Coaching Survey, 2008)

Coaching Research Project 2005 touched on this question and identified the following (Bresser, 2006a, 2006b):

∎ The prevailing coaching approach in Germany in 2005 was directive. Many clients required specific expertise from coaches in the field in which they were coaching, and expected advice in the coaching session. This contrasted with the Anglo UK understanding of coaching, which provided a much clearer distinction between coaching and consulting, and was much more, if not purely, process-oriented.

∎ Also, at that time, coaching in Germany was primarily only discussed and implemented in the form of one-to-one and team coaching, whereas in the United Kingdom, coaching was already also a hot topic in the context of leadership and business and management culture.

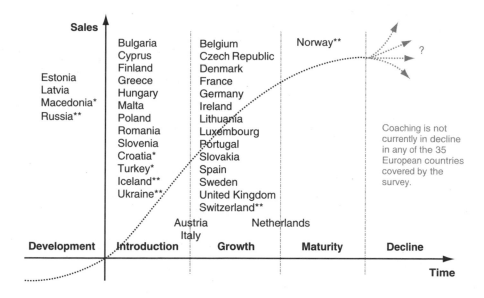

Figure 2.2 Current product life cycle stage of coaching in EU and other European countries (* = EU-candidate country / ** = non-EU country)
(Source: European Coaching Survey, 2008)

Now, interestingly, the results of the European Coaching Survey do not fully confirm this any more, as far as Germany is concerned. The typical, predominant coaching style in Germany cannot be regarded as just directive any more, but is today undecided between directive and non-directive. Also, the concept of coaching cultures is now – as opposed to some years ago – increasingly becoming known and used in Germany (also confirmed by Bresser and Schollmeyer, 2008).

France, Italy, Netherlands, Belgium, Luxembourg
All founder countries of the European Community (with West Germany) have well-developed, growing coaching industries. However, coaching in Luxembourg and Italy is less advanced when compared with the others. The Netherlands are the only EU country where the coaching market is starting to reach maturity now.

Regarding typical coaching approaches, an overall more international way of coaching can be found in Belgium, Luxembourg and the Netherlands due to their highly international, multicultural environment. Coaching in France is closer to psychology than in other countries, and a good code of ethics is seen as particularly important. Finally, in Italy, you find a high preference towards face-to-face coaching.

Spain, Portugal, Greece, Malta, Cyprus, Turkey
In this region, we find an ambivalent situation: the advanced coaching industries of Portugal and Spain contrast with the rather poorly developed ones of Greece, Cyprus, Malta and Turkey (eg coaching bodies don't exist and there is no commonly agreed or discussed 'best practice'). What is common to this region, however, is that supervision doesn't play a major role in any of these countries, and the number of coaches is generally low (Portugal: 30; Spain: 300).

In this region, you find a predominant directive coaching style, and a number of cultural pitfalls to avoid: in Portugal, for example, a coach must be able not only to understand, but also to feel, the traditional national culture and values. In Turkey, face-to-face sessions are preferred, the age of the coach is a factor and a number of subjects are culturally taboo (eg with regard to relationships with the opposite sex, including business relations with the opposite sex, and political and religious subjects/beliefs).

Denmark, Sweden, Norway, Finland, Iceland
It is sometimes suggested that within Europe the Scandinavian culture would be the nearest to and most compatible with the ideal of coaching. The coaching industry is highly developed in Sweden, Denmark and Norway (the Norwegian coaching market has even reached maturity). This is less true for Finland, however, and even less so for Iceland. The number and density of coaches in Scandinavian countries is high, but not the highest within Europe (eg Sweden: 500; Norway: 200; Denmark: 50). Supervision plays an important role in Denmark and Iceland, but is of less significance in Sweden and Norway and is still less used in Finland.

Interestingly, there is no directive coaching approach prevailing in any of these countries. In terms of local characteristics of coaching, the cultural values of dialogue, good relationships and balance of interests in this region play an important role, and overall support the idea of coaching. It is finally also worth highlighting that Norwegians like to do things in their own way and like coaching skills to be Norwegian, so foreign coaches may find it difficult to enter the market.

Eastern Europe (former communist countries)
After the fall of the Berlin Wall, coaching slowly started to reach the former communist countries. The figures today suggest that coaching in Eastern Europe is generally less advanced than coaching in Western Europe. Only about 3–4 per cent of all EU coaches are based in the area of the former communist EU countries (although these states represent about 20 per cent of the EU population). In none of the countries of this region (examined by the European Coaching Survey) is coaching today widely accepted and used as a business tool.

However, coaching is progressing steadily – particularly in the Czech Republic, Slovakia and Lithuania, where it is in the growth phase and fairly accepted and used as a business tool. What's more, international coaching conferences took place in Slovakia and the Czech Republic in 2006 and 2007.

Apart from these exceptions, coaching still has a long way to go to become a real profession in Eastern Europe. It can be observed that the coaching industry in Eastern Europe is facing very similar issues and challenges today to those that many Western European countries encountered when they began to introduce coaching in the past. More region-specific issues like the heritage of the communist era as well as reservations about coaching as an originally Western tool may also sometimes hinder the progress of coaching.

Other countries (Ireland, Austria, Switzerland)
Ireland
Ireland seems to have the highest density of coaches in the EU after the United Kingdom (500 coaches = 1 business coach/8,000 inhabitants). Besides professional coaching associations, an Irish Coach Development Network has been founded that supports the co-development of an independent, national framework for the development and accreditation of coaches. Interestingly, the prevailing coaching approach in Ireland is fairly directive and supervision doesn't play a major role.

Austria and Switzerland
Though Austria and Switzerland have some parallels to Germany as part of the German-speaking area, the Swiss coaching industry is much more advanced than the Austrian one (eg there are 300–500 Swiss coaches as opposed to just 50 coaches in Austria, where coaching has just started to enter the growth phase).

An overview of the European position

Overall, there is a clear west–east and a slight north–south divide in the development of coaching within Europe. The Anglo region, the founder countries of the European community and Scandinavia have an overall well-developed coaching industry. This is less true for the Mediterranean region – and even less the case for the former communist area. Within each of these regions, however, the practice and development of coaching may also differ enormously.

WORKING IN THE MULTICULTURAL ENVIRONMENT OF EUROPE

As each country goes through its own evolution and acceptance of coaching, with unique differences and diverse approaches, how does one go about coaching successfully in Europe?

This section attempts to touch upon that question, taking a closer look at wider global research regarding culture and leadership that we can apply effectively to our work. Equally, it suggests ways to deepen our level of awareness and appreciation to help us become better coaches when working in multicultural environments.

1. Understanding cultural differences

As culture, without doubt, is a key determinant in the way coaching is defined and delivered in different regions and countries within Europe, let us shed light on more of the culture-specific dimensions:

a) Hofstede's cultural dimensions

Hofstede (1980, 2001) identified five key dimensions of culture on the national level:

1. power distance;
2. uncertainty avoidance;
3. individualism (/collectivism);
4. masculinity (/femininity);
5. long (/short)-term orientation.

When we look at the underlying principles of coaching, we would argue that the ideal of coaching stands for low power distance, rather low uncertainty avoidance, medium individualism/collectivism, medium masculinity/femininity and medium long/short-term orientation.

When we compare this with the cultural values of each European country and region, plausible explanations can be identified for the development of coaching within each state. For example, the Scandinavian cultural values highly correspond to these coaching values, so this may help explain their natural openness to coaching.

b) Trompenaars' cultural dimensions

Trompenaars identified two further dimensions that are worth mentioning (Trompenaars and Hampden-Turner, 1997):

1.   universalism–particularism;
2.   neutral–emotional.

Continental Europe is generally seen as rather particularist, which may explain the enormous, fragmented diversity of coaching approaches within Europe.

Coaching is highly based on emotional intelligence. Accordingly, national cultures that are traditionally less emotional than others may need more time to adopt it. Or, they define it in a more rational, narrow way at the beginning (like in Germany).

c) Rosinski's cultural orientation framework

Rosinski (2003), in his *Cultural Orientations Framework* (COF), groups cultural dimensions into seven different categories from a coaching perspective. These include:

1.   sense of power and responsibility;
2.   time management approaches;
3.   definitions of identity and purpose;
4.   organizational arrangements;
5.   notions of territory and boundaries;
6.   communication patterns;
7.   modes of thinking.

In particular, time management approaches and communication patterns are two important categories that are useful in understanding the current coaching practices in the various parts of Europe.

d) MRG's leadership and culture

One of the largest studies to date in leadership and culture comes from the Management Resource Group (MRG, 2007). This was an extension 10-year study of cultural leadership practices, surveying over 50,000 leaders in 20 countries, including 6,000+ organizations across 30 industries. This was a self-assessment using MRG's Leadership Effectiveness Analysis (LEA).

While it's important to recognize the existing cultural strengths and differences, as shown in the above research, it remains vital to recognize that cultures are not homogeneous, and that country and culture are not synonymous. There are many subcultures within a culture, and significant cultural variations exist within the individual countries mentioned.

Table 2.2 Top strengths of manager leaders for a selection of countries within Europe (based on the LEA terminology)

▮ Belgium: *Consensual*

▮ Denmark: *Feedback*

▮ Netherlands: *Excitement*

▮ France: *Persuasive*

▮ Germany: *Tactical*

▮ Ireland: *Management focus*

▮ Italy: *Dominant*

▮ Sweden: *Innovation*

▮ UK: *Strategic*

(Source: MRG Study, 2007)

2. Practical applications

There is wide agreement across the profession that coaching is indeed systemic. In other words, all parties involved in a coaching relationship – the individual, the team, the sponsor, the coach – are all greatly influenced by the systems they have been brought up in. Added together, this creates a wider context to coach around.

If we also factor in the multicultural complexities, this creates an even greater challenge to coaches to learn and develop. Culture and country-specific differences create opportunities to further examine our own assumptions and beliefs about:

▮ coaching and being a coach;
▮ our coachees and the client relationship.

By using an appreciative inquiry-led approach when experiencing cultural differences, coaches can role-model cross-cultural competence, build effective relationships, and support clients in developing cross-cultural skills (Amend 2005). In our view, a coach who works across the EU, or any global organization where multinational cultures are paramount, will be required to hone their skills in this area, as a core coaching competency.

a) Self-assessment

A good place to start is with the self – by first understanding our values, our drivers and what motivates us – all of which informs our coaching, at one level or another. In this context, there are a number of specific assessment tools that can give us, as well as those we coach, further insight into some of these areas. These have been explored in *Psychometrics in Coaching* (Passmore, 2008a). In summary, here are some ways in which the coach can gain this personal insight into themselves:

- *IDI (Individual Directions Inventory)* looks at drivers and motives – helping to understand where an individual gains the most satisfaction.
- *LEA 360 (Leadership Effectiveness Analysis)* looks at 22 leadership practices, which can be compared to country-related norm data.
- *FIRO Element B* looks at interpersonal needs, including how people manage their hopes and fears.
- *MQ (Motivational Questionnaire)* looks at patterns of motivation; factors which may influence our approach to/within the coaching relationship.
- *CTT (Cultural Transformation Tools)* looks at organizational values and how they align with individual values.
- COI *(Cultural Orientations Indicator)* looks at individual cultural preferences, with potential culture-based risk and success factors.
- *IDI (Intercultural Development Inventory)* looks at attitudes and behaviours related to cultural differences.

Since our motives and values operate at a deeper level, using a well-researched instrument that goes 'below the iceberg' is generally more suitable than using personality or competency-based tools. Furthermore, it's useful to choose a tool that has European norm data, ideally country specific, and/or that factors in multicultural dimensions.

Although most of these tools require a qualified practitioner to administer – and have cost implications – views from many experienced EU coaches confirm that they are 'essential' for the cross-cultural toolkit (CAKO, 2007).

b) Self-awareness exercise

Looking more broadly, it's also helpful to consider what makes up our *social identity*. Social identity may be defined as 'the combination of elements – including age, ethnicity, race, religion, gender, sexual orientation, nationality, and socio-economic status – that marks us as part of various social groups. Some identity elements are obvious, others are less important' (Center for Creative Leadership, 2005).

How does our social identity impact our effectiveness as a coach, especially when coaching in multicultural environments? The exercise below (Table 2.3) is one that can be useful to heighten self-awareness around the

Table 2.3 A reflective exercise

Reflective exercise:

---

1. *In a quiet space, think about your role as a coach.*
2. *Reflect on the following questions:*

In what ways does my age, or the generation I was brought up in, impact my coaching?
....
....

How does my race, ethnicity or traditions influence my outlook when coaching someone from a different ethnic background?
....
....

In what ways do my religious beliefs affect my coaching? How might this show up?
....
....

How does my gender or sexual orientation influence those different from me? In what ways, if at all, do I coach male clients differently from female clients (or vice versa)?
....
....

In what ways does the nation I come from or my socio-economic status impact my coaching? What beliefs or values can I attribute to this?
....
....

3. *Looking at the above responses, what specifically do you need to be mindful of when coaching in multicultural environments?*

---

area of social identity – in particular that of the coach, which can then be expanded on in greater detail with their coach supervisor.

c) Appreciative Inquiry

Often compared with solution-focused coaching, in recent years, Appreciative Inquiry (AI) has become a popular approach used within coaching, in particular when working with diverse teams (Orem, Binkert and Clancy, 2007). Through appreciative questioning, AI brings out the best of 'what is' and creates possibilities of 'what could be.' It harnesses the strengths and highest qualities of another human being in a given system or situation (Rossi, Lustig and McKergow, 2003).

Therefore, this approach is highly suitable to implicitly make visible and leverage the potential of existing cultural differences. When coaching individuals or multicultural teams across the EU, using AI techniques can be a helpful way to gain greater commitment to change, with renewed energy.

In the box below are 11 questions which have their roots in AI principles:

---

1. What do you want more of (as a team)?
2. How will you (the team) know when the goal is reached?
3. What has been going well?
4. When have you (the team) been most successful?
5. What made it successful?
6. What was your unique contribution in this?
7. What do you value about yourself (the team)?
8. What do you value about your colleagues?
9. If anything were possible, and you couldn't fail, what would you (the team) be doing differently?
10. What would you be willing to do to make that happen?
11. What resources do you (the team) have to make this happen?

For further reading, *Appreciative Inquiry for Change Management* (Lewis, Passmore and Cantore, 2008) gives in-depth approaches for using AI practically in conversation.

TAKING COACHING FORWARD IN EUROPE

There is no doubt that coaching is here to stay. We have now passed the market test stage in Europe, with agreement amongst various professional bodies, academic institutions, businesses and individual sponsors of coaching that it is not just a passing fad.

Leading writers in coaching (Palmer, 2008; Whitmore, 2008) have expressed the view that coaching is now 'a profession', although others argue that while it has come of age, it still has more growing to do before reaching maturity (Passmore, 2008b). This growing maturity offers exciting opportunities to take coaching forward. This section explores ideas on how we might do this in Europe, while bearing in mind the different stages of growth and multicultural challenges stated previously.

1. Coaching alliances

Trading in today's global marketplace requires an ability to respond quickly to demand, while having the capability to deliver services and people resources locally. For many international firms, sending an expatriate to a foreign land for their expertise or knowledge transfer is common practice. Over a longer period of time though, this can be costly, especially when sent overseas or longer distances.

This is no different for coaching. While commuting back and forth within the EU is certainly possible in terms of cost, and is a frequent practice for a number of cross-cultural coaches, overall, having the ability to provide coaches locally is preferred. This is not just for the practical reasons (eg costs, accessibility), but for the ability to demonstrate a strong grasp of the language, culture and customs.

As the market continues to grow across Europe, we see an opportunity for more coaching alliances to form, across national boundaries. Although it is still early days, this is already starting to occur with a selected number of coaching providers and consultancies.

Features necessary for building a trusted coaching partnership include having a:

1. strong values alignment;
2. clear win-win business and remuneration model;
3. collaborative v competitive ethos;
4. high degree of communication;
5. openness to share each other's IP (Intellectual Property);
6. strong understanding of the team and of each other's strengths;
7. focused strategy on how to cross-sell each other's services;
8. initial review/trial period, with key milestones and an exit strategy;
9. written agreement, to include 'what if' scenarios;
10. willingness to invest time to grow and nurture the relationship.

When done well, a successful coaching alliance can offer a seamless and even greater level of service to the client, while solving the urgent demands that arise for experienced, local coaches in Europe.

2. European meetings and events

A second opportunity to take coaching forward in Europe is to encourage a greater amount of dialogue. Hosting meetings or events such as 'European Summits', 'Think Tanks, 'Open Forums' and 'Roundtables' are good ways to share understanding of specific cultural or country contexts, and provide opportunities to discuss 'what works' in practice in different cultural contexts.

This approach should yield high results, based on success factors so far. Engaging in open dialogue with peers is perhaps easier to do in coaching than in other industries, as coaching by its very nature has key qualities that support this (despite where each region or country is at in the market/coaching life cycle). These qualities are illustrated in Figure 2.3.

Interestingly, the words in Figure 2.3 all begin with 'co-', which by definition means 'joint, or working together' (Dictionary.com, 2008). Additionally, *co*-coaching and *co*-supervision are two other elements that are attributable to the profession.

Already, across the EU, coaching communities are coming together to share insights, for continual learning, and to gain further understanding of coaching best practice. Many are also aligned with a common purpose – to achieve coaching excellence or enhance the coaching profession – that is collaborative, not competitive.

Within the Association for Coaching, for instance, peer or *co-coaching forums* are one of the fastest growth areas (held monthly, in 25 regions), and are deemed by members to be a valuable way to 'learn other approaches', 'appreciate coaches' styles', 'gain feedback', and maintain their continuing professional development (CPD).

Another example is the *Coaching Roundtable*, made up of not-for-profit, professional coaching bodies, which meet quarterly. As a result of this collaboration, the Coaching Roundtable issued a *Statement of Shared Professional Values* (2008), with a favourable response from the market. To date, this has been mainly UK-based; however, there are currently discussions about this initiative widening into further parts of Europe.

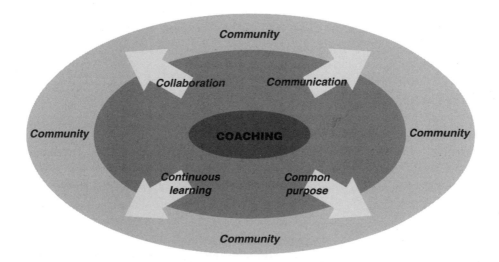

Figure 2.3 Key coaching qualities

There are other examples, too of strong collaboration and dialogue. This includes the *Global Convention on Coaching* held in Dublin in 2008. This was a year-long process, and involved a number of key stakeholders worldwide gathering together to discuss the key issues that impact professional coaching. Furthermore, the ICF have hosted successful European Summits, which specifically looked at coaching within the EU.

To build on this, and take coaching forward in Europe, what further areas would be helpful to focus on at a more local level, particularly for coaches and organizations? Table 2.4 lists some possibilities.

3. New technology

For today's professional, especially those working with multicultural organizations, the ability to use and adapt to the latest technologies is also important. Innovation has accelerated at such a rapid pace and the adoption of new technologies at work has been spurred on as *Generation Y* (those born between 1982 and 2000) have entered the workplace.

Although different cultures have varying attitudes to and beliefs about using technology as a replacement for face-to-face coaching, this section

Table 2.4 Moving forward together

For coaches:

---

1. Link up with 5–8 coaches who have each worked with clients from different parts of Europe. Share learning and approaches.
2. Host a cross-cultural forum, inviting coaches from different countries to set up a 'stall' to share nuggets on 'what works' when coaching in their culture.
3. Run an open event, under the theme 'Successful coaching within the EU'. Capture key points and distribute to all attendees.

For organizations:

---

1. Run a series of regional/country forums for internal coaches, where collectively results are shared across the company, appreciating the different approaches and styles.
2. Host a European Coaching Think Tank (no more than 8–12 participants), inviting in colleagues from different countries/regions to share coaching best practices.
3. Organize or sponsor a Coaching Summit, specifically aimed at organizations that are implementing coaching throughout Europe.

---

mainly looks to explore ways we can advance coaching in Europe by maximizing new technology to support this change.

Technology checklist

As a quick exercise, in the second and third columns of Table 2.5, on a scale of 1–10, rate:

1. your *level of knowledge* of these (from a user perspective);
2. your *current use of* these (mark '0' if not at all).

While there is a case to be made to first master second-generation technology (ie laptops, the internet, e-mail, memory sticks, LCP projectors, etc), what possibilities can open up for us if we make further use of technology?
   Below we have listed some initial thoughts:

▌ CPD opportunities – greater access to speakers (ie with expertise in multicultural coaching) via *podcasts, webcasts, digital audio.*
▌ Supply issues – greater access to EU coaches (ie with 'real time' availability and/or threaded by location, experience, country) via *online forums, smartphone.*
▌ Open-learning events – run a low-cost virtual forum for sharing knowledge and 'EU coaching nuggets' via *web conferencing, blogs, teleconferencing.*

Table 2.5 Technology checklist

	Level of knowledge	Current use of
1. Smartphone		
2. Videoconferencing		
3. Web conferencing		
4. Podcast		
5. Webcast		
6. Skype (voice over internet)		
7. Blog (web log diary)		
8. Digital audio player		
9. Teleconferencing		
10. Online forums		
11. Social networking websites		
12. 3D virtual communities		

▊ Group coaching sessions – connect with clients based in other parts of Europe via *videoconferencing, smartphone.*

▊ Coaching alliance meetings – at a very low cost, make frequent contact with EU or global partners via *Skype™ or other voice-over internet tools.*

▊ Special interest groups – create communities based on special interest groups or topics that pertain to coaching within Europe via *social networking websites, 3D virtual communities.*

▊ Corporate collaborative space – where internal sponsors of coaching can exchange ideas and thoughts with people with similar situations via *online forums, web conferencing, podcasts.*

These are just a few possibilities, which would be dependent too on the uptake on the receiver's end, the technology providers continuing to support these platforms, and the market as a whole.

As with any new technology, such possibilities won't be without their challenges. To help mitigate these, there may be a further need to establish technology etiquette and protocols, guidelines for coaches or facilitators to ensure cross-cultural differences are appreciated, along with a clear way to deal with technology glitches.

However, with the current forces of change and as we begin to coach Generation Y, this emerging client population may be making the demands before we do!

4. EU Coach Accreditation

As coaching in Europe evolves, is there a specific accreditation that needs to be developed for an EU Accredited Coach? Or for a Global Coach, for that matter? At present, the accreditation schemes offered by the main, not-for-profit professional bodies, such as the Association for Coaching, the International Coach Federation, and the European Mentoring and Coaching Council, don't seem to account for this.

Some comments and questions we may need to consider in further dialogue are:

▊ Bearing in mind the difference in approaches and stages of growth mentioned in this chapter, is one European coaching standard possible, necessary, or even valued?

▊ If so, what are the coach competencies of a coach who works across the EU? Shall we be looking at a competency model or establish other means?

▊ To take this forward, imagining we will have the collaboration, technology and resources necessary to support this idea, what needs to happen next?

We are interested in exploring these concepts further. Please e-mail eustandards@associationforcoaching.com if you are interested in taking part in a special interest group. Or contact us directly – Katherine Tulpa: ktulpa@wisdom8.com and Frank Bresser: info@bresser-consulting.com.

SUMMARY

In this chapter we have tried to pull together some views on the developing state of European coaching, drawing on research and giving some thought to the future as cultures and countries move together through technology and through the growing scale and scope of the EU. If you are interested in these ideas, we would be interested to hear from you.

References

Amend, S (2005) *Five Coaching Lessons from Europe and Asia*, Kultur & Management

Bresser, F (2006a) Coaching erfolgreich implementieren. *ManagerSeminare*, **96**, pp 66–73

Bresser, F (2006b) Coaching-Kultur, *Coaching at Work*, CIPD & People Management, May

Bresser, F (2005 and 2006c) Best implementation of coaching in business, *Coach the Coach*, **20** and **21**, two-part article

Bresser, F and Schollmeyer, U (2008) Gemeinsam zur neuen Organisationsform, *Personalwirtschaft*, **01/08**, pp xx

Bresser Consulting (2006) *Coaching Research Project 2005: Executive Summary* [online] www.bresser-consulting.com/implementation-of-coaching.html

Bresser Consulting (2008) *Report on the Results of the European Coaching Survey 2007/8*, [online] www.bresser-consulting.com/europeancoachingsurvey.html

CAKO (2007) Czech Coaching Association Conference, *Workshop on cross-cultural coaching* facilitated by K Tulpa

Center for Creative Leadership (2005) *Identity: A New View for Leading in a Diverse World*, [online] http://www.ccl.org/leadership/enewsletter/2005/JULissue.aspx. Adapted from *Leadership in Action*, **24**(3) (CCL/Jossey-Bass/August 2004)

Coaching Roundtable (2008) *Statement of Shared Professional Values* [online] www.associationforcoaching.com/news/M80221.htm

Dictionary.com (2008), Lexico Publishing Group, LLC [online] http://dictionary.reference.com/

Hofstede, G (1980) *Culture's Consequences: International differences in work-related values*, Sage, Beverly Hills

Hofstede, G (2001) *Culture's Consequences: Comparing values, behaviours, institutions, and organisations across nations*, 2nd edn, Sage, London

Lewis, S, Passmore, J and Cantore, S (2008) *Appreciative Inquiry for Change Management*, Kogan Page, London

Orem, S, Binkert, J, and Clancy, A (2007) *Appreciative Coaching: A positive process for change*, Wiley, San Francisco

Palmer, S (2008) Keynote conference paper, Association for Coaching International Conference, London, *Embracing Excellence* [online] www.accconference.com

Passmore, J (2008a) *Psychometrics in Coaching: Using psychological and psychometrics tools for development*, Kogan Page, London

Passmore, J (2008b) Conference paper, Association for Coaching International Conference, London, *Embracing Excellence* [online] www.accconference.com

Rosinski, P (2003) *Coaching Across Cultures*, Nicholas Brealey, London

Rossi, K, Lustig, T and McKergow, M (2003) *A Comparison of Appreciative Inquiry and Solution Focus – an Overview* [online] www.lasaev.com

Trompenaars, F and Hampden-Turner, C (1997) *Riding the Waves of Culture: Understanding cultural diversity in business*, 2nd edn, Nicholas Brealey, London

Whitmore, J (2008) Keynote Conference paper, Association for Coaching International Conference, London, *Embracing Excellence* [online] www.accconference.com

Further reading

Barrett, R (2008) Coaching for Cultural Transformation (CCT), in *Psychometrics in Coaching*, ed J Passmore, Kogan Page, London

Childs, R (2008) Coaching with FIRO Element B, in *Psychometrics in Coaching*, ed J Passmore, Kogan Page, London

ICF and PWC (2007) *Executive Summary of ICF Global Coaching Study*, Feb [online] www.coach-federation.org

Peters, H and Kabacoff, R (2003) *Going Global: What U.S. and European Leaders Need to Know About Each Other*, Management Research Group [online] http://www.mrg.com/documents/GoingGlobal.pdf

Useful websites

COI (Cultural Orientations Indicator), www.tmcorp.com
CTT (Cultural Transformation Tools), www.valuescentre.com
European Mentoring and Coaching Council, www.emccouncil.org.
Executive Summary of ICF Global Coaching Study, available at ICF Headquarters, www.coach-federation.org
Global Convention on Coaching (2008). Dublin, www.coachingconvention.org
Intercultural Development Inventory (Bennett and Hammer 2000); www.intercultural.org/
Management Resource Group, *Individual Directions Inventory* and *LEA 360*, www.mrg.com
Wisdom8 (copyright 2008) www.wisdom8.com, London

3

Coaching in North America

Dr Mary Wayne Bush

INTRODUCTION

The development of multicultural coaching across the United States has been paralleled by its rise in Canada, and many of the same trends are evident. The coaching markets in both countries are large and growing. There is evidence that these two regions comprise the largest coaching market in the world, with approaching 20,000 coaches working in the field within North America.

This chapter provides an overview of coaching in the United States and Canada, in terms of its development, practitioners, clients, challenges and potential future trends. Coaching practices, contracting and selection are covered. In addition, aspects of multicultural coaching in the United States and Canada will be highlighted. Lastly, some of the current debates and issues among coaching organizations and practitioners in the United States and Canada are discussed.

THE NATURE OF COACHING IN THE UNITED STATES AND CANADA

North American coaching is generally practised using a combination of observation, assessment and conversation. For personal coaching, these can take the form of dialogue, even when the coach is observing or assessing the coachee. However, it is common for personal coaches to use assessment instruments such as the Myers-Briggs Type Inventory (MBTI), the Enneagram, or other tools that assess and help the client clarify values, aptitudes and other important aspects of personal development. In the organizational setting, coaches often rely on multi-rater assessments and objective personality tests (Liljenstrand and Nebecker, 2008). These instruments can be customized by the organization based on their internal competency models, or chosen from among the many commercial products that are available. It is also common for organizational coaches to conduct personal interviews as multi-rater assessments, so that they can ask questions and follow the conversational path to deeper and more informative levels of detail about the coachee's situation.

While the general North American conceptual framework is that coaching is non-directive, there is much debate about this within the organizational coaching arena. Many coaches agree with the International Coach Federation (ICF, 2008) that coaches 'seek to elicit solutions and strategies from the client; they believe the client is naturally creative and resourceful. The coach's job is to provide support to enhance the skills, resources, and creativity that the client already has.'

However, as Vikki Brock (2008) notes: 'Minority voices in the coaching community believe that clients hire coaches to provide specific knowledge, experience and timely counsel as well as coaching. Many business coaches subscribe to the notion of not providing advice, and when asked directly admit that what they provide is consultative coaching to their clients.' The balance between 'directive' and 'non-directive' remains with the individual coach to work out with the coachee.

Coaching can be contracted for one session, such as giving feedback about an assessment instrument, or for longer periods. Many coaches use a retainer for contracting, offering a specific number of monthly sessions (usually two to four) for a fee paid monthly or annually. Others, especially business and executive coaches, contract for a coaching engagement, the length of which is agreed upon by the coach, the coachee and the organization. The length of these engagements is largely determined by the issue being coached: if a specific skill is being developed, or a behavioural issue being addressed, the coaching engagement can last for several months. However, if coaching is being offered for other issues, such as leadership development, strategic planning or executive transition, the engagement can last 18 months and beyond. In their study of organizational coaching, Underhill *et al* (2007) found that the most common coaching duration is 6 to 12 months. A study of coaches who worked with small business owners and entrepreneurs found that 'Typically, a coach will work with a client between three to six months (33.2 per cent) or six to twelve months (33.2 per cent), although 53.2 per cent work with their client for longer than six months' (Grant and Zackon, 2004). And a study by The College of Executive Coaching found that 59 per cent of organizational coaching engagements lasted four months or more (Auerbach, 2005).

Coaching contracts are likely to include agreements about the goal of coaching, the number, length and timing of sessions, the delivery method(s) to be used (ie telephone, e-mail, in person, group or individual sessions), contact between sessions, and the cost of the sessions. In a study of 2,529 professional coaches, Grant and Zackon (2004) found that 'Coaching is primarily conducted over the phone (63 per cent), followed by in person (34.3 per cent) and electronic means, eg e-mail (1.4 per cent). Overall, most [coaches] use electronic means, at least sometimes (63.6 per cent)'. Another study found 'North America is the only region where telephone coaching exceeds face to face coaching. In this region, over half of all coaching (56.2 per cent) is conducted by telephone, with 40.1 per cent conducted face to face' (International Coach Federation, 2007).

The evaluation of coaching engagements is more common in organizational coaching than in personal coaching, though recent statistics show that less than 10 per cent of organizations do any kind of analysis. In organizational coaching, there is sometimes an evaluation component specified in the contract, such as a multi-rater survey or 'pre-post testing' (testing the coachee both before and after the coaching engagement) to identify progress and goal attainment. One well-known US coach, Marshall Goldsmith, offers a 'results guarantee' for the success of his coaching: if the coaching does not produce the agreed-upon outcome, his coaches will not accept a fee.

The length and number of sessions in a coaching engagement can vary dramatically, depending on the locations of the coachee and coach, and the issue being addressed in coaching. Many personal coaches offer three to four telephone sessions per month, with each session lasting from half an hour to an hour. In the corporate arena, coaching sessions can range from a short 'laser coaching' exchange with an on-site coach to a longer shadow-coaching experience where the coach observes the coachee for extended periods during the workday.

Current research (Underhill, 2007) indicates that most coaches are selected by referral, although one study found that in organizations, the majority of coaches are selected by Human Resources (Fanasheh, 2003). In the executive market coaches are selected through multiple methods, as evidenced by the following statements from a recent study by Auerbach (2005) on behalf of The College of Executive Coaching:

> We issue a Request for Proposals with specific criteria. We interview the coaches and make a panel of approved coaches. Then employees contact and select coaches from that list.

> I receive the request for a referral. I request coaches' resumes and certification information. I interview the coaches and consider their values. I give the names of three coaches to the employee, then the employee chooses their coach.

> Usually the coach is a referral from someone we regard well, then we interview the coach with senior management.

Large companies that employ multiple external coaches, such as Sony, WalMart and Texas Instruments, are increasingly utilizing assessment centres to evaluate potential coaches. In these processes a coach will be invited to an assessment centre for a half-day or full-day process that can include interviews with senior decision makers, psychological or personality inventories and demonstration coaching sessions so that the decision makers can evaluate their coaching. In addition, there is often an orientation session or presentation to help the prospective coaches get to know the company, its goals and its culture.

CURRENT STATE

According to a recent study of the global coaching market by the International Coach Federation (2007), 'it is possible to estimate that the revenue generated by the coaching industry globally is close to $1.5 billion. The United States market accounts for approximately half of all global revenues.'

Of the 5,415 respondents, 60 per cent were from North America. Given this figure, we can claim that the study results are broadly applicable to the United States and Canada coaching markets. The study conservatively estimates the number of coaches to be 30,000 worldwide. Therefore, a conservative estimate of the number of US and Canadian coaches would be 18,000 (15,000 US, 3,000 Canadian). The study also found that North America has the most mature coaching profession, with almost half of all respondents (48.1 per cent) coaching for more than five years. Coaching is currently a predominantly female profession: the United States and Canada had very high levels of female respondents (73.2 per cent and 71.9 per cent, respectively) (International Coach Federation, 2007).

Respondents from North America had one of the highest average annual coaching revenues: $50,458. One in seven respondents from North America (15 per cent) stated that their annual coaching revenue exceeded $100,000. Assuming that there are around 30,000 coaches globally, the study estimates that the United States, with the largest presumed number of coaches, would account for just under half of all the global 125 million professional development dollars spent.

Survey results indicate that coaches are highly educated. Just over half of all respondents (53 per cent) had obtained a third-level education (ie an advanced degree such as a Master's or PhD), with a further 35.2 per cent of respondents holding a university degree. In addition to being highly educated, the survey respondents are making a significant investment in their professional development. Almost two-thirds of all respondents (64.5 per cent) had received coach-specific training through a programme accredited by ICF, with a further 30.1 per cent receiving training through a programme not accredited by ICF. Of all survey respondents, only 5.2 per cent had not undertaken any kind of coach-specific training (International Coach Federation, 2007).

There are two main branches of coaching: personal, or 'life' coaching, and organizational coaching, which includes executive coaching, business coaching and leadership coaching. While personal coaching is most often a relationship between the coach and coachee, an added complexity of organizational coaching is the need to include other stakeholders, such as the coachee's manager or team. So organizational coaching often presents itself as a triangular relationship between the coach, the coachee and the client company, where the coach must ensure that the goals of both are met. In addition, there are hundreds of speciality coaching 'niches', including wellness coaching, content-specific coaching (such as presentations coaching, writing coaching, etc), academic coaching, spiritual coaching, personal image coaching, and relationship coaching.

Coaching is now offered at many levels in organizations, not just the executive ranks. Many companies such as Dell, IBM, Wachovia Bank, Northrop Grumman, Johnson and Johnson, and EDP use internal company coaches as well as hiring external coaches to work with leaders. Organizations are also using other forms of coaching, such as team coaching and peer coaching, as well as training their managers to coach employees. Organizational coaching is increasingly being used for developing talented, promising personnel, rather than dealing with problem employees. 'This shift from hiring coaches for struggling employees to focusing on the rising stars has decreased the stigmatization of receiving coaching services and has in turn increased the demand for such services' (Liljenstrand and Nebecker, 2008).

The rise of coaching in North America has led to a proliferation of coach training schools, publications and professional associations (see Figure 3.1). Canadian Rey Carr, of Peer Resources, notes that 'Since 1995 the field has grown from two coach training schools to 273, from three professional associations to sixteen, and from zero magazines and journals focusing on coaching in the year 2000 to eleven in 2008.' (Rey Carr, personal communication, 22 January 2008).

The field of coaching is growing, and is in the process of defining itself. Coaching organizations such as the International Coach Federation (ICF), CoachU, and the Hudson Institute of Santa Barbara offer coaching certification programmes. The popularity of coaching has encouraged the proliferation of coaches, coaching organizations, training programmes, coaching conferences and professional coaching associations.

Credentialing and appropriate coach-specific training are cornerstones of professionalism. Currently the ICF and World Association of Business Coaches (WABC) are the main North American professional associations offering coaching certification, but many coach training schools offer credentials and certificates. More colleges and universities are also offering coaching training and certifications, such as programmes at Royal Roads University and Ryerson in Canada, and Georgetown University, Babson College, Fielding Graduate University and the University of Texas at Dallas. Supervision of coaches most often takes place within coach training organizations, as a prerequisite for graduation, or in organizations, where it is used to standardize coaching practices and ensure quality of coaching.

Several recent studies indicate that most North American coaches hold some kind of credential or certification (Gale *et al*, 2002; Grant and Zackon, 2004; International Coach Federation, 2007), and one study noted that 'those who have been providing coaching services longer also see less of a need for licensure or certification. Perhaps their experience and past success make it less important' (Liljenstrand and Nebecker, 2008). Grant and Zackon (2004) found that North American coaches in their study were well trained: 'Coaches in this study had overwhelmingly graduated from or have been enrolled in a coach training program (90.3 per cent), with the majority having graduated (71.7 per cent). Most are graduates of an ICF accredited training program (70.3 per cent).' And the ICF Global study (2007) found that 'seven out of ten (72.4 per cent) respondents in the North American region had received coach specific training through a program accredited by ICF, the highest proportion in any region. The level was particularly high in Canada, where almost four out of five respondents stated that they had received training through an ICF accredited program.'

Currently, there is no government or professional regulation of coaching in North America, since coaching does not fall within Mental Health/Behavioural Health guidelines or statutes. However, there is strong

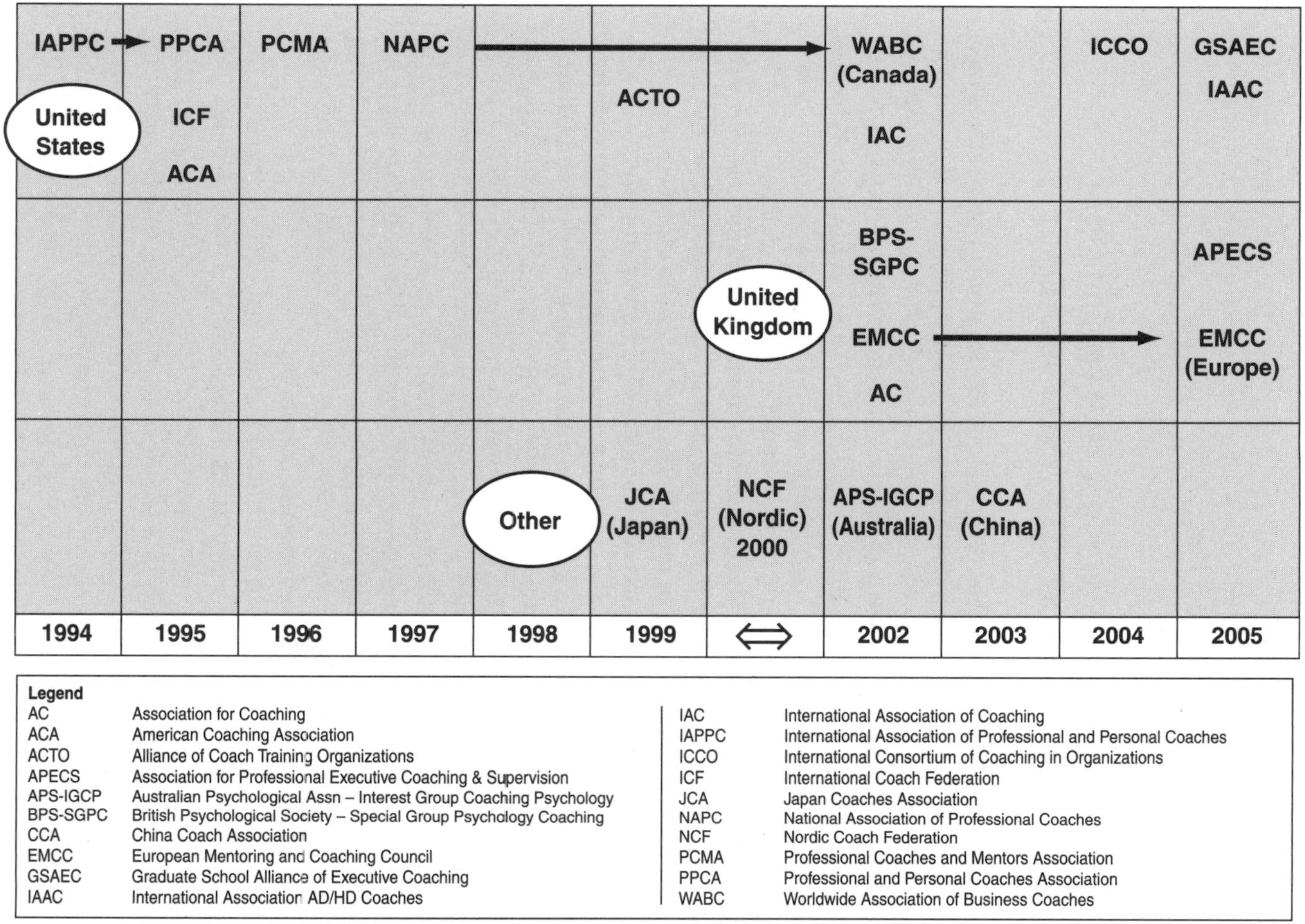

Region	1994	1995	1996	1997	1998	1999	2000	2002	2003	2004	2005
United States	IAPPC → PPCA	ICF, ACA	PCMA	NAPC		ACTO		WABC (Canada), IAC		ICCO	GSAEC, IAAC
United Kingdom								BPS-SGPC, EMCC, AC	CCA (China)		APECS, EMCC (Europe)
Other						JCA (Japan)	NCF (Nordic) 2000	APS-IGCP (Australia)			

Legend

AC	Association for Coaching
ACA	American Coaching Association
ACTO	Alliance of Coach Training Organizations
APECS	Association for Professional Executive Coaching & Supervision
APS-IGCP	Australian Psychological Assn – Interest Group Coaching Psychology
BPS-SGPC	British Psychological Society – Special Group Psychology Coaching
CCA	China Coach Association
EMCC	European Mentoring and Coaching Council
GSAEC	Graduate School Alliance of Executive Coaching
IAAC	International Association AD/HD Coaches
IAC	International Association of Coaching
IAPPC	International Association of Professional and Personal Coaches
ICCO	International Consortium of Coaching in Organizations
ICF	International Coach Federation
JCA	Japan Coaches Association
NAPC	National Association of Professional Coaches
NCF	Nordic Coach Federation
PCMA	Professional Coaches and Mentors Association
PPCA	Professional and Personal Coaches Association
WABC	Worldwide Association of Business Coaches

Figure 3.1 Professional coaching associations timeline (used with permission from Vikki Brock)

interest in this issue within both the coaching and psychology communities, and recent questions have arisen in Colorado and Ohio about official regulation for the field (International Coach Federation, 2005). There is also confusion in the public arena about the differences between coaching and therapy, and this confusion may grow as more and more psychotherapists become coaches (De Meuse and Tang, 2007).

WORKING ACROSS A MULTICULTURAL UNITED STATES AND CANADA

Coaching itself developed from multiple professions and perspectives (see Figure 3.2) and can be characterized as 'cross-disciplinary, multi-disciplinary or inter-disciplinary – that is, a hyphenated field rather than one that is "owned" by any one existing academic discipline' (Page, 2006). In North America, multicultural coaching is a relative newcomer to the field. Whereas organizational coaching has long been used to facilitate employees' orientation and assimilation into different corporate cultures, coaches have also been working with global teams, corporate citizens on foreign assignments, expatriates returning to North America, and leaders wanting to develop increased cultural sensitivity in the workplace.

Linked to the growing awareness of cultural diversity in businesses and governments, as well as rapidly changing demographics in both countries, multicultural coaching aims to promote understanding, respect and cultural sensitivity in individuals, teams and organizations. It is estimated that, in the near future, over half of the population in some US states will be comprised of ethnic minorities (Turner, 2007). Many large companies are working internationally, developing global markets and even outsourcing work to other countries. Demographic shifts like this change both workplace and systems dynamics, and have an impact on the coaching market, adding incentive for coaches to work with individuals on communication, openness to change, and cultural awareness and acceptance.

North American definitions of culture include aspects of the self, the personality, the environment, organization and society, as well as sources of inequity, power, dominance or differences in the way people approach important areas of life or work. In a recent study on cross-cultural coaching, Barbara St. Claire-Ostwald (2007) examined the cultural awareness of professionals working in organizations. She concluded that: 'The building blocks of improving cultural awareness and developing cross-cultural skills therefore have much in common with the key skills associated with building rapport as a coach or mentor. For the coach or business organisation, it is therefore about understanding the processes involved with the different

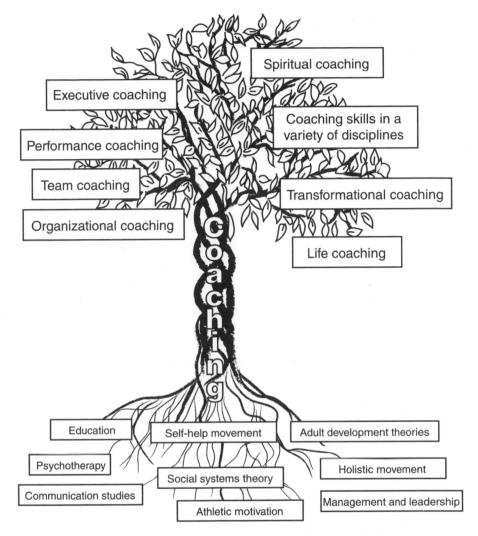

Spiritual coaching

Executive coaching

Coaching skills in a variety of disciplines

Performance coaching

Team coaching

Transformational coaching

Organizational coaching

Life coaching

Education

Self-help movement

Adult development theories

Psychotherapy

Holistic movement

Communication studies

Social systems theory

Athletic motivation

Management and leadership

Figure 3.2 The field of coaching studies: draws from many 'roots' and supports many 'branches'

ways in which we negotiate social interaction, and the elements of the various models of culture.'

Currently, no North American professional coach association specifically organizes for multicultural coaching, nor do any of the major US and Canadian coaching organizations have programmes or special interest groups in this area. However, some of the well-known coach-training programmes, such as the one offered by the University of Texas at Dallas, offer coursework in diversity as an aspect of coaching. UT Dallas's course in 'Coaching for Diversity and Inclusion' highlights workplace, gender and generational workplace diversity issues, and educates students on both US and Canadian anti-discrimination laws. (Brock, personal communication, 14 January 2008).

The following are examples of a range of positive steps that coaches are taking to adopt a multicultural approach to coaching within North America.

Team coaching

One of the ways that multicultural coaching takes place is with teams. Whether the teams work together face to face or virtually, via phone and internet, cultural differences can cause misunderstandings and communication breakdowns that can negatively impact both morale and productivity. Michael Detlefsen, President of Maple Leaf Foods, a Toronto-based food processing company, worked with Candice Frankovelgia, the Colorado-based coaching practice leader from the Center for Creative Leadership, to coach a team where each member ran operations in a different country:

> Once per quarter, the team members travelled to corporate headquarters and spent a week working intensively on issues that affected them all. Because of the different cultural norms governing communication, especially around sensitive topics, some team members had trouble working effectively with their team counterparts, and vice versa. For the Western members of the team, their Eastern colleagues were too reticent in expressing their honest opinions. For the Eastern team members, the bluntness of their Western counterparts was confrontational and disrespectful. To facilitate communication that would inform and illuminate yet not offend, the group created a communications template that invited people to describe three things they liked about a proposal as well as three weaknesses they saw in it. The idea behind the template, says Detlefsen, was to allow team members to point out potential flaws in a way that would not be perceived by anyone on the team as harshly critical (Field, 2007).

Expatriate coaching

As organizations from the United States and Canada continue to develop international markets, more and more employees are offered the opportunity to work overseas. In addition, more workers are coming to North America from other countries. Multinational companies have previously offered cross-cultural training and preparation for their members going to – and coming from – foreign countries, but coaching is now being added in many cases. Coaching provides a customized programme of learning and application for the coachee, targeting specific, real-time issues and situations that arise. As Larry Lee (2006) writes, 'Coaches can also help clients discover which steps are appropriate to take next and when to take them.'

Carol Braddick, an executive coach who works with expatriates, says this investment ultimately benefits the company: through cross-cultural training, ongoing learning and coaching, expatriates build indispensable skills and can invest these skills to their own and to the company's benefit. She says that coaching may also help lessen the 'culture shock' and stress for the employee living abroad, favourably affecting productivity, morale and retention: 'Working with an intercultural coach allows the expatriate to become aware of her/his map of the world and to deal productively with challenging differences when they arise' (Braddick and Tilghman, 2003).

Rosinski (2003) has outlined a Global Coaching Process designed to bring the client's cultural orientations – which are often unconscious – to the surface. He cites the example of an executive who shifted from a 'same rules, same generic processes around the world' mentality to being more flexible on local market needs. He then supported his team in developing a new product for the local market. This product became an important revenue source for the region and was ultimately adopted by other markets.

Diversity coaching for leadership development

Another emerging application of multicultural coaching is in leadership development. Large, global companies invest in providing training, mentoring and executive coaching for their leaders. While the current trend is for organizational coaching to be developmental rather than remedial, there is still coaching that is provided for leaders who are not performing to the expected standard. Sometimes, these performance issues can be traced to cultural issues, whether the leader is lacking the cultural sensitivity to interact well with others, or needs to become more aware of his or her own cultural biases.

Larry Lee (2006) argues that coaching is a natural adjunct to organizational diversity training programmes, which are 'important, but not the first consideration.' One aspect of diversity coaching for leaders is to support them in stepping up to, and deepening, their role as champions of engaging the diverse workforce:

> Changing individual executives in the core group changes the group and changing the group changes the organization. It works from the inside out. It requires personal, prudent courage to challenge existing practices. Coaches are instrumental in assisting clients to identify their own courageous direction

and also in creating prudent pathways together. In terms of diversity, it means helping your clients address diverse issues or diverse communities with diverse-wise action steps.'(Lee, 2006)

Non-profit organizations are facing the same demographic issues as larger corporations. A study of non-profit executive directors found that 'Racial and ethnic minorities represent a rapidly growing segment of the population, but executive directors are overwhelmingly white' (Peters and Wolfred, 2001). The same study found that 90 per cent of respondents were involved in some kind of professional development, and one in four said they had worked with an executive coach. In fact, the executive directors ranked funding for executive coaching and professional development in the top 10 potential funder actions. The study concluded with a recommendation to provide a pool of executive coaches for the non-profit executive directors.

Government offices are also employing multicultural coaches to help deal with cross-cultural awareness issues. Donna Karlin, a Canadian executive coach, works with diplomats as well as other officials and expatriates on issues ranging from appropriate cultural sensitivity at high-level meetings, to building acceptance of differing cultural norms. For instance, she has worked with the Canadian government on broader acceptance of the cultural norms of the 14 First Nation peoples in White Horse, Canada. She advocates against any tendency to ignore differences, and helps organizations 'find out, value the differences, celebrate and embrace them, then acknowledge and move on' (Karlin, personal communication, 21 January 2008). Donna frequently works as a Shadow Coach, a process that she developed to help leaders be mindful of cultural implications in their everyday work. Since Canadian law stipulates that all Federal government communication is bilingual, Karlin works in both French and English.

Coaching for individual multicultural development

In this leading-edge work, a coach works with a client to assess and develop his or her own awareness of culture and appreciation and acceptance of cultural differences. Coachees can be recent immigrants to North America or corporate or government employees who wish to expand their own understanding of how multiculturalism affects their lives and work. Patricia Comley, a Toronto-based coach, works with individuals and groups to develop inter-cultural competencies, and believes that the root of cultural competency begins in self-reflection. She recently completed an action-research project, coaching multicultural university students to help them develop awareness and sensitivity and to integrate and transform their cultural knowledge. Organization and government leaders are also seeking coaching to develop their own skills in dealing with the global diversity they are experiencing.

As organizations across North America strive to develop and maintain high-functioning, diverse and cross-cultural workgroups, coaches are asked to support both leaders and teams in dealing with these issues. Fortunately for the field, awareness and interest in multicultural coaching is growing. Many executive coaches today find themselves working with leaders from a variety of cultural backgrounds, as well as coaching leaders who work with culturally diverse teams. It is therefore increasingly important that coaches understand the role of culture in their work (Peterson, 2007).

TAKING COACHING FORWARD IN THE UNITED STATES AND CANADA

As coaching grows in popularity in North America, so do concerns about how it is practised and understood. With the possibility of government regulation looming in this expanding market, the North American coaching community must carefully examine any unresolved issues in the field. Although there are many professional coaches, the field itself is not yet considered a profession (Bennett, 2006) and suffers from a lack of consistent definition, as well as a body of knowledge upon which to base its theories, methods and approaches. Dr Esra Ozkan (2007), an anthropologist who studied the field of coaching in North America, noted:

> Professional coaches have different and often conflicting opinions about defi-nitions of coaching and the kind of educational and professional background necessary to practice as a coach. … More often than not coaches have defined coaching by what coaches don't do and how they don't do it rather than what they do and how they do it. They have emphasized that what they do is not consulting, not psychotherapy, not teaching and not mentoring.

One source of ambiguity is that coaching is decidedly cross-disciplinary with coaches coming from a number of prior professional and occupational backgrounds. Grant and Zackon (2004) note that:

> This diversity is both a strength and a liability. The diversity of prior professional backgrounds means that the emerging profession of coaching has the oppor-tunity to draw on wide range of theoretical and methodological approaches to coaching. However, this diversity also means that defining the field of coaching is fraught with complexity. Furthermore, each subgroup of coaches may perceive 'their way' as being the 'right way', dismissing other approaches as non-coachlike, irrelevant or ineffective.

There is also currently no barrier to entry for coaches in North America, nor is training or certification mandatory. This puts the onus on professional associations, coaching schools and individual coaches to maintain and monitor high standards of ethical behaviour and appropriate practices. Wasylyshyn (2003) states that if sustained behavioural change is the goal, coaches need training in clinical psychology.

In addition, the rise of multicultural coaching in North America may challenge our particularly Western view of the world. 'We need to open ourselves to the possibility that our own cultural values, assumptions, or backgrounds may potentially inhibit our effectiveness with a client' (Rosinski, 2006). The true work for multicultural coaches is to understand and acknowledge deeply held values, beliefs and assumptions – not only in the coachee, but in ourselves. We must also remember that in coaching, we are working with another human being, not simply another 'culture' or stereotype. As David Peterson (2007) observes:

> Culture is a social- or group-level phenomenon, and coaching occurs at the level of the individual. The coach's challenge is to get to know the person they are working with, regardless of whether that person was shaped by culture, social status, family background, life experiences, education, profession, personality or other factors. Certainly culture may be a potent force in shaping people's identity and behaviour, but it is an unpredictable and unreliable factor in determining the character, values, or behaviour of any particular individual.

SUMMARY

Coaching is gaining in popularity in North America, and as global changes and demographic trends highlight interactions between cultures, there is an increasing need for multicultural coaching. Whether this takes place in organizations, between governments or among indigenous peoples and new immigrants, the aim of coaching remains the same: to foster understanding, insight, awareness and action. Peterson (2007) puts it well: 'regardless of the amount of cultural knowledge a coach has, the best coaches will always be those who coach with an open attitude of curiosity and interest, who meet people where they are, who accept them for what they are, and who project a genuine desire to be helpful to each person on their own terms.'

It is interesting that coaching as a field arises from many other disciplines, and it is perhaps this fact that makes coaching so well suited to address the variety of issues associated with inter-cultural or multicultural situations. And, as with cultural diversity, the diversity inherent in the field of coaching can be both a strength and a liability. As Grant and Zackon (2004) note: 'the emerging profession of coaching has the opportunity to draw on wide range of theoretical and methodological approaches to coaching. However, this diversity also means that defining the field of coaching is fraught with complexity.'

Perhaps the rise of multicultural coaching can show the way, not only for individuals and organizations, but for the field of coaching as well.

References

Auerbach, J (2005) *Seeing the Light: What organizations need to know about executive coaching*, Executive College Press, Pismo Beach, California

Bennett, J (2006) An agenda for coaching-related research, *Consulting Psychology Journal: Practice and research*, **58**(4), pp 240–9

Braddick, C and Tilghman, T (2003) Valuing the international work experience: The hidden benefit in expat packages, *FocusNews*, June, pp 2

Brock, V (2008) Unpublished dissertation manuscript, Institute for Life Coach Training, Ft. Collins, Colorado

De Meuse, K and Tang, K (2007) [accessed 3 January 2008] Literature Review of Media References on Coaching [online] http://thefoundationofcoaching.org/files/review.pdf

Fanasheh, H (2003) The perception of executive coaching among CEOs of America's top 500 companies, *Dissertation Abstracts International*, **64**(03), pp 736 (UMI No. 3086669)

Field, A (2007) Coaching your team's performance to the next level: How team coaching can reduce conflict and increase collaboration – and hence a team's productivity, *Harvard Management Update*, Harvard Business School Publishing, Boston

Gale, J et al (2002) [accessed 15 December 2007] Executive Summary of Coaching: who, what, when, where and how? [online] http://www.coachfederation.org/Downloads/docs/exec-summary-2002.pdf

Grant, A and Zackon, R (2004) Executive, Workplace and Life Coaching: Findings from a large-scale survey of International Coach Federation members, *International Journal of Evidence Based Coaching and Mentoring*, **2**(2), pp 1–16

International Coach Federation (2005) [accessed 12 December 2007] ICF Regulatory Updates [online] http://www.icfnycchapter.org/national_regulatory.php

International Coach Federation (2007) *Global Coaching Study Module 1: Profile of coaching industry*, International Coach Federation, Kentucky

International Coach Federation (2008) [accessed 2 January 2008] What is Coaching? [online] http://www.coachfederation.org/ICF/For+Coaching+Clients/What+is+a+Coach/

Lee, L (2006) Personal Diversity Management: A praxis approach to diversity and decision-making, *International Journal of Coaching in Organizations*, **4**(2), pp 40–51

Liljenstrand, A and Nebecker, D (2008) Coaching services: A look at coaches, clients, and practices, unpublished manuscript accepted for publication in *Consulting Psychology Journal: Practice and research*, **60**(1)

Ozkan, E (2007) Unpublished dissertation, Massachusetts Institute of Technology, Boston

De Meuse, K and Tang, K (2007) [accessed 3 January 2008] Literature Review of Media References on Coaching [online] http://thefoundationofcoaching.org/files/review.pdf

Page, L (2006) Thinking outside our brains: Interpersonal neurobiology and organizational change, *International Journal of Coaching in Organizations*, **4**(2), pp 22–31

Peters, J and Wolfred, T (2001) [accessed 1 December 2007] Daring to Lead: Non-Profit executive directors and their work experience. Compass Point Non-Profit Services [online] http://www.compasspoint.org/assets/5_daring.pdf.

Peterson, D (2007) Executive Coaching in a Cross-Cultural Context, *Consulting Psychology Journal: Practice and research*, **59**(4), pp 261–71

Rosinski, P (2003) *Coaching Across Cultures: New tools for leveraging national, corporate and professional differences*, Nicholas Brealey, London

Rosinski, P (2006) Cross cultural coaching, in *Excellence in Coaching*, ed J Passmore, pp 153–69, Kogan Page, London

Stein, I F (2004) Introduction: Beginning a promising conversation, in Proceedings of the First International Coach Federation Coaching Research Symposium, eds I F Stein and L A Belsten, pp viii–xii, Paw Print Press, Mooresville, NC

St. Claire-Ostwald, B (2007) Carrying Cultural Baggage: The contribution of socio-cultural anthropology to cross-cultural coaching, *International Journal of Evidence Based Coaching and Mentoring*, **5**(2), pp 45–52

Turner, R (2007) Culture Wars in the Workplace: Interpersonal subtlety, emotional expression and the self-concept, *Consulting Psychology Journal: Practice and research*, **59**(4), pp 244–53

Underhill, B (2007) High impact executive coaching research findings. Paper presented at Conference Board Executive Coaching Conference, 25 January 2007, New York, NY

Underhill, B et al (2007) *Executive Coaching for Results: The definitive guide to developing organizational leaders*, Berrett-Koehler Publishers, San Francisco

Wasylyshyn, K M (2003) Executive Coaching: An outcome study, *Consulting Psychology Journal: Practice and Research*, **55**(2), pp 94–106

Further reading

Brock, V (2006) Who's who in coaching? Who shaped it? Who's shaping it? *Proceedings of the Fourth International Coach Federation Coaching Research Symposium*, International Coach Federation, Kentucky

Rosinski, P and Abbot, G (2006) Coaching from a Cultural Perspective, in *Evidence Based Coaching Handbook: Putting best practices to work for your clients*, ed D R Stober, and A M Grant, pp 255–76, Wiley, Hoboken, NJ

4

Coaching in Australasia

Jodie Anagnos

INTRODUCTION

As a new and developing field, coaching has given little consideration to the impact that culture has upon the process and efficacy of coaching from a business and life-coaching perspective. Due to the limited nature of the coaching literature, knowledge is drawn from related disciplines such as teaching, psychology and consulting, to supplement and contribute to current understanding of multiculturalism in coaching. This chapter considers how coaching is conducted in Australasia, with consideration of the modalities utilized and processes undertaken during sessions. It further reviews the current strengths and weaknesses exhibited in the coaching field, and reviews the state of coaching with reference to regulation, training and methodology. Consideration is made of Asian cultures, individualistic versus communist culture and indigenous populations, with comment on the methods that coaches may use to enhance the effectiveness of coaching in these cultures.

THE NATURE OF COACHING IN AUSTRALASIA

Coaching is a facilitative approach that uses questions and challenges to initiate the coachee to find solutions, combined with a belief that the coachee has sufficient resources to find their own answers. No definitive coaching modality or approach has been identified within Australasia; however, the generally accepted definition of coaching is as a method that facilitates goal achievement (Green, 2007), and one that is collaborative, solution-focused, result-orientated and utilizes a systematic process (Grant, 2001). Anecdotal evidence suggests that whilst many coaches report adherence to these approaches in theory, the degree of practical application of a non-directive approach may vary, possibly due to the diverse backgrounds of coaches (many arriving to the field from advisory roles such as HR, teaching and consulting, bringing with them their skills sets and professional practices). It is important that coaches can support the models that they use and can provide evidentiary bases to support their claims of efficacy; however, a question mark remains regarding this because of the limited information that exists around the practices of coaches.

A key responsibility for any coach upon commencing work with a new coachee is to educate them about the process and ensure they have an understanding of the coaching boundaries. Some coachees may arrive with expectations that the coach will identify solutions, and it is necessary to impress upon the coachee the different roles that the coach and coachee will hold. Questions with a basis in motivational interviewing can be useful at this point, because they highlight the reasons why the coachee is seeking certain outcomes and pinpoint what stage the coachee is at in terms of actively seeking those outcomes. It is possible that the coachee is still contemplating the goal or even pre-contemplating the goal. Such an exploration can be useful as a means of identifying what the goals are. These goals may change as the sessions progress but it is important that the first session begins with a clear sense of direction and exploration. Ideally the coach will seek to make the goals specific and realistic.

Once an understanding is reached about the coachee's goals, the coach will discuss the structure of consultations, which are primarily private. They involve one to two hours and are individualized (Faraday-Brash, 2007), meaning that the duration of coaching depends on the progress achieved by the coachee.

Selecting a coach for a member of the general population is likely to occur via advertisements or through many of the flamboyant websites available; a search for 'life coaching' on Google Australia revealed 223,000 hits. To date there is no regulatory body that educates the public about how to select a competent, professional coach, although the International Coaching

Federation (ICF) and Australian Psychological Society (APS) provide some resources (www.coachfederation.org and www.psychology.au). A special interest group for coaching was created in Australia in 2002 and has been cited as the fastest growing unit in the APS, reflecting the current interest in coaching (McEwan, 2007).

Research into coaching practices and participation in New Zealand (Brookes and Wright, 2007) suggests that the market is in growth phase. Like in Australia, there is no registration and the main accreditation body, the ICF, had 30 members in 2006.

Executive coaching is not better monitored but sets a higher standard, possibly due to the experience of the commission agents who are increasingly seeking credentials, experience and outcome measures from coaches. The same organizations have become very savvy at ensuring goals are specific and measurable by linking them in with the greater organizational mission. This push will likely have a carry-on effect for private coaching as coaches are required to upgrade their skills and professional affiliations to continue obtaining the highly paid executive coaching.

An additional drawback of an unregulated industry is that ethical guidelines are not dictated and those followed are likely to stem from the myriad of backgrounds that coaches appear to hold. Most coaches are aware of the need for confidentiality; however, many are seemingly less conscious of the potential reasons to break confidentiality and their legal limitations to hold total confidentiality under all circumstances. It is worrying when a coach is unable to accurately inform the coachee.

Drawing from ethical principles outlined by the APS, a psychologist will promise confidentiality to the client with limitations. These include if the psychologist reasonably suspects the client will do damage to him- or herself or a third party. In contrast to the United Kingdom, Australians hold a legislative mandatory reporting responsibility if a child is suspected of being in danger. The psychologist is also aware that any notes taken during the session can be subpoenaed by a court of law.

CURRENT STATE OF COACHING IN AUSTRALIA

Coaching in Australia shares with many other countries problems of a lack of regulation around training and supervision. Grant and O'Hara (2006), in a recent study on 14 life coaching companies, found that some trainers had no qualifications and some claimed that coaching could be used to treat anxiety or depression. Grant and Cavanagh (2007) highlight the booming nature of the coaching industry; however, the associated levels of quality and effectiveness have not yet been fully investigated and the research conducted so far has been largely anecdotal or case study based. Further, the quality of training of many self-professed coaches is also being questioned. Green (2007) highlights the lack of regulation around coaching and calls for psychologists to use the term 'evidence based life coaching' to differentiate themselves from other coaches.

Coaching is a growing field in Australia but is plagued with the same problems present in the United Kingdom and Europe resulting from a lack of standardization. Whilst a regular flow of coaches are establishing themselves in small business, little is understood about the background or education they possess or the type of clientele and therapeutic models they utilize. Figures are largely unreliable, often referring to coaching as the largest growing industry in Australia and talking of 100,000 coaches, but the source of these figures has been linked to a press release from a coach training provider that was subsequently quoted in the popular press (Spence, Cavanagh and Grant, 2006). In contrast, Hyatt (2003) claims there are over 50,000 coaches globally, suggesting that the Australian figure is vastly overstated.

Helping professions such as social work, psychology and psychiatry are carefully governed within Australia and New Zealand and are regulated by bodies that dictate approved training and accredit members of the profession. Coaching to date is sorely lacking the necessary parameters that would monitor entry into the profession and regulate issues such as training and experience, and this absence has led to a real concern around the quality and delivery of coaching. Australia and New Zealand are experiencing a similar plague of 'how to coach' training programmes, merely requiring weekend attendance, which has only served to exacerbate this issue (Bluckert, 2004).

Currently, coaches in Australia have two professional bodies available to them: the International Coach Federation (ICF) and Australian Psychological Society (APS), which also contains the Special Interest Group for Coaching. Both groups require minimum hours of training and experience; however, membership of neither group is compulsory. Due to the lack of regulation, little is understood or known about the training and experience of coaches working in the field to date. Reassuringly, however, Spence, Cavanagh and Grant (2006) found that 90 per cent of Australian coaches have undertaken coach-specific training, though given the excessive and often dubious statements issued by coach training firms it is hard to identify what this training consists of. In fact, Kaufman and Scoular (2004) raised concerns that coach training has become simplified into a '6-steps to success' in place of a thorough application of behavioural investigation.

Like coaching itself, the coach training market is unregulated and routinely markets with sensational promises and extravagant 'masters' qualifications, often bearing no relation to any legislatively approved

Australian training body or tertiary facility. In fact, some training bodies create their own accreditation bodies and are therefore self-accredited (Carr, 2005). Surprisingly, Grant and O'Hara (2006) found in their investigation of 14 coach training schools that 11 had some form of meaningful accreditation and seven were accredited with the ICF, although they recommend that potential coaching candidates should seek a programme accredited with a government registered training organization equipped to assess the quality of the service. This study further found that the ability to obtain quality training relies upon the consumer being aware of accreditation bodies and other indicators of quality training centres such as experienced trainers. This is a competence that few potential students have in common, which allows training centres to prey upon uninformed and sometimes naïve customers. This only serves to reiterate the urgent need for a governing body equipped to approve training programmes and importantly to identify the necessary components within a programme needed to equip a competent coach.

The growth of coaching, and executive coaching in particular, can be seen from its increasing use in organizations and the level of commitment placed in its ability to enhance performance. A Melbourne-based study (Dagley, 2006) investigated the perceptions of HR professionals responsible for commissioning over 1000 coaching programmes and AUS$15.4 million in coach spending in the previous two years. The respondents were resoundingly positive about the effectiveness of coaching, most commonly reporting benefits in communication and engagement skills, ability to cope with stress, and a clearer understanding of both personal professional performance and organizational issues and how to resolve or overcome them. Half the participants reported organizational benefits related to performance management and remediation, and team cohesion. Less confidence was exhibited regarding the quality of coaches, with participants commenting that 'there are a lot of quacks in the business', 'lots of quantity but not necessarily quality' and 'it is very difficult to source appropriately qualified and experienced coaches'.

Only one member of the study considered the costs excessive, yet the costs are considerably higher than alternative interventions such as training. Costs were reported as ranging from $600 for a four-session programme, through to $45,000 for an 18-session programme, and the average hourly rate for executive coaching across all organizations was $717.

Only one out of the 17 participants reported instigating a formal measurement of return on investment. Whilst organizations are notoriously poor at assessing programme effectiveness, it does seem a risky use of funds to pay excessive lump sums for services that cannot themselves prove effectiveness or claim clear empirical evidence for their work from the literature. It will be interesting to observe whether organizations will begin to demand more valid means of measurement from coaches to justify their expense in the current economic climate of cost cutting.

Global organizations in Australia show that an additional area of coaching not extensively addressed in the current literature is the mounting cultivation of internal coaches by organizations to replace or supplement the expense of external coaches who are presumably more qualified. Slowly, this is pressuring managers to develop coaching skills and is expanding expectations of managers, requiring them to act as facilitators (Ezzamel, Lilley and Willmott, 1994).

There have been two large surveys analysing the state of coaching practice within Australia conducted to assess the market share of coaching and details around experience, training and client groups. Clegg, Rhodes and Kornberger (2003) reviewed the status of business coaching in Australia by surveying 42 small businesses, and found that business coaching firms in Australia 'tend to be young and small', with 65 per cent of firms in business for less than five years, 86 per cent employing less than five people, and more than 50 per cent working out of home offices. Firms offered mostly business coaching and some other services, such as executive coaching, life coaching, consulting, training or coach training. Surprisingly, they appeared to have little understanding of their competitors, with over half the respondents unable to name a single competitor.

This study clearly identifies the relative youth and small size of firms in the business coaching market; however, it fails to account for private coaches or life coaches. Spence, Cavanagh and Grant (2006) have reviewed the private coaching population and found, similarly to Clegg, Rhodes and Kornberger (2003), that the industry is very young. They found that only 12 per cent of respondents had more than five years of experience and a third of the sample had less than one year of experience, although they do report a small core of highly experienced practitioners. They further found that coaches were largely engaged in executive/corporate coaching (71 per cent) and reported three common issues: career/business-related issues, relationships/interpersonal skills, and direction/goal setting issues. 90 per cent of coaches reported training with a coach-training school, tertiary study in a coach-related field (eg psychology) or training in a help-related field. Reassuringly, only five per cent reported no coach-related training and only two per cent reported a form of short in-house training or intensive workshop.

Whilst these two studies begin to shed light on what is happening in this burgeoning field, more research and investigation is required into the coaches and their practices. What is lacking is a clear understanding of the preferred theoretical model and approach that coaches utilize, and the level of expertise they have in undertaking that model.

There is some worrying debate that coaching has become a socially acceptable alternative for therapy, with little sanction accounting for the different expertise of coaches versus psychologists and counsellors (Spence and Grant, 2005). It is worrying to consider whether the coach is equipped to deal with emotional problems or has the necessary training to identify when a client's presenting problem is beyond their capability and provide them with the necessary referral to a psychotherapist or psychologist – particularly as one survey reported only a small proportion of coaches (approximately 20 per cent) have a background of human services (eg counsellor, psychologist) (Spence, Cavanagh and Grant, 2006).

It is also necessary to consider the legal obligations and duty of care of the coach who treats clients not necessarily within their professional capacity. Grant and Cavanagh (2006) consider the associated legal obligations but report that no case to date exists regarding the litigation of a coachee against a coach.

WORKING ACROSS A MULTICULTURAL AUSTRALASIA

Global multiculturalism has seen changes in lifestyle, work and entertainment. Australasia has a long history with multiculturalism. Australia often considers itself an international leader in racial tolerance and cultural diversity. However, any multicultural society is not without challenges and coaching must consider the impact of culture on work with coachees and organizations.

Impact of multiculturalism on executive coaching in Asian business centres

The impact of multicultural issues from a business perspective cannot be denied as corporations see international joint ventures fail due to a lack of compatible and complementary leadership characteristics and effective skills and behaviours needed to cross cultural boundaries. As competition continues to increase in global markets, the importance of people resources and their management escalates. Organizations can't afford to lose revenue due to avoidable inter-office dynamics. The question is whether executive coaches are equipped to address these issues and how they can adapt their own skills to achieve the desired outcomes.

Inter-cultural effectiveness inescapably starts with awareness and an understanding that there is no 'normal' position in cultural matters. It presupposes an understanding of the coach's own culturally learned assumptions (Connerley and Pederson, 2005), perception being key to any appreciation of working in cross-cultural environments. There is certainly an argument that coaches need to actively equip themselves to work in cross-cultural areas to gain an understanding of the coachee's multicultural milieu and in particular constraints placed upon them by their primary culture.

Hong Kong and Singapore combine a melting pot of cultures working together in global organizations but the parent culture is most commonly Western. Despite the use of executive coaching in these cultures, little is documented about the application of coaching in a multicultural environment, particularly where the significant organizational and coaching issues are likely to centre around integration. There is some debate about whether the diverse cultural workforce invalidates the assumptions of universal theories such as leadership and job satisfaction other than in the cultures where they originated (Lewis, French and Phetmany, 2000). This places organizations in the difficult position of addressing a significant problem without the usual frameworks they rely upon and presumably utilize satisfactorily throughout the European Union, United Kingdom and United States. Likewise this debate raises similar questions regarding the efficacy of the executive coach's foundation in theories that are similarly grounded in Western culture and not necessarily translatable to a collectivist society such as Asia.

It is possible that the success of coaching in diverse cultures may result from embracing non-directiveness and a loosened grasp on the theories and models of goal setting that often dictate a coach's approach. Enhanced success might stem from greater openness and collaboration about the principles that guide the coaching process. Whilst this may test the boundaries of client-centred therapy for some coaches, if they primarily identify with the premise that coachees have the solutions within them, then structurally coaching changes very little as it continues to be facilitation informed by cultural awareness or perception.

Collectivist versus individualist societies

A primary component impacting coaching in diverse settings is the level of collectivist versus individualistic beliefs in the culture. This may not require alteration of the underlying coaching practice but a shift in strategy may be necessary; one that allows the coachee to account for the community and its associated impact more readily or prior to consideration of themselves. Interestingly, in a Western context the coach may be inclined to structurally lead the coachee back to consideration of themselves and view an overly community focus as an avoidance of the issue. Thus a culturally informed coach is more likely to work more successfully with the coachee.

An issue unique to some cultures that makes coaching more challenging and potentially less effective is one of communication. Renner (2007) notes that in non-Western cultures, face saving may be very important and a vertical head shake and smile or positive feedback may not necessarily mean 'yes' or 'good job'. Importantly, this communication style may cloud whether clients are in agreement with consultation approaches and suggests the need for more objective measures of opinion to ensure accurate communication.

An alternative proposition is that coaching may not be appropriate in some cultures and mentoring might offer a more effective intervention. This is particularly relevant in a traditionally collectivist society whose members are more willing to turn to a respected elder than a new and untested consultant. These cultures attribute authority and wisdom to the oldest living men and women in the community, and elders are usually sought out for advice and direction in almost every aspect of life, as opposed to a coun-sellor or psychologist, whose merit is based upon academic requirements set by the state or some other jurisdiction. Thus trust is an important issue in the process and coaching in these cultures might require more evident 'buy in' from senior members of staff whose endorsement might dictate the active engagement of more junior members in the process. Torrance, Goff and Satterfield (1998: 9) have found significant promise with mentoring in racially diverse communities.

Indigenous cultures

Like other collectivist cultures, indigenous people have different mechan-isms and norms for seeking assistance that relate to the potential effect-iveness of coaching. Aboriginal Australians, Maoris and Torres Strait Islanders all have cultural norms independent of each other and different to the European settlers. Some research has found that, when indigenous indi-viduals consult indigenous healers for assistance in living, the helping rela-tionship does not seem to be regulated by prescribed rules and regulations (Vontress, 1999). Inhabitants of these societies generally show great respect for their elders and other authority figures. The consultation process is not a democratic interpersonal dialogue with counsellors as might be expected in other cultures, but one where the counsellor is treated with deference and the applicant mostly listens. In many instances, clients do not even state the presenting problem. The head of the family, accompanied by other members of the unit, escorts the person in need of remedy to the healer, to whom he or she describes the problem (Vontress 2002).

Thus some coaches might expect to see a different engagement in the process than that to which they are accustomed, and the application of coaching must be carefully considered for optimal outcomes and possibly facilitated to include members of the greater group. Additional complications that inhibit the coaching of indigenous individuals by non-indigenous coaches include their method of sharing and learning. For example, traditional Indigenous teachings utilize a circular, holistic style as opposed to a linear approach to pedagogy more common in Western teaching methodologies, and like many collectivist cultures place generosity and sharing above materialistic gain for the individual (Brendtro, Brokenleg and Van Bockern, 1990). Greater success has been found in problem solving skills training when a culturally sensitive teaching style was utilized (Place and McCluskey, 1995).

Some work has been done to establish mentoring systems for indigenous children in Australian and New Zealand schools; however, little exploration has been conducted outside of education and negligible literature is available on its success. A Canadian group has developed a highly successful programme to address recidivism in prisons and found that 38.71 per cent of the mentored group re-offended within 12 months, compared with 90 per cent of the control group (McCluskey *et al*, 2001). The achievements of these 'Made in Manitoba' programmes and others conducted by the same group might provide advances for the Australian and New Zealand programmes and indicate that this type of programme may prove advantageous over coaching.

TAKING COACHING FORWARD IN AUSTRALASIA

Coaching is a new field and will take time to establish itself as a profession comparable with psychology and psychotherapy. The literature cries out for further empirical research and for regulation, so it is likely that current attempts to standardize the industry will continue unabated, particularly if government intervention is achieved.

Coaching is based on the premise that coachees are functioning individuals seeking enhanced life or work performance, as opposed to psychotherapy or counselling where the individual displays pathology and the process aims to raise them from partial or sub-functioning to a normal level of functioning. There is an argument that suggests coaching modalities may be useful in the successful application of therapy and that counselling approaches may lack a sufficient level of feedback and goal setting to facilitate quick recovery. Little exploration has been made of the use of coaching techniques in mental health patients, despite the popularity of solution-focused and cognitive–behavioural approaches, which are characterized by statements reflecting their apparent quick and short-term outcomes.

Substantial success has been found in the application of coaching programmes in patient care facilities and as a rehabilitation measure catering for a range of physical ailments such as cardiovascular disease and diabetes. Notably, the most significant success has been found in patients whose health and condition can be rapidly improved by medication compliance and behavioural changes such as dietary and exercise enhancements.

One particular programme is the COACH (Coaching patients On Achieving Cardiovascular Health), a training programme for patients with cardiovascular disease in which a health professional coach trains patients to aggressively pursue the target levels for their particular coronary risk factors while working in partnership with their own physician(s). In one study, this led to a 14 mg/dL (0.36 mmol/L) greater reduction in serum total cholesterol levels than did usual care (Vale *et al*, 2003).

Given the ever-increasing life expectancy, and the impact of a sedentary lifestyle and high level of obesity and their associated effects, the use of coaching to promote behavioural changes in lifestyle may be a cost-effective method of producing successful medical outcomes and reducing hospital and medical costs. It may also provide necessary support to elderly and uneducated patients who might not otherwise obtain sufficient understanding of their situation and the necessary adjustments to their lifestyle.

In Australia, the 1997 National Survey of Mental Health and Well-being of Adults found that almost one in five (18 per cent) Australian adults were affected by mental illness. In an attempt to address the costs associated with this, which include lost wages, medical costs and disability claims, emphasis has been placed on a new government initiative. Recent national legislation in Australia has made adjustments to the National Health Service, Medicare, entitling Australians to a maximum of 12 subsidised sessions with a registered psychologist per year, resulting in an average AUS$23 out of pocket payment by the patient. It will be interesting to observe the impact that this facility has on the popularity of coaching, particularly for issues such as stress and relationship issues that might be as easily addressed by a psychologist as by a coach. Furthermore, it is anticipated that the increasing numbers of patients referred to psychologists by family doctors might result in a growing acceptance of mental health treatment and a subsequent reduction in the stigma attached to seeking psychological treatment, and so reduce the use of coaching as pseudo-psychotherapy. Thus, the onus for differentiating services may fall onto the coach, who may find it necessary to identify niche services not available from a psychologist.

The positive outcome may be that coaches will not fall into the trap of treating psychological illnesses or inadvertently providing therapy for coachees who are in need of psychological assistance, as these coachees will be increasingly likely to address their concerns to a GP, who can refer them to an appropriately qualified psychologist.

These changes will not affect the provision of executive coaching services to organizations and this may be the area that coaches will need to increasingly focus on for income. However, as organizations become more astute buyers of coaching and the drive for professionalism from experienced coaches becomes stronger, coaching is likely to evolve into a definitive intervention with boundaries and minimum standards. To achieve this, clear definitions around coaching and similar interventions are required, and failure to achieve this could result in the amalgamation of coaching with a host of other interventions.

To obtain a professional and regulated image and address the issues of regulation, coaching as an industry needs to develop a consensus on best practice. For these reasons, it is increasingly necessary to identify which competencies result in effective coaching outcomes. The development of explicit competencies for coaches allows for easier assessment of coach quality, a progression of coach levels, and development of frameworks for coach progression.

Despite the work of professional bodies and an enhanced understanding of organizations, the private coachee requires greater protection and this is unlikely to be forthcoming without government intervention. In both Australia and the United Kingdom, government legislation has been introduced to ensure that only accredited members of the profession can claim to provide psychological services. This has been achieved by the protection of the term 'psychologist' in the United Kingdom and Australia. Whilst this is by no means foolproof, a similar attempt to define and isolate coaching services with government support in conjunction with a regulatory body might enhance the professionalization of the coaching industry. Without the containment of coaching as a modality, it risks becoming a catch-all intervention without clear specifications, leading to manipulation of its use within corporate consultancies and potentially doing damage to coachees.

SUMMARY

The challenges faced by coaching in Australasia are not dissimilar to those faced in the United Kingdom and Europe and the United States. Coaching requires greater regulation and understanding of the processes currently utilized by practising coaches and increasing consideration of multicultural issues. These issues are especially important to coaches working in global organizations facing integration.

This paper has considered the appropriateness of coaching versus mentoring in some communities, and practices and considerations for coaches working within specific cultures. This paper has reviewed Asian and indigenous communities independently, but it is important to also consider them in the context of the larger Australian or New Zealand community in conjunction with European immigrants to address further complications of multiculturalism.

References

Bluckert, P (2004) The similarities and differences between coaching and therapy, *Industrial and Commercial Training*, **37**(2), pp 91–6

Brendtro, L K, Brokenleg, M and Van Bockern, S (1990) *Reclaiming youth at risk: Our hope for the future*, National Educational Service, Bloomington, IN

Brookes, I and Wright, S (2007) A Survey of Executive Coaching Practices in New Zealand, *International Journal of Evidence Based Coaching and Mentoring*, **5**(1), pp 42–57

Carr, R (2005) *A guide to credentials in coaching: Types, issues, and sources*, Peer Systems Consulting Group Inc, Victoria, BC

Clegg, S, Rhodes, C and Kornberger, M (2003) *An overview of the business coaching industry in Australia* (Working Paper), The Australian Centre for Organisational, Vocational and Adult Learning, Sydney

Connerley, M and Pederson, P (2005) *Leadership in a Diverse and Multicultural Environment: Developing awareness, knowledge and skills*, Sage Publications, London

Dagley (2006) Human resources professionals' perceptions of executive coaching: Efficacy, benefits and return on investment, *International Coaching Psychology Review*, **1**(2), pp 34–45

Ezzamel, M, Lilley, S and Willmott, H (1994) The 'new organization' and the 'new managerial work', *European Management Journal*, **12**(4), pp 454–61

Faraday-Brash, L (2007) Executive Coaching: Coaching, coaxing or counselling, *InPsych*, June

Grant, A M (2001) *Towards a Psychology of Coaching*, University of Sydney, Sydney

Grant, A M and Cavanagh, M (2007) Coaching psychology: How did we get here and where are we going? *In Psych*, June

Grant, A M and O'Hara, B (2006) The self-presentation of commercial Australian life coaching schools: Cause for concern? *International Coaching Psychology Review*, **1**(2), pp 20–32

Green, S (2007) Evidence based life coaching, *In Psych*, June

Hyatt, J (2003) *The Inner Game of Business – Thomas Leonard built a business out of the contradictions in himself*, Fortune Small Business

Kaufman, C and Scoular, A (2004) Toward a positive psychology of executive coaching, in *Positive Psychology in Practice*, eds P A Linley and S Joseph, pp 287–302, Wiley, Hoboken, NJ

Lewis, D, French, E and Phetmany, T (2000) Cross-cultural diversity, leadership and workplace relations in Australia, *Asia Pacific Review*, **7**, pp105–24

McCluskey, K W *et al* (2001) Creative problem solving in the trenches: Interventions with at-risk populations, *The Monograph Series*, Creative Problem Solving Group – Buffalo, Buffalo, NY

McEwan, A (2007) Report from the APS interest group for coaching psychology, *InPsych*, June

Place, D J and McCluskey, A L A (1995) Second chance: A program to support Native inmates at-risk, in *Lost prizes: Talent development and problem solving with at-risk students*, eds K W McCluskey, P A Baker, S C O'Hagan and D J Treffinger, pp 137–46, Center for Creative Learning, Sarasota, FL

Renner, J (2007) Coaching abroad: Insights about assets, *Consulting Psychology Journal: Practice and Research*, **59**, pp 271–85

Spence, G and Grant, A M (2005) Individual and group life coaching: initial findings from a randomised, controlled trial, in *Evidenced-based coaching: Theory, research and practice from the behavioural sciences*, Vol. 1, ed M Cavanagh, A M Grant and T Kemp, pp 143–58, Australian Academic Press, Brisbane

Spence, G, Cavanagh, M and Grant, A (2006) Duty of care in an unregulated industry: Initial findings on the diversity and practices of Australian coaches, *International Coaching Psychology Review*, **1**(1), pp 71–85

Torrance, E P, Goff, K and Satterfield, N B (1998) *Multicultural mentoring of the gifted and talented*, Prufrock Press, Waco, TX

Vale, M *et al* (2003) Coaching patients On Achieving Cardiovascular Health (COACH), *Archives of Internal Medicine*, **16**, pp 2775–83

Vontress, C E (1999) Interview with a traditional African healer, *Journal of Mental Health Counseling*, **21**, 326–36

Vontress, C E (2002) Culture and counseling, in *Online Readings in Psychology and Culture*, eds W J Lonner, D L Dinnel, S A Hayes and D N Sattler, Unit 10, Chapter 1, Center for Cross-Cultural Research, Washington

Further reading

Cavanagh, M (2005) Mental health issues and challenging clients in executive coaching, in *Evidence-based Coaching: Theory, research and practice from the behavioural sciences*, Vol. 1, eds M Cavanagh, A M Grant and T Kemp, pp 21–36, Australian Academic Press, Brisbane

Grant, A M (2003) *Keeping up with the cheese! Research as a foundation for professional coaching*, Paper presented at the First International Coach Federation Research Symposium, November, Denver, US

Kilburg, R R (2000) *Executive Coaching: Developing managerial wisdom in a world of chaos*, American Psychological Association, Washington, DC

Naughton, J (2002) The coaching boom: Is it the long-awaited alternative to the medical model? *The Psychotherapy Networker*, **42**, July / August, pp 1–10

Place, D J *et al* (2000) The second chance project: Creative approaches to developing the talents of at-risk native inmates, *Journal of Creative Behavior*, **34**(3), pp 165–74

Schwartz, S H (1999) A theory of cultural values and some implications for work, *Applied Psychology: An International Review*, **48**(1), pp 23–47

Trompenaars, F and Hampden-Turner, C (1998) *Riding the Waves of Culture: Understanding cultural diversity in global business*, 2nd edn, McGraw-Hill, New York

Part 2

Developing coaching practices

5

Coaching in South Africa

Craig O'Flaherty and Janine Everson

INTRODUCTION

South Africa has a unique, complex and rapidly evolving social, political and economic context that provides both possibilities and challenges to those who choose to live and work there. The purpose of this chapter is to show how an Integral Coaching perspective allows both coach and coachee to build bridges that can transcend the limitations and barriers that potentially exist in coaching due to challenges that are increasingly beyond those of race within a South African context.

We suggest that there are other dimensions to social identity that have equally significant impacts on people's choices and behaviours and that these need to be taken into account. This chapter explores how Integral Coaching transcends the challenges posed in coaching through such varied and complex situations and contexts. The chapter moves to explore various individual and systemic cases that reflect the impact that coaching can have, particularly in tackling issues of diversity.

HERITAGE TRADITIONS – THE FUTURE ISN'T WHAT IT USED TO BE

Social identity – beyond simply race

Recent shifts in South African social dynamics have created a social context that makes dwelling on the past both tiresome and inaccurate. The assumption that people will behave in certain ways based purely on their racial origins is something that has been disputed in worldwide research and is increasingly being challenged in the South African context. Social identity theory is a concept that emerged from social psychology research and was spearheaded by the French psychologist Henri Tajfel (1974). According to Burgess (2002: 4), 'It [identity] is an amalgam composed of the observable characteristics of a person, their values, lifestyle and social attitude.' Extending from this theoretical construct, observable demographic characteristics (eg race) represent only one of the components of social identity – the others being values and personality traits. However, before we look at the implications of the social identity lens as a means of understanding the South African context, a brief overview of South Africa's origins might be helpful to set the scene.

South Africa's history – a snapshot

The modern South Africa is a complex patchwork of racial, language and cultural groupings. That patchwork has threads that are both indigenous – over some 10,000 years – and settled – over some 350 years. South Africa has 11 official languages and a multitude of racial groupings. Extracting some of the threads of history gives some hint to this complexity. The earliest representatives of that diversity – at least the earliest we can name – were the San and Khoekhoe peoples (otherwise known individually as the Bushmen and Hottentots or Khoikhoi; collectively called the Khoisan). Both were resident in the southern tip of the continent for thousands of years before its written history began with the arrival of European seafarers.

Other long-term inhabitants of the area that was to become South Africa were the Bantu-speaking people who had moved into the north-eastern and eastern regions from the north, starting at least many hundreds of years before the arrival of the Europeans. Their existence was of little import to Jan van Riebeeck and the 90 men who landed with him in 1652 at the Cape of Good Hope, under instructions by the Dutch East India Company to build a fort and develop a vegetable garden for the benefit of ships on the Eastern trade route. Later governors encouraged immigration, and in the early 1700s independent farmers called *trekboers* began to push north and east.

Inevitably, the Khoisan started literally losing ground, in addition to being pressed by difficult circumstances into service for the colonists.

The descendants of some of the Khoisan, slaves from elsewhere in Africa and the East, and white colonists formed the basis of the mixed-race group now known as 'coloured'. It is noteworthy that the slaves from the East brought a potent new ingredient to South Africa's racial and cultural mix, in the form of Islam. As the colonists began moving east they encountered the Xhosa-speaking people living in the region that is today's Eastern Cape. A situation of uneasy trading and more or less continuous warfare began to develop. By this time, the second half of the 18th century, the colonists – mainly of Dutch, German and French Huguenot stock – had begun to lose their sense of identification with Europe. The Afrikaner nation was coming into being.

In 1820 some 5000 newly arrived British settlers were placed on the eastern frontier as a supposed defensive buffer against the Xhosa – a strategy that failed when many of them gave up the struggle with unco-operative land and turned to other occupations in Port Elizabeth and Grahamstown.

The early decades of the century had seen another event of huge significance: the rise to power of the great Zulu king Shaka. His wars of conquest and those of Mzilikazi – a general who broke away from Shaka on a northern path of conquest – caused a calamitous disruption of the interior known as the mfecane. Ironically, it was this that denuded much of the area into which Trekkers now moved, enabling them to settle there with a belief that they were occupying vacant territory. But this belief was by no means accompanied by an absence of conflict with the Zulu armies and others.

By the mid-1800s the tiny refreshment post at the Cape of Good Hope had grown into an area of white settlement that stretched over virtually all of what is today South Africa. In some areas the indigenous Bantu-speakers maintained their independence, most notably in the northern Natal territories, which were still unmistakably the kingdom of the Zulu. Almost all were eventually to lose the struggle against white overlordship – British or Boer.

The Indian community were also suffering under viciously racist treatment – in 1891 they had been expelled from the Orange Free State altogether. Mohandas Gandhi, then a young lawyer who had arrived in South Africa in 1892, had become a leading figure in Indian resistance. The struggle against the Indian poll tax in Natal involved a mass strike in which a number of Indians were killed, but achieved success when the tax was removed in 1914 – the year Gandhi, then known as Mahatma, left the country.

The Nationalist Party, however, was gathering strength and, in a surprise result, gained power in the 1948 election – power that it would not relinquish until 1994. Apartheid became official government ideology. The 1950s were to bring increasingly repressive laws against black South Africans and its obvious corollary – increasing resistance.

The Group Areas Act, rigidifying the racial division of land, and the Population Registration Act, which classified all citizens by race, were passed in 1950. The Pass Laws, restricting black movement, came in 1952. The Separate Amenities Act of 1953 introduced 'petty apartheid' segregation, for example, on buses and in post offices (Southafrica.info, 2007).

THE INFLUENCE OF TRADITIONS ON BEHAVIOUR, SELF-PERCEPTION AND RELATIONSHIPS

Burgess (2002) has highlighted the emergence of the term 'tribes' to describe not ethnicity or culture, but rather a typology of 16 South African groups. He relates this to their consumer and political behaviour.

Burgess's research used in-home interviews with a nationally representative sample and focused on social identity characteristics, including value priorities, personality traits and demographic characteristics such as race, gender, standard of living, participation in the financial sector and type of dwelling. He used cluster analysis to separate respondents into 16 groups based on their social identity characteristics. The groups, which have been called tribes, were then related to brand choice, product category participation, political party choice, and social attitudes. The results show that social identity is highly predictive of all of these phenomena, revealing an ability to predict brand choice with 85–95 per cent accuracy in the product categories tested. Business and government decision makers can take note that instead of using ethnicity or culture, social identity is a far more useful way to think about how individual differences influence the types of human behaviour that interest them.

Although emphasizing the importance of social identity, Burgess concedes that the racial component of this social construct is emphasized and retains an exaggerated influence due to the influence of apartheid. 'An artificial sense of racial identity, reinforced by this pernicious legacy of unequal employment, is Apartheid's most spoilt fruit. Ignoring racial identity can have very negative and unintended consequences, among which is the accentuation of perceived differences as individuals "defend" their perceived identity'. The point of this work is to stress that we need to look beyond the obvious but limited distinction of race as a way of understanding the differences between people from different population groups. It also suggests, however, that there are many characteristics, perspectives and values that people across racial groups are likely to share. Burgess is emphatic on this point. 'Although racial identity has influence, there is no evidence to suggest that it is a pre-potent influence on behaviour. In fact there is much evidence to suggest racial identity is a very weak influence on behaviour in most situations, even in a country where it is artificially exaggerated by one of the most powerful social engineering and propaganda campaigns in human history (Apartheid).'

So, having moderated the focus away from purely race as a predictor of differences in the social context of South Africa and suggested the possibility of social identity as a greater determinant and predictor of behaviour, what are the likely effects of differences in social identity between various groupings in South Africa?

IMPACTS OF SOCIAL IDENTITY

What are the likely impacts of social identity – particularly from a coaching point of view?

As Burgess (2002) noted, social identity serves a function in how people see themselves in the world – an image of who they are and who they want to be. It also affects the internal conversations people have with themselves and the conflicts that need to be resolved through internal dialogue and negotiation.

From a coaching perspective, many of the issues that arise in coaching are triggered by how people perceive who they are in their role as a member of a relevant and valid social group or category. Coaching topics relating to staying in an organization, profession or roles come to mind here. Other issues arising in coaching relate to the role a person decides to play in a particular social grouping, for example, a family or team.

There are a range of implications that extend from how people see themselves. These include the challenges people have and the efforts they put into trying to create and sustain a *positive social identity* for themselves or the groups they are part of, as well as the challenges around *social mobility* as people attempt to shift their identity between various social groupings.

Social conflict has three key causes. Firstly, social conflict arises when people actively challenge the desirability of groups and set out to overturn an existing or imposed order. A second factor giving rise to social conflict is the relationships between groups. When social identity is triggered, inter-group behaviour results. This is usually in the form of biased treatment of in-groups and out-groups. This 'us and them' situation is where issues such as discrimination and favouritism can emerge. These are issues that can show up often in a coaching context – particularly in a country like South Africa. A third factor is the behavioural differences between individuals.

The research shows (Tajfel, 1974) that actual or perceived group identity leads to different behaviours. From a coaching perspective, it's important for the coach to begin understanding what the perceived or desired group identity of their coachee is and how this impacts on the choices they make and the places that they may get stuck in or diverted by. This can give important guidelines for how the coaching dialogue needs to unfold.

COACHING APPROPRIATELY IN A CULTURALLY DIVERSE CONTEXT – A STARTING POINT

Coaching in a culturally diverse context like South Africa is not without its challenges and is a process that needs to unfold with awareness, openness, a commitment to challenging assumptions and flexibility from both coach and coachee when coaching across social identity boundaries.

At the core of the theory is an assertion that our social identity functions as a perceptual lens that causes us to categorize what we see into schemas that we make interpretations about. Categorization helps us to learn and choose ways to respond to others, providing us with various mental shortcuts. It improves our ability to recall from our memory and saves cognitive resources, allowing us to perform better, particularly when we are stretching ourselves, such as when we are performing multiple tasks. It assists us in fulfilling our need for meaning and coherence in life by providing a platform for shared comparisons.

The advantage of considering people in a complex society such as South Africa as having compound and intricate social identities is that it offers powerful possibilities in working with them as coaches rather than simplifying their membership into racial identity groups. The benefit of social identity theory comes from the fact that people are aware of and act from multiple identities and that these identities act as an integrating and predictable influence on their choices and behaviour. Moreover, responses to various social and situational cues often happen without conscious thought, allowing the selection of an appropriate identity from amongst many – mother, daughter, wife, sister, sports fan, violinist, friend, colleague.

When we translate Tajfel's thinking into how this might play itself out in reality, we begin to understand that how people respond to different situations, issues and people is a product of their social identity. We also see that people's social identity in turn is informed by their values, personality traits and categorical attributes, eg race, gender, age. The way we see the situations we encounter, the assumptions and the evaluations we make, and ultimately the choices and actions that result are thus filtered through this personal, social and relational identity and are encouraged and reinforced by it.

CHOOSING A COACHING MODEL

Choosing a skilful way of responding as a coach in the context described above requires identifying a coaching philosophy and model with the capacity to absorb and integrate these considerations, as well as having the flexibility to grow and change with our experience and ongoing learning.

One way of responding to this is through use of a model to guide the coach. The Integral Coaching model offers such a suitable framework, which we use in our practice (Flaherty, 1999). In selecting this framework we were looking for a model with an underlying philosophy that allowed for the capacity to absorb the nuances and continua of meaning that a social identity lens would require, as well as being able to allow the coach to interact meaningfully in the 'digest of selves' that they were likely to experience, without necessarily being familiar with or having these selves as part of their own social identity. The Integral Coaching model's greatest contribution to powerful coaching is the strong focus on understanding the underlying assumptions prevailing in the person's way of seeing the world and being able to trace how these might be driving the person to a particular action, or precluding them from others – because they might not be aware of them.

We've chosen three cases to highlight the three impacts that social identity can have and how coaching addressed these.

CASE STUDY – ANDILE: HOW PEOPLE SEE THEMSELVES

Background
Andile is a black executive in one of South Africa's financial services organizations. He was appointed to head up the business development team for a key division in the organization. After six months in the role it was decided to provide him with an executive coach to help navigate a difficult set of circumstances that had arisen.

Problem statement
Andile had begun to come up against the consequences resulting from Employment Equity[1] legislation. He had begun to feel that his team did not respect him and that he was perceived by them as a 'token placement' put in place only to satisfy the legislative requirements. This had caused him to lose his confidence and feel that he was not able to lead with authority and purpose.

Coach's approach

Having spent time building a relationship with Andile, the coach began to approach the issue of his confidence directly. The first line of enquiry that the coach explored was the basis on which Andile was making this assessment. Andile's response was to point out that he had noticed several things. One was that the organization had recently conducted a strong advertising campaign proclaiming their success in meeting Employment Equity targets. Nobody had mentioned or discussed this with him, leaving him feeling unsure of the context and thinking behind this comparison. Another aspect that was causing Andile discomfort was that the members of his executive team had recently started to go extremely quiet in meetings and he was having difficulty making progress on issues. Finally, he revealed that he had recently had discussions with peer executives in other organizations who were experiencing similar problems.

The coach spent some time with Andile trying to gain a sense of the facts that Andile was basing his assessment on and began to consider the possibility that Andile was making some powerful assumptions based on his sense of identity rather than on a factual base. The coach and Andile designed three exercises to verify what was happening. Firstly, the coach conducted a 360-degree survey consisting of interviews to probe how people saw Andile as a leader, what they valued and how they thought he could improve. Secondly, the coach sat in on a series of management meetings to observe the dynamics directly. After a couple of these, the coach quickly disappeared into the background as he became part of the scenery. Finally, the coach suggested that Andile do a series of one-on-one interviews with his management team to find out from them how they were feeling about his first six months on board.

The results of these three exercises were resoundingly similar and confirmatory. The leadership team was delighted to have a new leader on board because their previous experience of an autocratic leader, who was white, was deeply unsatisfying. Overall, the team felt that Andile had started positively, but had seemed to 'retreat into himself in the last two months'. They were not sure why. When the management team members were invited to express what they wanted from Andile, the very clear response was that they were looking to Andile to provide strong guidance and direction – matched with flexibility and responsiveness.

With the coach's help Andile was able to see how the 'filters' that his social identity had placed around him were causing him to misinterpret how his team felt and to assume that they would be prejudiced towards him. They instead were excited by the new possibilities that his leadership held but a little confused by his reticence. Andile was able to start working on a series of self-observations to help him notice when he started seeing actions and words in the wrong way and a series of practices that could help him to fashion a new identity for himself as a legitimately placed and authentic leader, rather than being a token.

CASE STUDY – RELATIONSHIPS BETWEEN GROUPS

Background

The next case relates to a leadership team of an organization in the FMCG industry. The team was newly formed under a recently appointed Chief Executive. It consisted of a variety of different executives from different backgrounds: white executives, who had traditionally held positions of power under the old dispensation in South Africa, coloured[2] executives, who had experienced rapid career development in South Africa's new dispensation, and black executives, who had experienced even more radical advancement.

Problem statement

The team had started off well in terms of fashioning its strategic intent and objectives. Recently, however, the early momentum had wavered as the team became divided on issues and started to become fragmented and act in anything but a cohesive manner. The coach was given the mandate to restore unity to the team.

Coach's approach

Instead of embarking on a typical team-building approach – where issues often get discussed and raised in a catalytic way and where progress seems to be made in a pressure cooker environment, but fades very soon afterwards – the coach tried something radically different. She decided to use a 'slow-burn' approach where relationships would be built over a longer period of time and people allowed to navigate the issues of trust and disagreement more genuinely.

She decided to use 'Coaching Circles' – an approach developed by Brassard (2002). Coaching Circles were set up and prepared for by putting the executives through a three-day training process on Coaching Circles in which they were invited to give each other honest feedback on how the team was doing as well as share with each other how each of them was doing. Once this was complete, training was given in the basics of how to conduct coaching conversations and how to listen, question and respond in ways other than managing or problem solving. Finally the executives were grouped into a Coaching Circle where each person was responsible for bringing an issue to the circle and the group was tasked with coaching each person through their issue, assisted by the coach, who would intervene to keep the discussion value-adding for the person and a true coaching dialogue.

After the three days, the group met every six weeks for a full day to repeat the Coaching Circle process, where each member would report back on progress made since the last session and request coaching on the developments relating to the issue.

The strategy adopted by the coach was threefold: firstly, to start breaking down the differences between groups by showing them how in many cases the issues they brought were similar. Secondly, to start having them feel a shared sense of commitment towards helping each other progress through their challenges and, finally, to introduce a common language – the language of coaching, that could help to bridge the social identity differences between the various groups.

CASE STUDY – LEBO AND DHESAN: BEHAVIOURAL DIFFERENCES

Background
Lebo (black) and Dhesan (Indian) were two partners in a professional services firm, both responsible for leading teams on client work. Both had ascended to the partnership at a similar time and the senior partners in the organization believed that they could both benefit from having an executive coach to work with them.

Problem statement
The partnership of the organization believed that both Lebo and Dhesan were on a fast-track and wanted the coaching to support this. They felt, however, that they were markedly different, particularly in their handling of teams. Lebo was seen as considered and thorough. He was widely consultative within his team and was not above holding long meetings to resolve issues. He would use the traditional name for such meetings – an imbizo – a meeting of chief and villagers to discuss the future of the village. His team respected him deeply and were extremely loyal. The senior partners were wondering about the possibility of Lebo accelerating and amplifying his style of leadership.

Dhesan, on the other hand, was extremely fast-moving in terms of decision-making. He would often make decisions on the run and it wasn't unusual for him to be seen in the corridors of the office with a trail of team members behind him trying to take instructions and rushing off to execute them. The senior partners felt that Dhesan could benefit from becoming more thoughtful and reflective and that this might help him to make better decisions.

Coach's approach
After a few sessions, the coaches, with the permission of the coachees, got together to compare notes. It was clear that their two coachees approached

their common role in very different ways. Each was effective, but could benefit from rounding out their approaches. The coaches decided on a unique approach. They decided that the best way they could demonstrate to each coachee what might complement their current way of working was to let each spend a day shadowing the other and simply watching and observing what they did. They then designed a self-observation exercise for each where they observed their own way of being for a period of a few weeks. Also, they suggested they get some feedback from team members, peers and clients as to what they could do to improve. Over time they began to get insights as to the shifts they could make and often conferred with each other as to progress made. While each retained their core way of behaving, they began to experiment with new and different approaches and became regularly referred to as examples of successful coaching in the organization.

The coach's strategy here was to encourage the coachees to observe and become aware of their own way of interacting. Once they were more self-aware, they were asked to compare their chosen way of interacting with another behavioural model, in order to see what other possibilities might exist. Over and above the insights they gleaned from this exercise, they were encouraged to use feedback to decide what changes they could make. Finally, ongoing support for each coachee emerged through their newly-acquired habit of conferring with each other on their leadership style and choices.

SUMMARY

This chapter has sought to explore the reasons for coaching having had such a positive impact in a country as complex and diverse as South Africa. The theoretically grounded and well-researched concept of social identity has been discussed in order to contextualize a shift away from what some might feel ought to be an intense focus on race and the South African racially divided past. Social identity theory shows that race is an element of this symbolic, interactive dance that we all engage in; however, it is simply one of the many cues and clues that people refer to in deciding how to interact with one another.

The chapter then focused on exploring a type of coaching called Integral Coaching that can be shown to allow for engagement even at the deepest levels with issues of social identity or structure of interpretation. Equally importantly, this type of coaching allows for the development of the various physically embodied competencies a coachee would require in order to be able to engage with the world in a fundamentally different way. This in turn opens the gateway to experiencing greater fulfilment and meaning in life.

References

Brassard, C (2002) *Action Learning Groups – A guide for practitioners*, self-published booklet, Impact Coaching, Ottawa, Canada

Burgess, S M (2002) *SA Tribes – Who we are, how we live, what we want from life*, David Phillip, Cape Town

Flaherty, J (1999) *Coaching: Evoking excellence in others*, Elsevier Butterworth-Heinemann, Boston

SouthAfrica.info (2007), all-in-one official guide and web portal to South Africa [online] www.southafrica.info

Tajfel, H (1974) Social identity and intergroup behaviour, *Social Science Information*, **13**(2), pp 65–93

Further reading

Everson, J M C *et al* (2006) Inspired moments – Possibilities beyond management through integral coaching, *Acta Commercii*, **6**(6), pp 75–86

Hogg, M and Abrams, D (1988) *Social Identifications*, Routledge, London

O'Flaherty, C M B and Everson, J M C (2007) *Embedding a Coaching Culture – A research survey into the impact of One Leader*, unpublished report, Centre for Coaching, Cape Town, South Africa

Tajfel, H (1984) *The Social Dimension: European studies in social psychology 1*, Cambridge University Press, Cambridge

NOTES

[1] A policy implemented in South Africa to increase and balance the proportion of people from previously disadvantaged backgrounds in organizations. Targets and timelines for companies of various sizes have been set.

[2] The term 'coloured' in South Africa is an official term and strongly owned by the people it refers to – namely descendants of the interaction between white settlers and indigenous peoples.

6

Coaching in Brazil

Silvio Celestino and Ingrid Faro

INTRODUCTION

In which country can you find the following palaces: Alvorada, Plateau, Justice and Buritis? Not in a present-day monarchy, but in a republic – Brazil. From the president's official residence, to the highest court of justice, the word 'palace' appears frequently in Brazilian life. In the corporate world, organization charts too reflect this attraction towards the monarchical structure. Brazilian business leaders often expect to be experts in leadership, without receiving the feedback that many other cultures see as useful and valuable in the developmental process. The disruption that this monarchical culture causes to the operations of Brazilian companies, and the ability of coaching to transform it, are the focus for this chapter.

HERITAGE TRADITIONS

In a play, the actors can only move within the limits of the scenery. However, simply moving between objects on stage is not enough. The actor also needs to know how to interact with the props to get across the full effect. In the same way, within organizations managers need to know not only how to be the boss, but also how to make full use of the resources available to them. Changes in current technology mean that a formidable amount of information is now available to senior managers, which could be used to enable them to have an overview of the business and to steer its direction. Brazilian businesses experience backlogs, postponements and, in some cases, disastrous delays as problems are not identified and shared with the key people within the organization.

To understand this cultural phenomenon, we should travel back through history to 1808, and more specifically to the events that brought the Portuguese royal family to Brazil, causing a major transformation to what had originally been Portugal's largest and richest colony. In that year Napoleon Bonaparte invaded Portugal, and the Prince Regent of Portugal, João, fled to Rio de Janeiro, taking with him both his court and the whole government bureaucracy – around 15,000 people, including employees and family. They also brought documents of state, the Royal Library and the public treasury (Wilcken, 2004).

João, who later became Don João VI after Napoleon's defeat, did not return to Portugal immediately; he raised Brazil to the position of a kingdom united with Portugal and remained in Brazil until the Court demanded he return to Lisbon. Don João left his son, Pedro, as Prince Regent, and he, in 1822, declared Brazil to be independent and crowned himself Don Pedro I (Rodrigues, 1975).

Unlike the situation in Spanish-speaking Latin America, where there were universities that trained local professionals, Brazil had no such institutions. From the beginning, the new country depended on men educated at Coimbra University in Portugal to carry out state and judicial functions. It therefore relied on employees and bureaucrats who held firm central authority in high esteem (Carvalho, 1982). Along with the national elite, lawyers and judges were also educated in Roman law, and shared a belief in the virtues of centralized power (Burns, 1968). This idea of a strong, centralized State did not arise just from a coercive structure (Faoro, 1975), but also from an intellectual and moral outlook that permeated professions during the formative years of the nation, an outlook that is still found today within organizations.

If in the beginning there was an implicit gain from this vision of a centralized State, in commercial businesses the demands of competition and the need for constant rapid evolution have turned it into an anachronistic and inadequate model (Anderson and O'Gorman, 1991), which is not suited to Brazil's emerging status (Goldman Sachs, 2007).

Implicit within this are deep-seated Brazilian ideas about society and above all about the preservation of relationships. In this mindset, lower hierarchical levels were expected to be capable not only of carrying out their roles but of doing so in a harmonious way, preserving relationships with their peers and, principally, not disturbing the highest levels. In the Court, a messenger who brought bad news ran the risk of being blamed by the king. Within companies, this has encouraged a commonly found culture of hiding away bad news rather than sharing it openly with a focus on resolving the issue, as employees fear being blamed for the problem.

The experience of many executive coaches is that the more senior the executive, the more likely they are to be a contributing factor to the organization's problems. Their style is often contributing to a culture of keeping bad news secret. Just like a monarch, this senior executive's main interest is not in developing themselves as a leader but in fixing problems in the team, which is where they perceive all problems to start. As a result, the Brazilian coach may often begin the relationship by investigating whether the executive is a suitable candidate for coaching. Is he or she capable of carrying out the tasks, assuming responsibility for the results, creating actions that lead in the same direction, and receiving and taking action on feedback from the coach?

For executives at board level, such as vice-presidents, directors and senior managers, the relationship in the coaching process should be clearly differentiated from other relationships. One of the main focuses of an executive at that level is organizational improvement, and it is worth noting that this will be treated as an extension of their abilities. At this level, in some organizations, the coaching process is seen as a recovery programme for under-performing executives. In these cases, the relationship from the outset should value the achievements of the executive, and the process should be presented to them as an opportunity to polish their competences, because their abilities are clearly valuable since they have brought them this far in their career (Hudson, 1999).

For middle managers, general managers, divisional managers and department managers, the relationship is more often supportive. It provides opportunities to explore the nature of leadership and how leadership operates in cultures outside Brazil. At this level, executives are generally successful in their careers, but have not had the opportunity to learn leadership competences, particularly those related to people management.

Across the organization, the relationship should be reflexive. MVE (mirroring, validation and empathy) techniques can be useful in encouraging senior managers to recognize their own contributions to organizational problems. Brazilian professionals can sometimes seem paradoxical. They will not commit to the purposes of the organization; they have a tendency to avoid stating their dissatisfaction with an event or person. Within the coaching process, their concern is often about passing responsibility to others and avoiding critically reviewing their own performance.

The coach needs to challenge these behaviours while maintaining strong personal relationships, which is critical for business in general within South American cultures.

THE INFLUENCE OF TRADITIONS ON BEHAVIOUR, SELF-PERCEPTION AND RELATIONSHIPS

These traditions of a monarchic organization are reflected today in the following patterns of behaviour, self-perception and relationships.

It is very common for senior executives to consider that their time is more important than the time of all the other people in the organization. Due to this, interrupting their subordinates in meetings or even in external or private situations it is seen by them as natural behaviour in their position: everyone else should give them immediate attention. This view is closely associated with their success, especially financial. The logic is, if I am in this position and making so much money, I must be right. They tend to have a vision that is tightly focused on control and on financial results. In some cases, they ignore rules if this will help them achieve results. They have great difficulty in expressing the assumptions behind their statements and in explaining how they reached decisions. Often decisions arise from intuition, sense of opportunity, and personal networks. Their relationship with their subordinates is there to meet their needs. At times, personal needs are put before customers, which can lead to poor service and poor business decisions. In family companies, this type of behaviour increases and in some cases generates a highly negative organizational climate due to an excess of rules, idiosyncrasies, emotional behaviour and work overload among their subordinates.

At the closest level to the main executive, which mostly consists of vice-presidents, directors and in some cases senior managers, standard behaviour is intense defence of the position achieved. Initiatives are rare and carefully implemented. It is common for them to think that they are at the summit of their career and therefore that their main objective, rather than taking the last step up to the highest level, it to protect their achievements. The relationship with the president is careful and governed by rapidly supplying him with what he requests, while making sure not to reveal details that may lead to unpleasantness. At this level, it is common for careful behaviour to be exaggerated, so that problems are only presented when the solution is to hit the road. They understand, above all, that it is better not to mention problems to the top level and in some cases not to the team, either. Their relationships with their peers are usually cautious, but when necessary they mark out their territory in tough discussions. They make heavy demands on their teams, and they tolerate little or no feedback. They generally provide little space for feedback to be provided, and in the rare organizations where it is provided it tends to be formal, distorted and lacking in depth or evidence. Frequently, there is no careful monitoring of improvements in performance from one year to the next. Their self-perception is that they have been successful due to their qualities, which are frequently concealed behind highly politic behaviour.

At the second leadership level, formed by general managers and division or department heads, the tradition of the company being seen as a monarchical structure causes constraints. Brazil does not train its managers well enough to meet its needs, and it is therefore common for these executives to have a team that is lacking in the number of people able to perform their roles effectively (Rodriguez, 2008). It is not unusual for senior managers to act as though they are responsible for the whole company's overall success or failure. They often have great vision of the scope of their activities and principally of the consequences of failing to carry them out. At times, they hide weaknesses in their team, as they believe that will be seen as a problem related to their personal leadership. First-line managers in Brazil are often highly focused on short-term results. Their aim is for swift recognition. Many have a self-belief that is far greater than their actual contribution to the organization. They move quickly from area to area, and so cannot present comparable year-on-year results. In general, they place high demands on their team, and are mainly concerned about their meetings with higher levels of management. They believe that their knowledge and principally their intelligence are their main differentiators. They have a critical vision of the top levels, and can sometimes end up in problematic situations by failing to recognize the internal political sensitivities of an issue. For instance, when dealing with their peers and in some cases even with senior levels, they observe time limits and rules with excessive rigidity. To move ahead in their career they often need to improve their relationship skills and emotional control.

Our experience of female managers is that they are often better trained than their male counterparts at the same level are. However, they often lack self-confidence, so can restrict themselves to more junior roles or hold back from applying for promotion opportunities. They have a high ability to integrate, and difficulty in managing their emotions. In many companies, they are the only woman on the board, and in some cases the first one to hold such a position. They are pragmatic and extremely committed to their roles and to the company. They have a holistic vision of success that encompasses the personal, mental and spiritual spheres alongside the professional and financial – the last two being considered the most important to male success. They are often excellent in relationships focused on the aims of the company, the department and the task, but they struggle with the political issues of the company. This is especially true of the youngest executives or those most recently promoted to leadership positions. They are not usually the most effective when dealing with paradoxes, which are understood here to be events or actions that are contrary to the aims of the organization, such as political situations within the company or with external bodies such as the government and unions.

At all levels, it can be seen that the leaders feel a great deal of pressure from their responsibilities. They work extremely long hours. Research into the lives of 678 Brazilian managers showed that 38 per cent were afraid to go on holiday. The main reason for this concern was that important company decisions would be made in their absence, or changes to their role while they were away. This means that many do not take holidays and instead prefer to stay at work. Such a culture of long working hours and reduced holidays is likely to be detrimental to both health and performance.

Their physical presence and dedication to the company are seen as signs of loyalty, even if in certain situations technology can give appropriate options for communication and decision-making at a distance. Once again, the situation is more critical in family businesses. In some cases, they have a low and inadequate take-up of technology, but a high level of bureaucracy, filled with controls and impositions that generate a lot of work, but do not contribute to the end result of the company.

DEVELOPING CULTURALLY APPROPRIATE COACHING

The main implication of these cultural characteristics is that the communication among the professionals is not clear. The most common and relevant focus in the coaching process is to offer the clients an effective communication tool to be used by them day by day, which can address some of these common cultural features.

Of particular help is getting managers to focus on following five themes: Purpose, Objectives, Scenarios, Options and Criteria. This method can be also be used by the manager in their dealings with employees and with customers.

The first theme to explore in any discussion is the purpose. In the coaching session, the aim is to help the manager to state explicitly the purpose of the company. It aims to explain the reason for the existence of the company or the department. The purpose should be broken down into a series of successive objectives to be reached.

The Latin culture does value emotions. The coach needs to help the manager to talk about their emotions, but also about their actions, and about how these are connected. The use of the method 5W2H – what, where, when, who, why, how much and how (Ishikawa, 1990) – or SMART (Specific, Measurable, Achievable, Relevant and Time-bound) goals (Drucker, 1954) is helpful, as are cognitive–behavioural-based approaches.

Once a clear purpose and objectives have been established, the next stage of the process is to help the coachee to consider the options and to help them evaluate these. In a typical coaching session this may involve discussion about people, structures, investment and timing. By being open, the manager reduces the risk of encountering problems with employees about what is required. Further, by encouraging the manager to reflect on their emotions and behaviour, the manager can become more self-aware and thus recognize their contributions to successes and failures, as well as recognizing the value of others.

Another situation that causes problems within organizations is the communication style of the senior manager, specifically in giving good quality feedback. This is the task that many executives try to avoid. This is partly due to the fear of the embarrassment that it can provoke, but mostly because the executive does not recognize when their employees have done a good job, and instead believes this is due to their own contribution. The coach needs to work with the executive to help them recognize the contribution of others, and be willing to be specific in both identifying individuals and what they have done that has helped achieve a successful outcome.

CASE STUDY: GABRIEL

Gabriel is a manager in a medium-sized import-export business. He took up a new job and during the first year made savings of US$1.2 million. However, to deliver this he took dramatic steps, cutting staff and parts of the operation. The result was that staff became very unhappy, and a coach was invited in by more senior managers to help him address his way of working.

The coach and Gabriel spent time talking about the importance of securing staff commitment, of listening to staff, and of providing feedback, both positive and developmental. Over the course of the year, Gabriel began to change his communication style. He paid more attention to other people's contribution, rewarded his good staff with praise, and involved them in looking for further savings.

By the end of the second year, the team had identified a further US$1.7 million of savings, granting the executive the recognition as the best manager of the year in the company.

SUMMARY

Brazilian culture significantly affects the way managers in Brazilian business act and think. If the Brazilian coach ignores these factors, the coach has only half the canvas with which to work.

With the continued growth in the Brazilian economy and its growing involvement in global markets, coaching will become an established and common tool. Its potential for working one to one is great, allowing senior executives to receive the personal feedback and development they need, but in a way that does not threaten their perceived status or power.

References

Anderson, B and O'Gorman, R (1991) *Imagined Communities: Reflections on the origins and spread of nationalism*, 2nd edn, p 61 Verso, London

Burns, E B (1968) *Nationalism in Brazil: A Historical Survey*, Praeger, New York

Carvalho, J M de (1982) Political elites and state building: The case of nineteenth-century Brazil, *Comparative Studies in Society and History*, **24**, pp 378–99

Drucker, P (1954) *The Practice of Management*, Collins, London

Faoro, R (1975) *Os donos do poder: Formação do patronado político brasileiro*, 2nd edn, Editora da Universidade de São Paulo, SP

Goldman Sachs (2007) [accessed 24 April 2008] *Brick and beyond*, Goldman Sachs, London [online] http://www2.goldmansachs.com/ideas/brics/BRICs-and-Beyond.html

Hudson, F (1999) *Handbook of Coaching*, Jossey-Bass, New York

Ishikawa, K (1990) *Introduction to Quality Control*, Productivity Press, New York

Rodrigues, J H (1975) *Independência: Revolução e contra-revolução*, Francisco Alves, Rio de Janeiro

Rodriguez, A (2008) *Knowledge and Innovation for Competitiveness*, World Bank Publications, New York

Further reading

Araujo, A (2006) *Coach: um parceiro para seu sucesso*, 10th edn, Gente, Sao Paulo

Celestino, S (2007) *Conversa de Elevador: uma fórmula de sucesso para sua carreira*, Sedna, São Paulo

Celestino, S (2008) *Coaching, lideranca e desenvolvimento de executivos*, [online] http://www.enlevo.com.br/

Covey, S (2004) *The 7 Habits of Highly Effective People*, Free Press, New York

Diniz, A (2006) *Lider do Futuro: A transformacao de lider coach*, Crescimentun, Sao Paulo

Di Stéfano, R (2000) *Manual do Sucesso Total*, Elevação, São Paulo

Di Stéfano, R (2006) *O Líder-Coach: líderes criando Líderes*, Qualitymark, Rio de Janeiro

Garfield, C (1989) *Peak Performer*, Harper Paperbacks, New York

Graham, R (2001) Constructing a nation in nineteenth-century Brazil: Old and new views on class, culture, and the state, *The Journal of the Historical Society*, **1**(2–3), pp 17–56

International Stress Management Association (2008) *Research Paper: Brazilian professionals and vacations* [online] http://www.ismabrasil.com.br/

Wilcken, P (2004) *Empire Adrift: the Portuguese court in Rio de Janeiro, 1808–1821.* Bloomsbury, London

Useful websites

ABRACEM (2008) *Brazilian Association of Executive and Business Coaching*, http://www.abracem.org.br/English

ICC (2008*) International Coaching Community*, http://www.internationalcoaching-community.com

ICF (2008) International Coach Federation in Brazil, http://icfbrasil-sp.org/icfsp/

ICI (2008) *Integrated Coaching Institute.* http://www.coachingintegrado.com.br

Lambent do Brasil (2008) *South America Coaching Training and Consultancy Network*, http://www.lambent.com

7

Coaching in China

Catherine Ng

INTRODUCTION

As we enter the 21st century, China is emerging as one of the most important economic powerhouses in the world. Since 1978, when Deng Xiao Peng announced the open door policy, China has experienced tremendous economic growth at a furious pace. China represents staggering potential business opportunities for coaching companies and coaches, with its enormous population and expanding economy. Developing and implementing a successful business strategy for this Chinese market requires an accurate, pragmatic understanding of both the risks and rewards.

Part one of this chapter will review some of the differences that have an influence on corporate management. Part two will give an analysis of the specific issues affecting current corporate management in terms of Chinese traditional culture and historical background. The third part will briefly summarize the values of coaching for corporate management in China and will discuss the matching points between Confucian ethics, the core of Chinese traditional culture, and coaching. Finally, we will demonstrate, with two coaching examples, how Confucianism-based coaching has helped Chinese enterprises improve their management despite cultural differences.

HERITAGE TRADITIONS

There are many cultural differences between China and Western countries. Such differences will not be listed one by one in this chapter. Instead we will focus only on those cultural characteristics and concepts that affect corporate management.

Firstly, the traditional Chinese view of value puts society and groups higher than individuals, forming a strong link between personal value and family or country. The teachings of Confucius contain some descriptions of this, such as 'personal cultivating, family regulating, state governing, and kingdom tranquility and happiness' (修身齐家治国平天下) (Zhu, 2004: 6). The traditional culture asks Chinese people to make contributions to society as a whole, paying little attention to personal rights and interests. Personal improvement is for the purpose of serving family and the country. This is in strong contrast to the individual-based Western culture that highly values personal rights, giving consideration to group and public interests only after satisfying personal interests.

Secondly, according to Chinese traditional social morphology, family members commonly share the same house; as a result the interests of family members are closely related. Therefore, the whole society has strong family concepts, characterized by the belief that family members are more trustworthy than others, and that family members are responsible for helping each other and making their family flourish. In Western society, family members tend to be more independent of each other, with weaker family ties, thus encouraging a greater focus on personal interest than on family glory.

The third difference is Confucian ethics. These were accepted as the official doctrine in ancient China, meaning Confucianism, which is mainly about state-governing methods, became the main thought and ethics system in society. The rational scientific method that has dominated Western development has been seen as a valueless technique.

Fourthly, in traditional Chinese society, people's hierarchy and order was considered of considerable importance, and their nobleness or humbleness was classified according to their sex, age and job. Strict official systems were built up. This contrasts with Western development, where human rights and equity have served as the basis of social culture, developing from the Judeo-Christian tradition.

Finally, Chinese traditional culture highlights interpersonal harmony, with the solidarity and peace of society and family foremost. Close attention is paid to self-effacement instead of competition between individuals. And being decent and polite is highly praised, forming a strong 'face' concept and a gentle and tactful communication manner. In contrast, Western culture tends to highlight interpersonal competition and think highly of aggressive individual performance, worrying little about conflicts and communicating in a direct and simple manner.

Compared with modern Western management philosophy, Chinese traditional concepts show some shortcomings that have negative effects on corporate management. Nevertheless, the long-standing Chinese traditional culture is broad and deep, and has many concepts that match with the most advanced management theories, and that can be used in management by Chinese enterprises.

THE INFLUENCE OF TRADITIONS ON BEHAVIOUR, SELF-PERCEPTION AND RELATIONSHIPS

Traditional culture has some adverse effects on modern corporate management in China. Chinese enterprises only began to develop after the Cultural Revolution some 30 to 40 years ago. During this short time, due to a unique traditional culture, corporate management in China has encountered some problems.

1. Bureaucracy concept

In China the general view has been: 'Officials valued, but commerce ignored' (重仕轻商); China has been an agriculture-based country since ancient times. All dynasties in Chinese history followed an economic policy that stressed agriculture while restraining commerce. Rich merchants were less respected than peasants in society. The group enjoying the highest social status were the officials, who controlled abundant social resources and public power, and who could easily influence other social groups.

The concept of valuing officialdom and ignoring commerce meant that Chinese people in ancient society were not proud of being in business. Those who could afford education always strived for a governmental position to become an official. Under such social concepts, a large number of outstanding talents 'flowed' into government to facilitate the development of bureaucratic systems and culture. Officials became examples for other social groups. By contrast, traditional businessmen mainly came from family members and lower-class people who had no opportunity to obtain an official position. The indifference to commerce and lack of talent attracted to the area resulted in commerce failing to move forward with the pace of other economies. In contrast, China excelled at developing government practices, which are still visible in the following ways in modern Chinese enterprises up to the present.

Firstly, in Chinese enterprises people pay particular attention to interpersonal relationships. Employees regard superiors as those who determine their career development, and hope to build up friendly private 'relations' with them. Generally, they don't offend their peers to avoid superiors' opinions being against them due to negative comments from these peers. The business between Chinese enterprises also highlights the concept of 'relations'. Businessmen always think friends and acquaintances are more trustworthy, instead of specifying strict requirements about the professionalism of their partners.

Secondly, leaders and employees are unequal in status. Influenced by traditional concepts of hierarchy, leaders are likely to look on their management position as 'official', and often develop a kind of superiority complex over their subordinates, making them fail to genuinely respect their employees. Employees highly respect their superiors while keeping distant from them. They are likely to put the leaders and themselves into the roles of 'official and civilian' or 'management and obedience'. They often choose to be a follower instead of showing their own opinions confidently when facing their superiors, and this makes for a wide credibility gap and a communication obstacle between leaders and employees.

2. Family concept

Family is the basic unit that forms Chinese society. The concept of family plays a core role in the Chinese traditional culture, which has a far-reaching influence on the development of traditional commerce in China. As commercial activity was viewed as of secondary importance, businesses recruited new staff from among their wider family. These practices led to a less competitive commercial sector, with specific problems.

Firstly, family members are more readily promoted to important positions, and non-family member employees may therefore unite to exclude family members, which may result in conflicts between the two parties. In addition, family members also take priority in getting a good salary and training opportunities. Such unfair treatment is detrimental to attracting and managing outside talent.

Secondly, family members are not always qualified for their positions. But due to their special identity, such family members are difficult to manage, leading to weakness and disorder in team management. This, together with the resulting talent loss, causes an inevitable decline in corporate efficiency.

3. 'Face' concept and indirect communication patterns

Since ancient times, dignity and decency in public have been very important to Chinese people. The concept of 'face' is important. As a result, communication is frequently indirect, without direct references to issues or to individuals. For example, many corporate leaders avoid criticizing their subordinates in public or in private to avoid making them lose 'face'. Personal opinions are not expressed directly among team members. As a result, communications can be ineffective, as feedback and challenges are avoided.

4. Special historical background

Traditional culture in China has had an influence on modern enterprises through continuation of tradition. Special historical background also has an impact on corporate management in terms of the practical environment and the personal qualities of business owners.

Chinese enterprises, especially private ones, came forth and developed after the 'Cultural Revolution', which is a very special period in Chinese history. From the 1960s to the 1970s, China's economy was in a 10-year stagnation due to the Cultural Revolution. Little from the outside business and management world permeated Chinese borders. After the Cultural Revolution, when the Reform and Opening up began in 1979, social demands and foreign investments boomed, with many opportunities and easy profits. This created a large number of entrepreneurs. At that time, most entrepreneurs were born in the 1950s or the 1960s, and the majority of them failed to receive a proper education due to the impact of the Cultural Revolution. With delayed study and development opportunities in their youth, they followed out-of-date management concepts. At the same time, they remembered the scarcity of materials and commodities during the 1960s and the Cultural Revolution, so were eager for development and success once opportunities came up. At the beginning, they looked on 'profits' as the only standard to measure success, and this brought forth the following issues to many enterprises.

Unclear corporate visions

Businesses lacked specific goals and planning for long-term development. Correspondingly, little attention was paid to employees' personal visions and values.

Lack of talent cultivation

Entrepreneurs treated their staff as a tool used to earn money, ignoring the talent development and career development of the staff. As a result, employees would focus on their salaries, without planning for their long-term development. This meant that staff lacked loyalty and sense of belonging.

Short of competitive edge

Most owners of private enterprises adopted a centralized or imperative management style. Leaders paid little attention to, or were poor at uncovering, employees' potential. The personal abilities of the business owners set an upper limit on the development of their enterprises. Furthermore, these enterprises paid insufficient attention to the development of core technologies and self-owned brands. They preferred to seek short-term profits by imitating, or even copying, technologies and products.

DEVELOPING CULTURALLY APPROPRIATE COACHING

The manufacturing and production sectors of the economy are leading the thriving growth in China. But due to the lightning speed at which China has seen its economy grow, a proper business environment has failed to emerge. Many of the entrepreneurs do not know how to approach the basic issues that most growing companies need to confront. These include difficulties with human capital, business innovation and continuous growth. As a result of these problems, a strong desire has arisen to learn Western management concepts, as these are perceived to be well developed with proven records based on the success of lots of Western corporations.

The history of coaching in China can be traced back to the mid-1990s, when the term 'coaching' was introduced into mainland China. It was unfamiliar to most Chinese enterprises. Coaching came into being in the Western cultural environment, whereas Chinese enterprises have their own traditional culture and historical background, which are different from those of Western countries. For those who are committed to popularizing coaching in China, there is a need to recognize the differences as well as the similarities between Chinese and Western priorities and ways of working.

Compared with traditional management theories, coaching stresses people over corporate regulations. Coaching theory highlights people's values, goals and potential. Coaches encourage, guide and help the coachees to become more self-aware and set aspiring goals. As a result, coaching has the potential in China to help break the belief barriers that can hamper development and growth. Three examples will illustrate this point.

Firstly, coaching helps Chinese enterprises set up value consciousness and social responsibility to make corporate visions clear, leading Chinese enterprises towards long-term development. It also helps enterprises enhance core values to create a corporate culture and brand.

Secondly, coaching enables leaders to correctly understand people's potential, highlight talent cultivation, and drive their enterprises to become learning organizations. It can increase consciousness of breakthrough and innovation, improve corporate capabilities in innovation and promote sustainable development.

Thirdly, coaching provokes direct and effective internal communication, building up mutual trust and a harmonious atmosphere, and enhancing execution and cohesion.

Coaching originated in Western countries, and consequently it will take some time for it to become widespread in the special Chinese social and cultural environment. As mentioned at the beginning of this chapter, some concepts in Chinese traditional culture have an adverse impact on corporate management, but some elements can be incorporated into modern corporate management. Confucian ethics, the core of traditional culture, has advocated being people-oriented in management for thousands of years. In spite of the great impact of the Cultural Revolution on traditional culture, which affected the inheritance of those fine traditional values, many values of traditional culture have been preserved. Confucian ethics have been widely recognized in the field of corporate management in China, and there are some similarities between the Confucian ethics-centred traditional culture and coaching values. Here are some examples.

People-oriented

In a famous quote, Mencius says, 'If a king regards his officials as valuable as his own hands, the officials will regard him as their heart; if he regards them as humble as dogs, they will regard him as a countryman; if he regards them as valueless as grass, they will regard him as an enemy.' (君之视臣如手足, 则臣视君如腹心; 君之视臣如犬马, 则臣视君如国人; 君之视臣如土芥, 则臣视君如寇仇) (Zhu, 2004: 323). This old saying highlights that rulers cannot get support and loyalty in return unless they respect and cherish those below them. A similar meaning can also be found in the saying 'People are more important than rulers' (民为贵，君为轻) (Zhu, 2004: 404), which means the king should regard his people more noble than himself, advocating a 'people-oriented' concept.

The above two sentences reveal that recognition of individuals was recognized as an important feature by Confucianism as early as the Chunqiu and

Warring States Period in ancient China. Being 'Ren-focused' (Huang and Liang, 2007: 7) asks corporate leaders to include employee-oriented guidance, inspiration and management in their coaching activities.

Everyone has the ability to succeed

'Everyone makes Emperors Yao and Shun' (人皆可以为尧舜) (Zhu, 2004: 373) is another saying from Mencius. Both Yao and Shun were wise emperors in ancient times in Chinese history. They are regarded as saints with perfect virtue. It is obvious from the saying that Mencius thinks everyone has the potential to become 'Yao'- and 'Shun'-like, in developing a perfect virtue. As a comparison, 'Focus on one's potential and future' (看人之大) (Huang and Liang, 2007: 69) is advocated as a key coaching technique, and at the heart of coaching practice is the desire to help the coachee achieve their full potential.

Achieve self-improvement through learning from others

The Analects of Confucius includes a saying that Confucius told to his pupils: 'When walking in the company of other men, there must be one I can learn something from. I shall pick out his merits to follow and his shortcomings for reference to overcome my own.' (三人行,必有我师焉。择其善者而从之, 其不善者而改之。) (Zhu, 2004: 112). This old saying shows us that we can review our own faults by observing other people's behaviours, and thus correct our weaknesses.

In the Tang Dynasty, Li Shimin, Emperor Tang Taizong, said 'With a bronze mirror, one can see whether he is properly attired; with history as a mirror, one can understand the rise and fall of a nation; with men as a mirror, one can see whether he is right or wrong.' (以铜为鉴可正衣冠, 以古为鉴可知兴替, 以人为鉴可明得失) (Ouyang and Song, 2003: 110). This saying suggests that using others as a mirror enables us to see ourselves, and our own weaknesses. The parallel in coaching is the coachee's use of the coach as their mirror. The coach can reflect back the coachee's real status and help adjust their attitude and behaviour.

Pursue truths and values of life

Confucius once said 'If a man in the morning hears the right way, he may die in the evening without regret.' (朝闻道, 夕死可矣) (Zhu, 2004: 80). Here, the 'way' means the truths of life. The individual can then use these truths to inform their own personal values and goals throughout their life. The parallel in coaching is the aim of the coach to help the coachee to reflect on their values, and recognize how these values can be expressed in who they are and what they do each day.

Examine oneself critically

Tseng Tzu said 'Each day I examine myself on three counts: whether or not I am loyal to those in whose behalf I act; whether or not I am trustworthy in my dealing with friends; whether or not I practice what is imparted?' (吾日三省吾身: 为人谋而不忠乎? 与朋友交而不信乎? 传不习乎) (Zhu, 2004: 55). This saying reminds us that every day we should review our beliefs and behaviour in accordance with certain standards and requirements. The parallel in coaching is that coaching calls for inner learning to help coachees continuously self-review themselves and make adjustments to keep their values and goals in line.

Practice is essential

Wang Yangming, a learned and famous scholar in the Ming Dynasty, once said that people should make 'unity of knowledge and action' during learning. This emphasizes that one cannot master any knowledge or make any progress unless he or she puts theory into practice. The parallel in coaching is that coaching too highlights people's experiences and inspires coachees to use these experiences as evidence to build confidence as well as to try out new things.

Emphasize values of life in two aspects, individual and social

The life ideals that Confucianism advocates are *'personal cultivating, family regulating, state governing, and kingdom tranquillity and happiness'*, which means that people should improve personal qualities, commit themselves to their family, and make contributions to their country and the world. Some aspects of coaching such as the Transpersonal approach advocate a similar path, paying attention to work–life balance and considering how one makes a difference to society.

Generally speaking, cultural differences result in problems that are different from those in Western countries during the application of coaching in Chinese enterprises. However, Chinese traditional culture has its own advantages, making it possible for coaching to enrich itself by combining with traditional culture to enable it to make an impact in Chinese enterprises.

In fact, over the past decade we have been using Confucianism to explain coaching theory. This approach has helped managers and workers to see that coaching is not a Western-style approach, but has many echoes in established Chinese ways of working and thinking. We found that such an approach made corporate leaders accept coaching quickly and encouraged the rapid spread of coaching culture through Chinese enterprises. Here are two representative coaching cases.

CASE STUDY: SUN QIMING

Sun Qiming, an entrepreneur in Shanghai, founded a small air compressor equipment factory early in the Chinese Reform and Opening up. Now the company has become one of the largest air compressor equipment manufacturers in China.

Sun Qiming formed a management team made up of his relatives and local people at the beginning. However, the family operation caused internal conflict and disunion in the team. To try to alleviate these problems, Sun Qiming gradually introduced professional managers into his enterprise. Nevertheless, he preferred to cooperate with his relatives and gave preference to them when choosing suppliers.

Sun Qiming thought that he should transfer some power to the new professional managers. He was afraid that intervening too much or imposing high requirements would make managers feel they were not trusted. For this reason, Sun Qiming tried to make no intervention and no condemnation, even if he was dissatisfied with what they had done. He seldom blamed employees for their faults, and made roundabout implications even if he criticized them to avoid making them lose 'face'. As time passed, Sun Qiming found it difficult to communicate internally and his management also became less focused. Such situations even had an influence on customer management, allowing the deferral of payment by the customers and affecting the company's cash flow.

Before Sun Qiming began to learn Chinese Confucianism coaching, knowing his past secondary school education was not enough, he had already taken MBA courses offered by the Renmin University of China, aiming to improve his management ability. However, he did not apply advanced management knowledge in practice because his solid family ideals and communication philosophy were unchanged. After having learned coaching in 2006, he began to realize the negative impacts of the traditional family concept in operating the company. He fired all unqualified relatives and became more cautious in handling the suppliers and clients who were relatives, daring to say no if necessary. He began to have requirements for his managers to fulfil and to communicate directly with his employees. At the beginning, his subordinates were strongly against such changes, thinking that Sun Qiming no longer trusted and recognized them. They were uncomfortable with straightforward and goal-oriented communication. But Sun Qiming insisted on his own practice while motivating his subordinates to study coaching. Eventually, he got successful results.

For example, one general manager, a non-family member of Sun, was once arbitrary in his work and tried to suppress the promotion of excellent subordinates for a long time due to fear of being replaced. Upon learning coaching, he recognized his shortcomings and got rid of his traditional domineering management style. He elevated competent subordinates and enhanced their loyalty by encouraging them to seek promotion.

Another successful result of the coaching was the effect on employees in his Xiamen Branch. The morale there was low and the staff lacked motivation to improve themselves besides working. However, after being taught coaching they were eager to begin self-improvement, and began to attend MBA courses offered by universities to enhance their knowledge of products and techniques. Coaching encouraged them to improve their personal qualifications in order to challenge for management positions.

At present, an atmosphere of direct communication has formed in Sun Qiming's enterprise, and he is willing to make an investment in order to support employees' learning activities. In response, the working attitude of his employees has become more positive and confident, which increases team management effectiveness. A well-improved training system is forming gradually, due to the change in attitude regarding the upgrading of professional skill. With the enhancement of internal management, the enterprise also improved its customer management.

According to Sun Qiming, learning coaching helped him not only improve corporate management, but also to realize the importance of attitude training and the harmonious soul in addition to corporate profits. Therefore, he pays more attention to Confucian ethics that highlight personal mental cultivation. Now he is trying to gain a further understanding of the essence of Chinese culture by making use of coaching, and integrating it into his corporate management and daily life.

CASE STUDY: LINING (CHINA) SPORTS GOODS CO LTD

Lining (China) Sports Goods Co Ltd, a leading sports product maker in China, with headquarters in Beijing, introduced professional management systems after a short period of family operation at the beginning of its establishment. Listed in Hong Kong in 2004, Lining is now preparing to develop further by using the opportunity of the Beijing 2008 Olympic Games. Lining defines its mission as 'to inspire in people the desire and power to make breakthroughs through sports'. Its vision is to become the world's leading brand in the sports goods industry and this is supported by its core value of 'athleticism (Integrity, Professionalism, Passion, Breakthroughs and Trust)'.

Lining took the lead in introducing advanced philosophy of management and talent cultivation. Therefore, unlike other private enterprises, Lining had already set up the Leadership and Development Centre in 2004 and created a talent model of their own before being introduced to coaching. However, a number of obstacles stood in the way of successful implementation of coaching.

Firstly, some established employees who experienced the early stage of the company's development became complacent and acted as though they were superior to newer members of the organization. Newcomers had difficulty getting along with the established employees and fitting into the corporate culture. In order to promote internal communication, the management team introduced the 180-degree appraisal system, but employees dared not communicate freely with their superiors when doing 180-degree appraisal. As a result the appraisal system failed to highlight or address the problems. In addition, core values and other corporate cultural concepts were not well communicated to employees, nor fully executed in practice.

To overcome these issues with established employees, Lining decided to develop the potential of 60 outstanding selected employees via coaching. The idea was to escalate their integrated abilities in order to embrace the opportunities brought by the Beijing Olympic Games in 2008 and to ensure sustainable development of the company. The first team coaching service in Lining was initiated in September 2007, with the focus on internal communication and employees' self-awareness. By combining traditional Chinese people-oriented concepts with coaching theory, we helped Lining's managers learn to pay attention to self-value and set up specific goals. We also demonstrated the importance of direct communication, feedback and experience-sharing inside the company with the old Chinese dictums 'with men as a mirror' and 'unity of knowledge and action'.

The team coaching went smoothly because Lining itself had a number of employees with management qualifications and who had an open-minded approach. According to coached employees, they understood the importance of learning and self-reflection. Some established employees began to listen to other employees' comments and also to reflect on their relationships with both established and newer colleagues.

All employees of Lining who participated in team coaching made a clear 'My Career Development Plan' to improve four aspects of their leadership: personal abilities, business/management skills, interpersonal skills and leadership skills. At the end of coaching, some employees said they had fulfilled their business goals. Internal communication was also improved. For example, an employee confessed that previously he dared not exchange opinions directly with his team and superiors as he was afraid of being wrong or having his ideas criticized. With the encouragement of his coach, he tried to express his ideas directly, and, to his surprise, he did not receive negative feedback, but instead got high praise from the team. This made him more willing to communicate directly and share his ideas, while increasing self-confidence in the team.

After the team coaching service came to an end, Lining had positive feedback. The team believed that coaching had been of great help in promoting self-learning, communication, cohesion and execution. In addition, coaches not only helped employees awaken their passion, increase their self-awareness and create an atmosphere of mutual trust via direct communication, but also enabled Lining's employees to fit well into its corporate culture of 'Integrity, Professionalism, Passion, Breakthroughs and Trust'.

In November of the same year, Lining started its second team coaching service and planned to cultivate internal coaches. Coaching culture is implanting into this famous Chinese enterprise with a positive momentum, and will have far-reaching influences on Lining.

CONCLUSION

The traditional cultural environment and the special historical background of Chinese enterprises created different problems and situations from those faced by Western enterprises when putting Western-based coaching in practice. Knowing the differences between Chinese and Western cultures will help us to better understand the current status of Chinese enterprises and solve problems in management. There are also some resemblances between coaching and advanced concepts of Chinese traditional culture. Therefore, if we seek such common points between coaching and traditional culture to make a unique combination, we will not only help Chinese enterprises better understand and make use of coaching, but we will also enable entrepreneurs to integrate and apply this advanced tool in management. Coaching itself will be enriched and supplemented to become universal in China.

Chinese entrepreneurs have realized the importance of improving management concepts, and have begun to learn advanced management knowledge and skills. As a coach, I can always feel the traditional Chinese character of modesty and studiousness when coaching them, as well as the modern spirit of courage and personal breakthrough. Therefore, I believe coaching will be gradually recognized by more enterprises in China, and will ultimately fit well into their talent management and their corporate spirit and culture.

References

Ouyang Xiu and Song Qi, of Song Dynasty (2003) *New Book of Tang*, Zhonghua Books, Beijing, China

Ronghua, H and Libang, L (2007) *REN Coaching Model*, China Social Sciences Press, Beijing, China

Zhu Xi (2004) *Variorum of the Four Books*, remarked by Chen Shuguo, Yuelu Publishing House, Hunan, China

Further reading

Gu, Zhengshen (2007) *Introduction to the Comparison between Chinese and Western Cultures*, Peking University Press, Beijing, China

Kai Alexander and Dr. Schlevogt (1999) *Chinese Organizations: An Empirical Study of Business Practices in China*, [online] Dissertation.com

Pengcheng, G (2006) *15 Sessions of Chinese Traditional Culture*, Peking University Press, China

Rudnicki, S (1998) *Confucius in the Boardroom: Ancient Wisdom, Modern Lessons for Business*, Dove Books, USA

Sun Jinghua (2006) *Management Logic of Chinese People*, China Machine Press, China

Wong, E and Leung, L (2007) *The Power of Ren, China's Coaching Phenomenon*, John Wiley & Sons (Asia) Pte Ltd, Singapore

Zhu, Xiying and Xu Shuxia (2007) *Introduction to Chinese and Western Cultures*, China Light Industry Press, China

8

Coaching in the Middle East

Tom Palmer and Dr Val J Arnold

INTRODUCTION

Coaching is essentially about behaviour change. We view coaching as the process of equipping people with the tools, knowledge and opportunities they need to develop themselves and become more effective. In most cases, and quite exclusively in organizational contexts, coaching focuses on adults changing aspects of their thinking and behaviour. Change is never easy, and as coaches, facilitating the learning and behaviour change of another, we draw on the science of psychology. Psychological processes influence culture, and in turn culture influences psychological processes. In the Arab world, where culture is such a strong foundation for how people behave, understanding the dynamic of how culture influences the psychological processes of behaviour change and vice versa is critical to an effective coaching relationship. Based on research and experience in working with organizations in the Arab world, this chapter aims to outline some of the key issues in coaching engagements and related strategies for achieving maximum impact and results.

HERITAGE TRADITIONS

All generalizations contain lies

To make sense of the world we look for patterns, for generalizations that help us to navigate. Generalizations, by their nature, are over-simplifications of the complexity within the group. We recognize that for every generalization or principle we discuss, there are as many or more exceptions. This fits with one of the basic observations within psychology, that people differ more within groups than we see in the mean differences between groups. As we talk about the ways that coaching is different with the Arab population, we must bear in mind that individual differences are so great that we need to focus as much (or even more) on what works for each person as we do on what's different because of culture.

In the context of our work in the Arab world we want to highlight four caveats to our coaching observations.

1. First, the leaders we have worked with represent a specific subset within the Middle East. All of our coaching is done in English, a second language for all of the people we've worked with. So we're talking about Western coaches working with Arab clients.
2. Our work has been done in large companies with significant Western history/interaction. Hence, leaders we work with spend their days in a Western business world/culture and their non-work lives in local Arab culture. Some of the organizations are multinational, others are local with global operations, but in all cases they are large organizations. There are many family-owned businesses as well as governmental agencies in the Arab world where we suspect that the coaching challenges differ substantially.
3. You'll notice we talk mainly about Arabs. There are many different groups of people in the Middle East. The experience we're referencing in this work is exclusively with the Arab peoples. Experiences with Persians, Kurds, Israelis, etc can be expected to be different. However, Saudi Arab culture is different from Omani Arab culture. Again, all generalizations contain distortions and need to be viewed with caution.
4. Finally, 90+ per cent of the people we've worked with are males. In Saudi Arabia, 100 per cent of the coachees are male, whereas in Oman or the UAE we have had the opportunity to coach female leaders.

The above generalizations having been considered and noted, there are important heritage traditions to take into account. From a coaching perspective there is an historical and socio-political context that is important in understanding differences in management approaches in the region.

Colonization, the Bedouin and tribal ancestry, the framework of Islam, the impact of socio-economic factors, and more recently the huge influx of expatriate workers and increased international exposure have all had their influence.

Firstly, the framework of Islam is fundamental to the culture. Obviously not all Arabs are Muslim and not all Muslims are Arabs; however, for the majority of Arabs the philosophy of Islam is one of practice and not just belief. Within Islam, there is no separation of religion and state, or of personal and political. To this end there is an expectation that good practice of Islam is what all Muslims do, and the practice of Islam underpins and guides business and leadership behaviours.

In addition, tribal traditions and their collectivistic culture profoundly influence Arab managerial styles. In our experience working in the Arab world we find organizations tend to endorse collective values and practices such as preference for personalized relationships, which emphasize the importance of the in-group. Leaders generally shoulder all the responsibility and centralize authority, at times at the expense of collaboration with other groups or departments (Abdalla and al-Hamoud, 2001). Given this centralized authority and collectivist approach, managers often display intense loyalty to their 'in-groups' and employees see their boss as the protector and caregiver, which reinforces a paternalistic viewpoint of what makes an effective leader. Indeed, researchers published in both Arabic and English (Muna, 1980; Atiyyah and Al-Hassani, 1981; Barakat, 1983; Leila, El-Sayed and Palmer, 1985; Abdalla and Al-Hamoud, 2001) agree that favouritism, nepotism and personal connections have a significant impact on how managers make their decisions. In the Arab world this is known as *wasta*.

When coaching in this region it is very important to understand, and be sensitive to, the extent to which interpersonal connections and networks affect the business environment. *Wasta* is Arabic for connections, or influence, and, although not often openly spoken about, it is seen as a contributing factor in decision-making (Cunningham and Sarayrah, 1993). Traditionally, *wasta* was the process by which the head of a tribe or family obtained for other, less senior family members that which would otherwise be unattainable. Those with good connections are described as 'having *wasta*' and can be perceived as having a smoother ride through complex, collectivist bureaucracies, where if you don't know the right people it can be very hard to get things done.

Another influencing factor is the influx of expatriate workers, and in some countries a colonial legacy, which has influenced native work methods and managerial styles. As such the present native managerial style is a hybrid of bureaucratic and traditional tribal methods.

THE INFLUENCE OF TRADITIONS ON BEHAVIOUR, SELF-PERCEPTION AND RELATIONSHIPS

Building on the premise that culture influences psychology and psychology influences culture, it is inevitable and quite appropriate that the Arab regional traditions are strongly evident in leadership behaviours. It may be helpful to view this within the framework of the 'What' and 'How' of results. In the Western business model the common commercial objective of obtaining business results drives toward similarities in the 'What' of results, ie managers irrespective of culture have similarities in terms of the business results they are expected to achieve, while cultural differences cause some differences in terms of 'How' things are done. Despite observed differences that may be culturally attributed, and empirically noted differences in leadership style (eg the GLOBE study, House *et al*, 2004), as coaches we need to be careful that we don't view non-Western leadership values and norms as being backward or unsophisticated compared to where we see ourselves.

The framework of Islam has a significant impact on leadership behaviours. Leaders expect to be obeyed, and in return they will look after the interests of their subordinates. The Holy Quran attests 'O ye who believe! Obey Allah, and obey the Messenger, and those charged with authority among you' (Surat An-Nisa, section 5 (59) *Holy Quran*, 1981). However, as Abdalla and Al-Hamoud (2001) point out, employees are only expected to obey their boss's orders if they are in line with God's orders. The system works when employees defer to the boss's orders and seek their guidance and the boss in return protects and ensures career progression or remuneration increases for their employees. Employees are unlikely to strongly oppose their boss and if the situation is likely to result in confrontation they most often choose to withdraw. This all reinforces a paternalistic work environment where authority is handled centrally and is power distant, although there can be an 'open door' for consultation. For example, the impact of this is that in some organizations we have worked for, we see senior leaders at vice-president level signing off on basic administrative requests that initiate many organizational levels below them. Accountability is constantly deferred upwards, and a culture of 'make no mistakes, and keep the boss happy' pervades. In an organization where power to decide is centralized and rarely delegated, initiatives from and opportunities for lower-level management can be restricted (unless you have *wasta*).

Arab culture is highly context-dependent and relationships are central to every aspect of life. Appropriate behaviour is crucial. It is important that business leaders live up to the ancient norm of hospitality. In a coaching setting this means that much more time must be spent on hospitality and getting to know each other, before getting into business. In fact, Angala (1998) reports that many managers are more concerned with the fostering of social networks than the job itself. This is in part supported through empirical personality research (Lewis, 2006), which shows that in Saudi Arabia personality characteristics that help maintain harmony and positive relationships are much more prevalent than in Europe or North America. Similarly, where action may depend on personal ties, trust and loyalty are vital; however, trust is a personal matter not a procedural one. Utilization of networks of relatives and friends is described by some managers in an Arab context as very legitimate; the family and tribal connections in the Arab world are the primary sources of *wasta* (Muna, 1980). With business affairs and personal life interwoven, loyalty is more important than cold, hard efficiency.

One consequence of the influx of expatriate workers and adoption of more 'Western' styles of management is that Arab managers are often caught in a paradox, particularly when required to adhere to modern Western organizational and productivity metrics such as selection and reward systems, whilst simultaneously ensuring that the needs of the in-group are protected. The paradox is further complicated as younger, better educated leaders find themselves responsible for leading older team members, a situation at odds with traditional cultural norms. One coachee we were working with found himself in the unenviable position of managing his own father, which from a cultural standpoint presented many challenges for both of them. Leading 'old-timers' is often cited as the biggest challenge for young upcoming leaders, and the paradox of cultural expectations to 'look after' your employees, whilst at the same time managing performance, is an area frequently raised in coaching sessions.

Finally, the authors come from low-context cultures where the responsibility for being clear and making sure there is understanding lies with the communicator, the sender. English, our native language, is fundamentally denotative and allows for explicit, clear and direct communication. The Arab cultures we work in are high context, where the responsibility lies more with the receiver to understand what is being communicated. Arabic is more connotative and evocative and often significantly less explicit than English. Put these together and leaders are often less than explicit or clear and it is the subordinate's responsibility to understand or figure out what is going on, what is meant, what is expected. Teaching a leader to adopt a Western, explicit, denotative style may fly in the face of what is expected behaviour from leaders. This may be expressed as: 'If I need to tell him, then he doesn't belong here…'. Being explicit can also run headlong into issues of impression management and saving face. Difficult messages delivered in a vague and roundabout manner allow face-saving through plausible deniability. For leaders, being coached this may mean they are much less comfortable with direct assertive responses; this may be especially true when asserting upwards, with older co-workers, and/or outside of family/tribal networks.

DEVELOPING CULTURALLY APPROPRIATE COACHING

As coaches, we firmly believe that effective coaching makes you more the person you want to be. Coaching doesn't work if you're faking it, especially if you're trying to be someone you're not. Coaching is most effective when it is consciously and overtly helping the individual align their behaviour with their beliefs and values. Given our point of view that the purpose of coaching is to help individuals change their behaviour, one key to culturally appropriate coaching is understanding and using what David Peterson terms the 'active ingredients' required for change and development. The Development Pipeline (Figure 8.1) describes the five necessary and sufficient conditions for change and serves as a guide to where coaching can provide the greatest value for a given individual (Hicks and Peterson, 1999a; Peterson, 2002; Peterson, 2006).

The Development Pipeline

1. Insight

The extent to which the person understands what areas need to be developed in order to be more effective.

2. Motivation

The degree to which the person is willing to invest the time and energy it takes to develop oneself.

3. Capabilities

The extent to which the person has the skills and knowledge that are needed.

4. Real-world practice

The extent to which the person has opportunities to try new skills at work.

5. Accountability

The extent to which there are internal and external mechanisms for paying attention to change and providing meaningful consequences.

Figure 8.1 The Development Pipeline

The pipeline analogy has development as a liquid flowing through the pipeline. It is harder for a liquid to flow where there is a constriction in the pipeline. Hence, in coaching it makes sense to focus on those areas of the Development Pipeline where there is a constraint to development. For example, little additional value will be gained by taking a 360-degree assessment as an initial diagnostic if your coachee already has Insight about what they need to work on. It may be more beneficial to focus energy on the Motivation segment – why they may want to change or do something different. We will now examine the five conditions within the context of the Arab world.

Insight

Cultures vary a great deal according to their willingness and ability to think in psychological terms. The Middle East countries didn't go through the same 1960s and 1970s human potential movement experienced in many Western countries. They don't tend to have a rich history or rich language of the internal dialogue, of psychologizing about motives, drivers and other psychological concepts/explanations for their own and for others' behaviour.

We've found more of a need to teach/cultivate a different kind of self-awareness or mindfulness than is typical within Arab culture. On the one hand, the high context culture requires a reading of the environment and careful choice of behaviour. On the other hand, this cultural expectation does not require a high degree of self-reflection on one's own or on others' motivations, emotional states, etc.

While the Development Pipeline as a model can work well with anyone's core beliefs, in the Middle East, the ubiquity of Islam and the attendant lack of separation between the religious, the personal, leadership and the government is an ever-present background to all you do. By definition, within Islam, there is no separation, nor should there be separation, between what the Quran says, what the coachee believes, and therefore how he acts.

This can be a strong lever in your coaching if you can frame your suggestions within Islamic tradition and/or with quotes from the Quran. Within your partnership, if you are working with someone with strong beliefs and knowledge of the Quran, you can explore the coachee's understanding of the Islamic perspective on everything you do. Coachees are often able to give supporting quotes from the Quran on development needs being worked on, such as the importance of seeking and using feedback, hence cementing their belief that working towards their goal is worthy and right. What often works well is to share any Western sayings or adages around an issue and explore whether there is a similar saying in Arabic.

To help the individual understand what needs to change, what needs to develop, the coach can leverage the cultural importance of impression management and maintaining status. The culture lends much more power to the views of others with high status/high value. One of the more powerful ways to start coaching and identify what to work on is to collect data from 'key others,' those persons with whom the coachee is most concerned. The quite common practice of a formal 360-degree feedback questionnaire can be useful; however, making contact with key stakeholders and interviewing in a 'verbal 360' approach adds greater value. While interviewing key individuals can be even more powerful in a Middle Eastern culture, the power of others' perceptions also includes 'what is the impact on impressions of me if I ask for feedback?'

Impression management is critical, so data collection must be framed in a way that both the coachee and their colleagues will accept and see as positive. Similarly the data gathering process must be managed carefully. The choice of who to interview can be a powerful conversation in itself, encouraging the coachee to think about who would be able to give good feedback and why.

Preparing the respondents is crucial, whether using a 360-degree questionnaire or stakeholder interviews. In a high power distance culture it can be a career limiting move to provide critical feedback to a superior, both in perception and at times reality. For example, one senior VP didn't believe the company should engage in this kind of coaching because asking questions about how someone is performing and gathering feedback suggested that the person might have weaknesses or that something might be wrong. When talking about the importance of giving and receiving feedback, there is a saying in Arabic that roughly translates to 'God blesses the one who provides negative feedback', and talking about this can help put in perspective the usefulness of feedback.

The coach needs to be aware of the increased power of perceptions and think through how any collected feedback is presented. High 'pride' sensitivity can cause the coachee to see negative feedback as an attempt to 'hurt me and my career' and therefore to see the source as an 'enemy'. The coach needs to explore all of this thoroughly so that data collection is constructive for all parties.

In order to achieve behaviour change, people need to want to change. Of course, coaching is easiest when the individual has a solid sense of how they want to use coaching. Coaching can be more straightforward when individuals have goals that build on their insight of what they want to change or what they need to develop to meet the expectations of their environment. For the coachee with low internal/high external focus of control and low 'psychological mindedness', data collection, a personal 360-degree assessment, may be valued less for gaining personal insight leading to change and more for understanding and guiding a response to the perceptions of others. The coach may need to be prepared to go with the importance of 'changing the perceptions of others' as the goal if the coachee isn't willing or able to identify the perceptions as meaning they need to change something about themselves. The coach's goal in developing insight becomes helping the individual articulate what perceptions they want to change and how perceptions are limiting their ability to do what they want or achieve their goals.

To leverage all of the forces above, the coach needs to work with the individual to identify whose perceptions matter.

▌ Whose perceptions matter to you, to your future, to your success?
▌ Whom do you trust? Whose perceptions will you believe?
▌ Who has the data? Who knows you well enough that they can answer the questions we pose?
▌ What are the questions?

The coach is seen as the expert, often having some of the same authority as the leader. The coachee may not have the answer to 'What are the questions?' and the coach may suggest something generic that allows effective follow-up probes.

Examples would be:

▌ What makes Ahmad most effective in his role/leadership/etc?
▌ What gets in the way of Ahmad being as effective as he is capable of being?
▌ What suggestions do you have for Ahmad's development?
▌ What skills, changes or development would make him more effective or help him to reach his potential?

Collecting the data must be done in a way that is seen as both supportive and constructive, building the individual's capabilities. The coach needs to be particularly careful about suggesting any focus on weaknesses. If the person being interviewed goes there, you can follow. Again, we've seen very broad differences in individuals' willingness to identify specific behaviours, strengths and especially development needs. However, this is our experience across many cultures, with more sensitivity to the issues in our Arab clients due to impression management.

Motivation

Insight is crucial to getting a coachee focused on development, but working on issues around motivation is where it is possible to inspire commitment to change. Motivation and trust are intertwined in any coaching situation and in particular in the Middle East, where we have found it crucial to demonstrate that we have the best interests of the coachee at heart. We have found the development diagnostic tool called the GAPS (Goals, Abilities, Perceptions, Success factors) Grid particularly helpful in working through issues of Insight and Motivation (see Table 8.1). We have used GAPS in the Arab world as part of standard coaching and development intervention with considerable success. This simple two-by-two grid examines where the person is now (left-hand column) and what matters most (right-hand column). Both issues are considered from the person's perspective (top row) and from the perspective of any significant others, such as boss, senior management, direct reports, peers, the coach and family (bottom row).

Table 8.1 GAPS Grid

	Where the person is now	*What matters*
The person's view	Abilities	Goals and values
Others' views	Perceptions	Success factors

Adapted from D B Peterson and M D Hicks (1996) *Leader as Coach: Strategies for coaching and developing others*, Personnel Decisions, Minneapolis, MN

The Goals and values quadrant refers to what matters to the person and what motivates their behaviour. Abilities refers to the person's view of their own skills, abilities and style. Perceptions refers to how others (eg boss, colleagues, direct reports, coach and family) see the person. According to Peterson (2006), by separating Abilities and Perceptions, the purpose of exploring GAPS information becomes understanding feedback from different perspectives rather than trying to get agreement between the perspectives. This can be a powerful tool in coaching, as discussed earlier. Often a coachee's view of their abilities will differ in important ways from other people's perceptions.

Success factors refers to the expectations of others regarding what it takes to be successful in various roles, such as the person's current or desired job, or their social role as team member, leader and family member.

In a cultural environment where low psychological mindedness and a high external focus of control can make determining motivational drivers a challenge, a GAPS conversation can be a very powerful tool. Discussing Goals and values is a good starting point as the coachee is most likely to readily answer questions and have the most energy. Through strategic questioning a coach can help the person articulate what is most meaningful to them. For example, using questions like:

▌ What do you care most about?
▌ What motivates you?
▌ What matters to you?

In a high impressing environment, a coach can expect that initially the coachees will want to make sure that socially desirable responses have been heard and the importance of these understood. Typical standard responses include: being a good boss, being a good father or family member, making a difference for company and country, doing the right thing, getting a promotion. However, don't stop there, press beyond the surface level to tap what is truly most important for the coachee. Acknowledge what you've got and probe further:

▌ What else is important to you?
▌ What else?

Continue probing and digging until they have to look deeper within themselves. If people are getting stuck it can help to put forward some additional suggestions, for example: 'Some of the things we often hear people say are money, teamwork, work–life balance, promotions – how important are these things for you?'

These prompts can often lead to more reflection and get the coachee to think deeper and harder about what they really value.

As coaches, we have to listen without judgement or evaluation, remembering there may be little separation between religion, family and work. Whether we agree with their values is irrelevant, and it is imperative that we not superimpose our own concept of what values a leader should have, eg business might not be a primary motivator or driver. Similarly it can be viewed as imperialistic, not to mention condescending, to dismiss management practices that do not fit with our Western view of leadership. What we want to understand, and help them understand, is what is most important to them, and how what they value links to specific development priorities that will have a high payoff for both the coachee and the organization. For example, one mid-level manager surfaced some issues regarding managing upwards. He brainstormed solutions with his coach and agreed on specific development actions. After this the coach asked, 'What else is important to you?' His response was that having talked about work, and having understood he could trust them, he now wanted to talk about a tricky family situation he was facing. This demonstrates how asking the right questions builds trust and surfaces the most important issues to focus on.

Sometimes high status needs can be channelled as a force for change, eg when a high-status person in the community (CEO, VP, family leader, etc) embraces the desired development. Time can be spent on the Perceptions quadrant of the GAPS Grid and motivation can be further leveraged by highlighting the high-status person as supportive of the coachee's goals for development and by appropriately keeping the source informed of change and development. The coach can be the conduit for observations of progress between the high status source and the coachee. To this end, the more that senior leadership can highlight their support and endorsement of coaching as a business critical strategy, the greater the buy-in and motivation.

For the high external focus of control individual, who doesn't tend to think in motivational terms, the emphasis may be more on social constructs than personal constructs. For example, identifying the leadership traits and behaviours expected by the culture, the Quran, and aligning them with the feedback from others about what the individual needs to do more of or less of, can be motivating. The issue for the coach can be avoiding spending too much time listening to the individual tell you that 'I'm already doing that...'. For the person unable or unwilling to embrace the internal need for change, the coach may shift to 'What do you need to do to get the key people to observe you doing xyz?' and leverage discrepancy between the Abilities and Perceptions on the GAPS Grid.

Even reasonably sophisticated and highly educated coachees may experience less 'self efficacy', the experienced confidence and power for making self-change, than in parts of the world where high internal focus of control is more typical. One of the large cultural differences between the Western coach and the Middle Eastern client is likely to be an external focus of control that can limit the coach's ability to facilitate change. The sense that things are done to me, that I'm the passive recipient of life, is captured effectively by the ubiquitous 'Insha Allah'; the attitude that what will be, will be and it will happen only if Allah wills it. This is a frequent theme in coaching sessions where when asking 'What motivates you?' the response is 'Promotion, but it's out of my hands.'

In conjunction with less psychological mindedness we find a lower sense of self-efficacy around personal change. It is often not a part of the individual's psychology that 'what I do or I can do' will impact my behaviour, skills, ability or my future. Like all generalizations, you will find broad differences, but the coach needs to be prepared – a strong external focus of control makes coaching very challenging.

An external focus of control can also lead to the view that coaching is something that is done to someone, not something participated in. In this case the responsibility for change is on the coach, not the coachee. Also, having 'gone through coaching', the person perceives himself or herself as now 'developed'. Actual change may not be seen as relevant.

Capabilities and real world practice

Capabilities refers to the extent to which an individual has the skills and knowledge they need. A highly social people, the Arabs love dialogue and they love to talk. In fact, talking may be preferred to action. In coaching this can be seductive; your coachee may tend to think a good conversation is development, that discussion or insight equals change. If we've talked about it, it's as good as fixed. The coach needs to help the coachee differentiate between insight/discussion and the demonstrated ability to do something differently than they have in the past. Beware of the cultural tendency towards 'Because we've talked about it, I now understand and have therefore mastered it.' For individuals who believe a discussion is as good as change, it is important to try and build skills in the here and now, and practice and role-play are essential.

Building skills and changing behaviour requires practice in the coaching session followed by 'real world practice' on the job. More than in other cultures, we've found the need to teach and get buy-in around experimentation. We have found that the sooner we can get into some role-playing or immediate practice the better. This helps get around the cultural approach of 'We've talked about it, so now the problem is solved.' As we work through the coaching session, we identify on-the-job opportunities for the individual to practise their new approaches.

Getting people to practise new behaviour with you is often difficult, but can be powerful. The best coaching reduces the coach's feedback as the individual develops the capacity for self-feedback. In a high context culture some things are to be 'understood' instead of stated. Being clear with negative information can be difficult; being indirect and giving subtle and roundabout clues as to the message may be more culturally appropriate. For the Western coach, working with an Arab coachee may require presenting an assertive or direct approach as 'one way' and then asking the coachee how they might deliver such a message 'in their culture', while always exploring implications for doing things either way. This isn't unique to an Arab culture, but high-context versus low-context cultural differences may require a very different approach.

As Westerners, we may teach skills or approaches that are too direct, or that do not project the culturally appropriate leadership image. The coach needs to build a partnership that allows putting out an idea or approach that might work elsewhere, followed by exploration with your coachee on how to accomplish the goal in his/her culture. As you would with any coaching, work closely with the coachee on how nuances can be used. Once the relationship trust and partnership are solid, you can begin with the direct/core issue, what they want to accomplish in a specific situation, and work through how that would be done in their organizational/national culture.

The complex drive towards social status and standing, gaining status while avoiding embarrassment, can be a powerful motivator, but it can also inhibit the willingness to practise anything that might make a person look weak, ineffective or culturally deviant. Coaching requires real world practice of new behaviours and the coach must find ways to help individuals manage the risk-taking that experimenting with new behaviours requires. In the Middle East, as elsewhere, we find that coachees have been most successful in developing through situations where they are willing to try small experiments in environments that feel reasonably safe. As the Gestalt therapists say, change occurs at the contact boundary. If I stay too safe, I can't learn. If I go too far, I'm paralysed or shamed. The coach needs to help the coachee find a situation where a small amount of risk can be taken, experimented with, and learned from.

High impression and status management leads to being more careful outside of the coaching session. It is usually more important to avoid mistakes than take risks in the social network. The coach therefore needs to work closely with the coachee to 'titrate the risk' or gauge the right amount of risk to make sure the coachee is willing and able to follow through on real world practice. Successful follow through requires finding the right place to practise, where people and the situation are supportive.

While these concerns are typical of coaching, the importance of saving face makes consideration of this even more important. If you are able to leverage a high-status person's support, one way to increase motivation for follow through of practice is to arrange for the high-status person to observe the 'change' or at least the practice of change. Having a high-status person observe 'practice' can be high risk. However, leveraging perception once behaviour has stabilized is powerful for the individual, and critical to getting the perception changed in the work environment. Change without acknowledgement from those of high status is not as valuable. So, a strategy of safe practice followed by real world demonstration of change tends to work best.

Accountability

Lower internal focus of control tends to mitigate against holding oneself accountable. However, the coach can leverage external focus of control and impression/status management by getting feedback from high-status respected external sources. In our work this typically means senior leadership within the organization or within the family. Whilst the process of coaching is a very individual process, coaching as an organizational intervention is something that must be endorsed from the top down. In addition, it can be useful to have in place some sort of measurable outcome. This may be a formalized learning plan or coaching plan with specific, measurable behavioural targets that can be endorsed by senior leadership or the coachee's boss.

Cultural and religious forces lead the Arab coachee to view the future as uncertain; therefore a coaching conversation may tend towards what has already been achieved rather than what to focus on for the future. Thus coaching becomes remedial and about fixing problems, a less productive focus. If we view Accountability as a constraint in the Development Pipeline for an individual, we want to move towards a focus on improving future performance. For example, a mid-level manager had difficulties with an employee who was older than him. The employee was unhappy with his work and unhappy with how his recent expatriate assignment had been structured. As his boss, the coachee felt responsible for this and for improving the benefits his employee received. The coach spent time talking with the manager about what had happened and who was responsible for what. Through questioning (based on the GAPS Grid) it became apparent that the real challenge was not the situation that had already occurred, but having a difficult conversation with someone perceived as being more senior. To highlight accountability, the coach encouraged the coachee to make specific commitments for action:

- ▌ When will you next meet this person?
- ▌ What do you need to do to ensure you have this conversation?
- ▌ When are you going to schedule it?
- ▌ What obstacles do you foresee?
- ▌ What if he returns to Saudi Arabia before you meet with him?
- ▌ So, when will you have this meeting?
- ▌ What specifically will you say?

Once there was a clear commitment to action, the coach could then begin practice and role-play what to say. As Peterson (2006) comments, the world is a messy, complicated place, and a lot of coaching is about navigating through that complexity to help the coachee arrive at a clear goal with specific commitment to action.

SUMMARY

Coaching in the Arab world is tremendously rewarding. Whilst the broader process of behaviour change does not necessarily vary that much from coaching in a Western setting, understanding the myriad of cultural and psychological differences helps build more culturally appropriate processes. There are numerous coaching models, but we have found the Development Pipeline analogy is a simple framework around which to position the differences we have noted in our work. In the Western context, Insight is more about 'me' and 'what do I need to work on?', whereas in the Arab world we have found that Insight can be about 'what perceptions do others have about me that I would like to change?'. Motivation in the Arab world can often be better leveraged through considering that the drive to change behaviour may be as much a social construct as a personal construct. Capability building and real world practice involve structuring coaching to help the coachee identify safe opportunities to practise skills, and altering the perception that the coaching session, by itself, is a panacea.

Finally, like coaching anywhere in the world, people differ greatly. The issues discussed above will help to build culturally appropriate coaching, but essentially we as coaches need to go where the energy is for a coachee. The role of the coach is to help the coachee determine clear goals and make a conscious choice (Peterson, 2003) about what they want to do differently. We find this to be the same irrespective of culture. We need to be aware of the cultural differences that underpin what goals are chosen and the cultural factors that are involved in making that choice conscious.

References

Abdalla, I A and Al-Homoud, M A (2001) Exploring the implicit leadership theory in the Arabian Gulf states, *Applied Psychology: An International Review*, **50**(4), pp 506–31

Angala, A A (1998) Management development in the Arab world, *Education & Training*, **40**(4) pp 179–80, MCB University Press

Atiyyah, H S and Al-Hassani, H (1981) *Public Agencies and the Public* (in Arabic), National Centre for Consultancy and Management Development, Baghdad, Iraq

Barakat, H (1983) *Contemporary Arab Society: An exploratory sociological study* (in Arabic), Arab Unity Studies Centre, Beirut

Cunningham, R B and Sarayrah, Y K (1993) Wasta: *The Hidden Force in Middle Eastern Society*, Praeger, Westport, CT

Hicks, M D and Peterson, D B (1999a) The Development Pipeline: How people really learn, *Knowledge Management Review*, **9**, 30–3

Holy Quran (1981) Arabic text and English translation, Islamic Seminary, Elmhurst, NY (Sarwar, translated version)

House, R J *et al* (2004) *Culture, Leadership, and Organizations: The Globe Study of 62 Societies*, Sage, London

Leila, A, El-Sayed, Y and Palmer, M (1985) Apathy, values, incentives and development: The case of the Egyptian Bureaucracy, *The Middle East Journal*, **39**, 341–61

Lewis, R E (2006) *Cultural differences in a shrinking world: Leadership implications*, Personnel Decisions International, Minneapolis, MN

Muna, F (1980) *The Arab Executive*, St Martins, New York

Peterson, D B (2002) Management development: Coaching and mentoring programs, in *Creating, Implementing, and Managing Effective Training and Development*, ed K Kraiger, pp 160–91, Jossey-Bass, San Francisco

Peterson, D B (2003) *Clear Goals, Conscious Choice, Compelling Culture: Three steps to fostering integrity and ethical behavior in organizations*, Personnel Decisions International, Minneapolis, MN

Peterson, D B (2006) People are complex and the world is messy: A behavior-based approach to executive coaching, in *Evidence Based Coaching Handbook: Putting best practices to work with your clients*, eds D R Stober and A M Grant, pp 51–76, Wiley, Hoboken, NJ

Peterson, D B and Hicks M D (1996) *Leader as Coach: Strategies for coaching and developing others*, Personnel Decisions, Minneapolis, MN

9

Coaching in India

Yogesh Sood

INTRODUCTION

In India, ambition is a highly personal issue and differs from person to person. Coaching as a concept is still evolving. In fact, until recently participating in executive coaching would carry a stigma, as it would tend to indicate some weakness that needed to be taken care of. In the Indian culture a person does not express his ambitions outwardly; instead people often reveal their ambition and passion through hints and suggestive communication. Though the societal fabric is undergoing a rapid change, it is still the norm for elders or bosses to consider themselves as natural coaches to their young colleagues or other team members. Generally there is a gap in putting mutual expectations forward and a lot is left open to the assumptions of the other party.

This chapter provides an overview of the state of coaching in India. I will first review the heritage of the country and how the different Indian traditions across this diverse nation influence the coaching relationships. In the second part of the chapter I will explore how these traditions influence behaviours, self-perceptions and relationships before finally considering a culturally appropriate model of coaching for India.

HERITAGE TRADITIONS

India as a country has a very long history. The dated records show references as old as 3000 BC. Perhaps the tradition of coaching started in India, in guided learning through conversations. The lives of all great rulers of ancient India were impacted by the powerful presence of their 'gurus' – individuals who, in many ways, were similar to modern-day mentors or coaches.

At one time the tradition of coaching was very prestigious, when the would-be kings and princes from powerful families were sent to Gurukuls (learning schools). These institutions were run by Gurus or Rishis and they would coach the disciples in the field of academic learning as well as the art of war. The disciples would treat their Gurus as Gods. From these early encounters, lifelong relationships were often formed, with disciples seeking the advice of their Guru on critical matters throughout their life.

In Mahabharata, the famous Indian epic, the Lord Krishna acts as a guide (coach) to Arjuna, the archery expert and a well-known warrior from the Pandava family (the Pandava family comprised direct descendents of King Bharat, after whom India was christened Bharat, thousands of years ago). The outcome of this dialogue between Lord Krishna and Arjuna was Gita – the Indian holy text. Arjuna faced an onerous task of waging a war against members of his own clan to regain the family kingdom from them. He was struggling with the very thought of fighting against his near and dear ones. Lord Krishna helped him to focus on the cause and not to worry about the consequences. In eighteen chapters of Gita, Lord Krishna coaches Arjuna on various aspects of life, war, religion, relationships, the journey of the soul and life. The result of that coaching dialogue was that Arjuna was motivated to fight the war for justice and eventually to win.

Another example from Mahabharata of how the coachee held the coach in very high esteem, and was willing to obey his or her command without question, is the story of Eklavya, the classic narration of devotion and dedication to one's coach. The story goes as follows: Dhroncharya, the famous archery coach, wanted the thumb of Eklavya – his best disciple – as his fee for coaching. Eklavya knew that his coach had an ulterior motive of disabling him, as he wanted some other disciple to be the best in the skill of archery; however, he still obeyed the command of his coach. Without any hesitation or remorse he chopped off the thumb of his right hand and presented it to his coach.

One area that is traditionally very common in India is what might be considered to be 'life coaching'. There are many self-proclaimed experts in this field, who help people to improve their health, wealth and life through a combination of activities. These activities include yoga, meditation, wellness plans and spiritual guidance. Another prevalent concept is coaching by elders. This may be more akin to mentoring, with the elder giving advice and guidance to younger members of the extended family on all aspects of life.

THE INFLUENCE OF TRADITIONS ON BEHAVIOUR, SELF-PERCEPTION AND RELATIONSHIPS

In India the coach is expected to be prescriptive rather than facilitative, directive rather than non-directive. If a coach does not provide the right answers then the coachee is likely to see the exercise as meaningless. Coachees tend to believe that the coach needs to offer guidance and direction on questions such as where to go and what to do in order to reach the goal. This contrasts with the UK and US coaching approaches, which are more facilitative in nature, and the role of the coach is to help the coachee to find their own answers.

Traditionally, in Indian families, children are discouraged from asking questions or challenging the view of elders. They are expected to follow the line of elders and obey the family hierarchy. When young people go to school or college, this cultural norm continues, with the teacher assuming the role of elder. The young student is expected to listen to teachers and not express conflicting views. However, after 20-plus years of learning this approach of deferring to elders, organizational life is very different. As they progress to more senior roles, the conflict becomes greater; they are expected to express their views and to challenge accepted wisdoms, particularly within global companies. Yet they habitually say 'yes' to what the more senior staff request and then face problems if the commitments are not met or deadlines are missed.

A typical analogy to coaching in India is student education. In the Indian education system the weaker students seek extra knowledge by going to a tutor and asking for guidance. From being a stigma a decade and a half ago, now it has become a fashionable practice to go to as many tutors as possible and tell others about this too. The kids from the well-to-do families engage more than one tutor and often pick and choose the ones they want to work with. This trend is also being seen in executive coaching. From being a matter of apprehension and concern at a personal level, coaching practice is being increasingly viewed as a sign of the importance of the manager. As a result, many of the senior leaders in Indian corporations are starting to use business gurus to get advice and help.

DEVELOPING CULTURALLY APPROPRIATE COACHING

Ironically, most of the modern Indian business leaders are still going through a learning curve. They have been very slow to incorporate coaching into their organizations compared with other countries, and as a result the state of development of coaching services is still in its infancy. Business coaching itself is very new in India, and is commonly viewed as yet another buzzword for consultancy and training services. Certified business coaches are almost non-existent. Where they do exist, they are active mainly in the corporate sector in large metropolitan areas. Most companies are hesitant to embrace coaching, and there is concern about the high costs of business coaching.

Still, there are many progressive Indian companies/organizations who are embracing this approach. To name a few of them – Aditya Birla Group, Godrej, and Mahindra and Mahindra have hired coaches to work with their high potential executives. These coaches help the target group to achieve that edge, think strategy and develop potential. The idea is to cut short the leadership learning cycle by building on the strengths and improving upon the weak areas of the individuals concerned. From the viewpoint of coaches, some common areas in which they need and seek help are: managing time, influencing others and garnering support across the organization, and motivating themselves and others, as people issues are becoming increasingly complex. Because of rapid economic growth in India, leaders find it extremely difficult to retain and engage talent, and striking a balance between driving business and effectively leading teams is emerging as a big coaching area.

Within this context, Indian economic growth is continuing at a fast pace, with a 499 per cent growth in Indian's equity markets between 2001 and 2007 (Goldman Sachs, 2007). Indian businesses are witnessing unprecedented and exciting global integration, as India's highly educated workforce are called upon to provide IT and customer service roles for global companies. In this context, managers are realizing that traditional management styles of deference and/or securing a coach for fashion reasons will fail to meet the demanding needs of the new climate. Organizations now need to attract and retain talent to keep pace and to develop their workforce in order to deliver results. Further, corporate leaders and entrepreneurs who have to manage in an increasingly complex environment are seeing the need to collaborate with someone who can help them navigate through these business challenges and realize their full potential.

While organizations will need the help of external coaching professionals to work with their leaders and managers, they will also need to help all their managers become more coaching-oriented in their style of management, so that an organization-wide coaching-oriented culture develops. There is also the first movement towards professionalization with the development of an ICF (International Coach Federation) chapter in India, and a developing membership. What is likely to follow is the development of coach training and also the emergence of a culturally appropriate style of coaching that suits both the Indian managers, recognizing their backgrounds and experiences, and also the needs of Indian and international organizations, with their desire for open cultures and their drive for performance and results.

CASE STUDY: RAM THE LEADER

Ram is a Team Leader in a business process outsourcing company and has been asked to attend the annual Team Leaders' meeting. The company is changing very fast and has acquired business in different parts of the world in the last two years.

Recently, Ram was allocated a goal to achieve 40 per cent increases in profits for the coming year and a reduction in the employee attrition rate, from 25 per cent to 15 per cent. Ram was requested to submit a plan that identified how he would achieve these goals. He faced several challenges – restriction on additional spending, a multicultural and multinational team to manage and a very results-oriented chief executive, who was from Scotland and had only recently been moved to take up this role.

Ram was confused – in the past, when he faced challenges, he would ask his team to work longer and harder. However, this time he knew that he must help his team arrive at the destination, and achieve this goal collaboratively, or risk making his employee turnover figures worse rather than better.

In coaching Ram over several months, Ram's coach helped him to start to think differently about the problems, and to realize that using hierarchical relationships or elder-based models of leadership might only result in higher turnover. The coach helped Ram to start to think about his new boss and what he might want and expect from the Indian operation. He also reflected on how he could help his boss to begin to understand the operation and the culture of the Indian business, and how this might differ from his previous experience in Europe. The second area they worked on was motivation. How could Ram motivate his team and get more commitment and more engagement from them? This was focused around getting Ram to think about his employees' needs and expectations, including their longer-term development needs and their aspirations for the future.

The outcome of the process, while not quite a fairytale ending with all targets achieved, did see both a reduction in turnover (although not quite to target) and Ram delivering his growth objective. However, the side benefit of Ram's stronger relationship with his boss, the result of Ram helping him to understand and settle into the new working culture, were harder to measure, but were possibly of longer-term benefit to both Ram and his boss, and to the company.

CASE STUDY: GATEWAY

Greatway India is a subsidiary of Gateway Inc USA. The company is in the business of fast-moving consumer goods. Indian operations are more than 10 years old and are headed by an American, Dane. He came to India six years ago, after a successful stint of managing sales operations in different countries. Being a man of action, he believed in setting clear goals and achieving the same. Under his leadership the company had been growing at an average rate of 10–12 per cent annually and had been ahead of the competition in many ways. However, in 2007, the parent company wanted Indian operations to grow at a rate of more than 25 per cent. The country head brought this news back to his team and there was a mixed reaction to it. Clearly there were two schools of thought – one made up of relatively new members of the team, who felt very excited at the prospect of doing things faster and bigger, and the other a group of senior leaders who felt otherwise.

Dane got frustrated after some time as he realized that things were not moving forward as he desired. He discussed the issue with Mohan, Vice-President of Human Resources, to try and find a solution. Mohan organized an assessment of the desired competencies at the senior leadership level and found to his utter dismay that many members of the leadership team (more than 50 per cent) did not score well and needed immediate help. He discussed this situation with the country head and together they decided to take immediate action, ie have one-to-one meetings with each member of the leadership team and apprise each one of them of his/her strong and development areas. Some of the members of the team, who had been working with the organization from the start, did not like the evaluation process and showed a high degree of passive resistance.

The group training and learning efforts yielded little result, and Dane and Mohan were forced to think about some tough choices. They were contemplating some extreme action, ie paving the way for the graceful exit of some of the leaders, but it was a difficult choice to make. Around that time Mohan happened to attend an HR forum meeting and came across the idea of one-to-one coaching to handle this kind of problem. While researching the idea, he zeroed in on a team of coaches who had helped other companies in similar situations.

The lead coach suggested that in the given situation, the first action was to work on the 'I'm fine attitude' of some of the leaders. These were the people who were also influencing others in the group and stalling the change initiative. Dane and Mohan drew up a list of six such people, who they thought needed to go through the coaching exercise. Together they engaged with these six leaders and explained to them the process, the requirements, the reviews mechanism, mutual commitments, timelines, desired outputs, rewards of success and consequences of failure, etc. The entire exercise was done in a transparent and collaborative manner. Then the coach drew up individual development plans and discussed them with each member of the group. Over the next six to eight months, through periodic but intense interactions, the coach was able to make significant changes in the attitude and competency of five of the six people. One of them eventually had to leave, but just one out of six.

The experience taught this organization a valuable lesson – that people can change if adequate focus is given at personal level and on a one-to-one basis.

Note: The name of the company has been changed for confidentiality reasons.

SUMMARY

Today's Indian business finds itself in the midst of unprecedented opportunities and complexities. It also finds itself under constant pressure from a most competitive and challenging environment. Leaders across industries are looking for wisdom, hand-holding and support to succeed in this environment. Indian organizations are also realizing that the significant limitations of traditional approaches to training and management development in driving performance improvement have hampered their success. Coaching offers a way to address some of these challenges and to unleash the Indian economy.

References

Goldman Sachs (2007) *BRICs and Beyond*. London: Goldman Sachs Global Economics group.

Further reading

Bhagavad-Gita (1972) translation by A C Bhaktivedanat Swami Prabhupada

Blanchard, S and Homan, M (2004) *Leverage Your Best and Ditch the Rest*, HarperCollins, London

Covey, S R (1989) *The 7 Habits of Highly Effective People*, Simon & Schuster, New York

Trungpa, C (1973) *Cutting Thorough – Spiritual Materialism*, Shambhala Publications, Boston

Wilber, K (1996) *A Brief History of Everything*, Shambhala Publications, Boston

10

Coaching in Russia

Julia Choukhno

INTRODUCTION

Over the last 20 years Russia has come a long way, from being a communist country with a strong ideological system and a planned economy, to a free market economy. The 1990s was the time when the 'iron curtain' was removed and Russian business had access to Western business ideas and training. As part of this process of opening up to new ideas and methods, coaching has emerged as a powerful business tool. Clients still have lots of questions about the nature of coaching and how it works, but step by step it is taking its place in private life, in business and in political circles. In this chapter I will explore the development of coaching in Russia and how current Russian coaching practice is rooted in the mythological consciousness that was part of the Soviet system.

HERITAGE TRADITIONS

What is Russia?

In the mid-1990s in Switzerland there was an international meeting to explore the development of school educational programmes. Participants were evaluating how long it would take each country to build a system where programme trainers could reach every schoolteacher and thus ensure every child received the material in its proper form. The Russian representative sounded most negative and sometimes even aggressive throughout the general approach discussion.

'What is so special about Russia?' he was asked. 'Why do you get so angry when we discuss the plans?'

The Russian team representative said 'Size does matter,' and explained 'You know what our six-person Russian team is dealing with? Our target is to get about 65,000 schools involved in the programme. This means nearly half a million teachers need to be trained. If each of us trains 50 people per day five days a week without a break and even a chance to see how they deliver what we train them to do it will take us nearly six and a half years. And this means we'll not see our families during these years as we will not have enough time to come back to Moscow. Russia is a country with the biggest territory in the world – nearly 10,000 kilometres long and 5000 kilometres wide. It is equivalent in area to more than 400 Switzerlands or more than 30 Frances! Many parts of our country are isolated and cold with unpredictable climates so it might take several days to access these parts of the country.

'Another issue is that we have nearly 160 different nations. Although all people speak one language, their mentality and attitude to the issue we raise is different and they require tailored teaching approaches. We have a very strong education system but people will not follow you if you sell them just a good idea. Without integrating this into the official system, creating the leverage, and building a proper training and communication chain as well as some follow-on system, the programme will take too long and will not be what we want it to be.'

That was more than enough for the other participants.

Eight years later, not only that particular programme but three more interconnected programmes were successfully implemented in Russia by the team.

This story can be treated as a typical one and reflects the widely held belief that Russia's size is an important factor in its culture. This factor affects the development of coaching as much as any other aspect of Russian life.

Russian identity

Ask any Russian national what he understands by the term 'Russia' and you are likely to get a poetic answer:

> You will not grasp her with your mind
> Or cover with a common label,
> For Russia is one of a kind –
> Believe in her, if you are able…
>
> (Fedor Tiutchev, translated by Anatoly Liberman)

Most Russians still believe that Russia is unique and that a common logic is not applicable to Russians. When considering coaching, in which the focus and target is clarity and transparency, Russians feel that their unique status is being undermined.

The impact of Russian history on the Russian psyche

Within the last 150 years, Russia has experienced many significant shifts in opposite directions in its political and economic systems. This history has had a sharp effect on the Russian psyche and can help us understand in part core dimensions relevant for coaching in Russia. These include: dominating outer locus of control; humility and self-sacrifice; dual attitude towards power and values; and trust and responsibility distribution, as well as management concepts (Russian Academy of Science, Complex Social Research Institute, 2004).

At the beginning of the 20th century, Russia was mostly an agricultural country with limited industrial development. It benefited from a strong economy, a powerful bureaucratic system and an Orthodox Church. The Tsar was the head of the country. Most of the population were peasants who had for generations lived under a feudal system.

In 1917, as a result of the revolution, political systems changed tremendously but the hierarchical power system did not change much. Instead of the Tsar, there was a communist party leader, and bureaucracy grew even bigger as the party sought to control the economic development and the population. Some groups of the population and even whole nations were either forced to stick to their place or to relocate to different areas appointed by officials.

A further issue that affects the Russian mentality is the impact of war. Each generation of Russians had their own war. The first part of the 20th century was dominated by the two World Wars, where Russia was one of the key players. Revolution and civil war separated these two tragic wars. These were followed by the period of the Cold War and more recently the separation of many of the former USSR states to create new nations including Ukraine, Belarus, Latvia, Moldova, Estonia, Georgia and Central Asian countries.

Forces of power

Russian history can also be viewed as a history of power, with a desire by Russia to control, protect and expand its territory. Partially due to a thousand years of Christian tradition, authority was anticipated if not sacred. The ruthlessness with which Russian authority executed its plans over hundreds of years added much to the feeling that a person is nothing compared to the system. Those who rebelled against the system, be they peasants or scientists or political leaders, were traditionally annihilated, or sent to unreclaimed territories to die or build a new life as far from the capital as possible.

Another power source was the Orthodox Church. This was accepted as an official religion about 1000 years ago and assimilated pre-Christian traditions. Step by step it became a powerful influencing tool for the authorities, until the revolution in 1917. Persecuted after the revolution, the Orthodox Church was again used as a power tool during the Second World War and remained half-underground until the 1990s, when it was officially welcomed by the authorities again.

A third source of power that should be taken into consideration is the power of family and community (Kantor, 2001). For this agricultural country where people used to have big families and live and work together, the community was sometimes the one and only source of support and protection. None of the terrible shocks the country faced through the last century could break this strong interconnection and interdependence between families and generations. Although nowadays families tend to be smaller, people still feel very much linked together.

THE INFLUENCE OF TRADITIONS ON BEHAVIOUR, SELF-PERCEPTION AND RELATIONSHIPS

Being a part of something bigger

During the 70 years of Soviet management, Russian citizens were told 'You are a small part of a huge and great country. The country is rich and powerful and if you behave well, do the right things, work hard and protect the country from enemies, it will take care of you and your children. Everything will change for the best for you.' This message had strong echoes from the feudal system that had dominated Russia for centuries before.

Between 1945 and the early 1970s, there was a period of time when things really changed for the better for most of the population. The country was exhausted after the Second World War but recovered step by step. A bright future seemed to be approaching fast during the 1960s. There was enough food and a high demand for qualified specialists for industry. The education system and science grew and developed. For those who wanted to achieve something in life there appeared to be a chance to get what they wanted. However, this was limited to those who were part of the system and were willing to abide by its rules.

In the post-war period, high motivation following the war victory was supported by propaganda. This developed the myth about how unique the country was. And the myth worked perfectly until the energy and enthusiasm of the majority of people started to fizzle out and the Soviet system collapsed.

Russian peasant and self-sacrifice role-model

If you look back at Russian history and culture you will find lots of hero figures where patience, staunchness, steadfastness, and the ability to overcome obstacles were presented as the dominating values. The myth of the Russian hero becomes reality when individuals in real life achieve something through suffering. This is seen as noble and truly Russian.

Some researchers attribute this attitude to the Russian climate and agricultural cycle. Long, cold winters with very limited resources were followed by summers of hard work in the fields, often with unpredictable results. Every harvest was a heroic feat. This was inevitable and the best thing people could do was to work hard and take things as they came and to pay attention to small details in trying to predict the future.

Self-sacrifice as a part of the worker's culture became highlighted and promoted during the Soviet period. Each daily newspaper or news programme contained various examples of the self-sacrifice of individuals who gave everything for their company or the Soviet system. Being acknowledged as a loyal and devoted person was seen as a great role-model, which others were encouraged to follow.

This generation had an accepted model: see what you do and the suffering you experience in doing it as more important than what is achieved at the end of the process. As a result, outcomes are seen as less important than the effort and troubles that must be endured.

Duality and sabotage

It's a well known fact that pressure provokes resistance. In the Soviet era, resistance could not be overt, but was still possible through the many small things that people could do. Here is one anecdote about six contradictions of the Soviet system that sharply reflects the reality of the 1970s–80s:

> All have a right to work, but nobody works
> Nobody works, but plans are over-fulfilled
> Plans are over-fulfilled, but there is nothing in the shops
> There is nothing in the shops, but everyone has everything
> Everyone has everything, but nobody is happy
> Nobody is happy, but everyone votes for the Party

This circle could not function for long. The communist system collapsed, but the thinking behind the model has remained in much of Russian society and business.

We are born to render a fairytale into being

The shift from the Soviet Union to a market economy caused tremendous changes in peoples' lifestyles and in the social structure. It seriously affected the image of the country and shook the values system again. The new system required skills very different from those Soviet Union citizens were trained in and expected to display. In fact, identity became a hot issue.

The mid- to late 1990s were a mixture of Al Capone, Cinderella and Ali Baba stories. Those who had access to real economic power and knew what was going on became owners of Soviet industry bit by bit, and those who had less access to the industry but an understanding of economics or an entrepreneurial mind started establishing their business. Within a few months, while some people became billionaires or well-known politicians, others lost all their possessions and even their lives. Criminal wars became part of life.

Those who missed the chance to get into the big economy sharing game divided into three major groups:

1. Those who suffered and complained but worked to survive, who stuck to Soviet values and refused to change, waiting for the old good times to come back or expecting that the new powers would pay them back for their loyalty.
2. Those who took the changes as a chance for a breakthrough and started small, usually family business.

3. Those who gained the freedom not to work within organizations but devote their lives either to the traditional Orthodox Church or other traditional religions (Islam, Buddhism, etc) or to other spiritual practices.

Each of these groups had its own trend in personal and professional development. Of course there was no hard demarcation strip between them, but there are visible differences in dominant beliefs and values (Russian Academy of Science, Complex Social Research Institute, 2004).

Surprisingly enough, that period had shown that for most of the population, money as such had no value. The Soviet Union has never been a consuming society, but rather a minimal requirements society, ascetic and intellectual. You could enter 90 per cent of the Soviet apartments and find typical wallpaper, furniture, typical plates, forks and knives and many books there. It was a fashion to have the collected works of famous writers, which you could get through special subscription associated with a waste paper collecting system.

The Russian elite didn't show off their wealth and there was no visible gap between the average worker, engineer and manager, although under the surface benefits differed a lot. The non-financial compensation system was highly developed, especially in the 1970s–80s. The system provided officials with the best apartments, cars with drivers, and special shops where everything was better quality and cheaper. To have a good life or have something done, a person needed to know the right people rather than have the money to pay for it.

DEVELOPING CULTURALLY APPROPRIATE COACHING

Coaching in Russia – first steps

Until the end of the 1990s hardly anybody in Russia knew what coaching was. The country's experience of the first five years of the market economy and new business owners resulted in recognition of the need for training and people development, if Russian businesses were going to compete. People wanted to gain new skills but the traditional education system was not able to respond. While there was a strong mentoring tradition in Russian industry, by the end of the 1990s this had all but collapsed with the fall of the Soviet era.

Short-term skills training, time management or leadership programmes became popular. Some of them were brought to Russia from abroad; others were created by Russian businesses that responded to the new era. Psychology as a science was pretty strong in Russia during the Soviet period but its achievements were not much applied to real life except in the political process. The shift of the system let applied psychologists use their skills in business, and training and development started to flourish.

When coaching was first brought to Russia, the proponents were mostly NLP practitioners. There were no books on coaching available in Russian and the whole concept was far from being understood. Coaching was often confused with therapy, and as a result some Russian businesspeople avoided it, fearing the potential shame of being seen to need 'therapy'. Others suggested that coaching should be treated as consulting, but this brought the expectation that the coach would be an expert in the field in which the manager worked.

In 2002 there were as few as 10 companies in Russia that offered coaching. Nowadays there are several hundred. Coaching has become a new fashion among consulting companies, with most offering this service. Unfortunately, the quality of coaching still leaves a lot to be desired and there is a need for coach training and the development of professional standards.

Russian business and management culture

Until thunderstorm starts muzhik [a man] will not cross himself

(Russian saying)

Russian business culture in general can be described as an ad hoc culture. Although the country had experienced a so-called 'planned economy' during the Soviet period, the 'plan' was seen more in terms of formality than as an action plan with real target setting. The fast changing business environment of the 1990s made planning redundant, as the focus was on responding to a dynamic, even chaotic emerging market. When things start falling apart people look for a solution. Coaching is now seen as a tool that can offer a magic effect on performance.

Although management as a scientific discipline existed in the Soviet Union, there was no entrepreneurial culture. The 1990s have shown a huge gap between knowledge and practice. The belief that anybody can manage economically and that management does not require any specific skills was a costly mistake, which many among the new generation of Russian businesspeople made.

The gap between knowledge and practice can also be described as a gap between culture and money. Those who had money hardly paid attention to any culture issues; those who had an understanding of culture had very little access to money and real management.

The process typical of the 1990s in Russia can be pretty perfectly described using the developmental journey (Whitmore, 2002). The gap between those who paid more attention to the spiritual side and those who focused on earning money grew until it became evident that really successful management can hardly develop and grow without both things being integrated. Of course there were businesspeople and companies that were closer to a middle, balanced direction, but unfortunately these were a minority. Those who had good theoretical knowledge had to gain real business experience and practise what they were talking about. Coaching became a good tool to build a bridge between the two groups.

Typical coaching clients and requests

Typical individual coaching clients in Russia can be described as three major groups:

1. International minds – usually have high-quality education and work experience in international or big Russian companies. Most of them speak foreign languages. Being pretty well informed about what coaching is, they treat it as a service and a tool for boosting their performance.
2. Innovation seekers – they are always ready to try something new to make their life better or to solve their problems. They treat coaching as one of several possible options and tend to try different coaching approaches. Typical coaching school students.
3. Person-oriented clients – they feel they need some tools to help them change their life but have little or no understanding of what can help them. Usually become clients when they meet a coach they like and trust.

Coaching requests vary from presentation or time management skills to personal development or finding a person's mission or purpose in the world, but there is a tendency for any initial request to transform into a more complex and personal mission pretty fast. Quite often, from the very beginning the client expects that a coach, as an expert, will tell them what they should do. It often feels as if the client expects a miracle. High client expectations mean he or she wants things to be changed fast and expects that the coach can bring this about. Sometimes it becomes a challenge for a coach to stay within the coaching frame and maintain a non-directive approach. When the difference between coaching and any other approach becomes obvious for a client, the coaching relationship gets stronger and more productive.

There are many requests from executives related to management issues and leadership skills, which require the systemic approach. As a result a more integrative and transpersonal coaching is appropriate, rather than a purely behavioural approach, which focuses on developing new skills. Sometimes insight and clear vision gained during a coaching session helps the client to make a real breakthrough. It might be creating a metaphor, which helps the individual to see things in a new way, or it can be about asking fundamental questions about what they want from their life.

CASE STUDY: ALEXANDER

Alexander is a middle-aged middle manager in a Russian media company. He decided to hire a coach when he felt that his professional life had got stuck. He had applied for several promotions but had been unsuccessful, and was wondering what he should do next to help him move his career forward. He had attended some training over the past two years but few of the sessions he had attended had helped much. He was looking for a new tool to unlock his potential and shape his new targets. He wanted to explore new opportunities, and wanted some clarification about whether he should continue to work hard and serve his current company, or should take the advice of friends and leave. Alexander contracted for four sessions.

During the coaching session the issue of duty and loyalty came up several times. Did Alexander need to suffer more for his company, accepting second-ments out of Moscow to other cities, before they would reward him? Did he fit in, even though he was not one of the group who dominated in the most powerful positions in the company? The session helped Alexander identify that his real passion was photography, and that while he could work in the wider media, he really liked design and managing the shoots. He decided to become a professional in this sphere, and left the company to set up his own photography business. Making this step, thinking through the barriers and hurdles he might face and making plans for how he might overcome them made good use of the coaching. While the new career went against many of the things that Alexander had been brought up to believe, it allowed him to move forward rather than feel trapped.

During the sessions he made a one-year detailed plan and defined check-points for the next five years. To support the move into the new business area, Alexander went back to obtain some further training. He combined this study with building the business during the first year, undertaking work as an event and wedding photo-artist at the weekends.

Where do coaches come from?

The first generation of Russian coaches were trained by Western trainers or coaches and were from a mix of different backgrounds, but mostly psychology, therapy, business or NLP.

Some therapy approaches, such as solution-focused therapy, are very close to coaching and as a result some therapists saw coaching as one way to diversify their business and attract more clients. This crossover between areas has also been true for NLP specialists, who have drawn on their NLP training to offer coaching. Both of these groups have struggled to understand the nature of Russian business, the distinctive nature of coaching and the role the Russian psyche plays in influencing the thoughts, feelings and behaviours of coachees.

Coaches from business and mentoring have focused on transmitting their knowledge. Their major weakness has been that they believe in 'right' models and ways to achieve things and pay less attention to the individual profiles of people and the different nature of business in Russia.

However, a second generation of coaching professionals is growing from the professional business trainers, businesspeople and HR professional environment. They are aware of the latest training and development issues and nowadays form about 60 per cent of a typical coaching school presentation's audience.

The number of coaching training programmes has grown significantly since 2005 and is expected to continue to grow through the rest of the decade. Coaching is now established, with coaching on offer as part of MBA programmes within universities and through private management companies.

CASE STUDY: RESO

It is difficult to find many companies in Russia where coaching has become a core part of their people development work. One example is the Russian-owned insurance company RESO, which has built the best insurance agent training school and has integrated coaching culture into the company management system. Led by the slogan 'Here you will be astonished by your abilities', they use a value-based and performance-focused coaching programme that has three levels differentiated by dominating coaching type.

The first level is 'executive' – top management coaching. The second one is 'partner' coaching for mid-management and business partners. The third level is so-called 'expert' coaching for sales staff. To unlock potential and maximize performance, the employees and the company should have common values and vision and coherent aims and targets, as well as efficient resource management and clear interpersonal communication. Each person at managerial level gets proper coaching skills training and each employee has an individual development plan that reflects his/her targets correlated with company targets and common values.

The growing telecom market in Russia became a field where high-level professional teams completely integrate coaching into the system. Beeline, one of three leading telecom providers, has pioneered this process, inviting Russian and British coaches to train their managers in coaching skills. Coaching is part of the high-performing staff retention programme at Beeline. It includes 'an introduction to the key coaching models; the development of core coaching skills; understanding how coaching fits into the workplace; using coaching as a tool to get the best out of others; understanding your impact as a leader; and developing a personal plan for implementing what would be learned on the course' (Sparrow, 2007).

It can also be seen as a trend that coaching becomes an entry point for organizational changes and strategy building. Owners who gain a clear vision and understanding of unused potential get interested in services that combine coaching spirit and business consulting. This quite often applies to companies that grow from small family businesses to mid-size organizations or from local mid-size organizations to national networks. 'Before we started changes using coaching in the company I had lots of doubts. The changes were necessary but it looked as though nobody had energy to start moving ahead. But it worked. I never knew my staff could be so involved and take responsibility for so many issues' – the words of an internet shop owner whose team increased performance by more than 25 per cent on average within two months during a team and individual performance coaching programme. 'We now know we are able to make dreams true together.'

SUMMARY

A massive period of transformation has affected Russia over the last decade. The emergence of new business has created a strong demand for coaching in the emerging business sectors.

In spite of this strong demand for coaching, it remains outside of the Russian business culture. To move forward, coaching in Russia needs to develop competent and local coaching solutions that match the psyche of Russia, not follow the trends from the West. It needs to clearly distinguish itself from therapy and consulting by creating a new lexicon and with increased coach training and professional standards. Thirdly, Russia is a big country and Russian coaches need to accept that change can be slow, and that spreading the word about the potential of coaching can take longer than in smaller nations.

References

Kantor, V (2001) Is Russian mentality changing? *Russian Journal*, 29 December
Russian Academy of Science, Complex Social Research Institute (2004) *Citizens of New Russia; What they feel they are like and which society they want to live? 1998–2004*, Analytical report, Russian Academy of Science (in Russian)
Sparrow, S (2007) Coaching challenges in Russia, *Training and Coaching Today*
Tiutchev, F I (1993) *On the Heights of Creation: Lyrics (Russian and East European Studies)* (translated by A Liberman), JAI Press Inc, New York
Whitmore, J (2002) *Coaching for performance*, Nicholas Brealey, London

Further reading

Belovitskaya, Y (2007) Don't be afraid of changes, interview with E Stacke, *Elite Personnel* (in Russian)
Ersov, A (2006) Coaching is freedom, interview with Myles Downey, *Elite personnel* (in Russian)
Klarin, M (2007) *Business Training and Development in Russia: Trends and Issues* (in Russian)
Kukushkin, M (2007) Coaching: Russian field for discussions, *Elite Personnel* (in Russian)
Menshikov, S (2004) *Anatomy of Russian capitalism*, Mezhdunarodnye Otnosheniya Publishers, Moscow
Rybkin, I (2005) *Coaching for social success*, Humanitarian Research Institute, Moscow (in Russian)
Savkin, A and Danilova, M (2003) *Coaching in Russian: Courage to wish*, Rech, Saint-Petersburg (in Russian)
Sorokoumov, A (2006) *Strategy of success in epoch of changes: Coaching players in business*, U-Factoria, Ekaterinburg (in Russian)

11

Coaching in Japan

Takashi Tanaka

INTRODUCTION

Coaching was introduced into Japan 20 years ago. Although it is now booming and bookstores are full of books about it, some people say that the concept of business coaching, as introduced from the United States and Europe, is not effective for Japanese people.

If it is not effective, is this due to the cultural, social and economic elements unique to Japan? What kind of knowledge and skills are needed to make coaching work effectively in Japan?

This chapter first describes the cultural characteristics of Japanese firms, followed by the specific Japanese cultural influence on business coaching. In closing, it discusses who needs coaching and what type of coaching is needed, based on such cultural influence, and seeks out coaching methods that can be used in different cultural backgrounds.

HERITAGE TRADITIONS

Traditional corporate culture

In Japan coaching is given to individuals in most cases. Business coaching is often more effective when the coach understands the working environment of the individuals, which includes the business philosophy, strategies and corporate culture of the firms they are working with.

There are two elements that affect and promote changes in the philosophy, strategies and personnel structure of Japanese firms. One is the Japanese socio-cultural element, exemplified by the groupism of Japanese firms, the homogeneous and single-race society and the lack of social grades resulting from non-elite education. Because this element is widespread among Japanese firms and resistant to change, it has led to a clear difference from other nations over a long period of time (Ishida, 1989).

Socio-cultural elements indirectly affect the whole system of Japanese personnel management, from the philosophy of personnel management to the personnel structure, as well as the values and behaviours of employers and employees.

The other element is economic and technological change. Business globalization, innovation of information and ecological technologies, slow economic development among developed countries, the emergence of newly developing economies, and yen depreciation and deflation are directly affecting the management strategies and personnel structures of Japanese firms. Such environmental changes also affect international firms working in Japan.

Economic and technological changes are also slowly but steadily changing traditional Japanese values and work ethic. For example, the declining birth rate and ageing of the population has changed the structure of the labour market, promoted diversification of the labour force and changed the homogeneous society. Business globalization has activated not only mergers and acquisitions among Japanese firms but also mergers and business partnerships involving foreign firms. This means an increase in firms with heterogeneous culture in Japan, which has at least some effect on the homogeneity.

The virtual working environment having emerged as a result of the innovation of information technology has enabled a variety of employee working styles and changed the group-oriented culture.

Groupism

In describing the traditional cultural characteristics that affect private firms, the first characteristic is the groupism in Japan. Groupism values the interests of the group before those of each individual. The workplace is not only considered a place where workers receive a salary as compensation for their labour, but also one for character-building through group activities and a place for self-realization by achieving the goal of the group. Groupism also sometimes restricts behaviour with the traditional practices unique to village society. It is also a stifling society; one in which people must be always concerned about their delicate interpersonal relations.

Homogeneous society

The second characteristic of Japanese culture is the homogeneous society. Japan, where more than 90 per cent of the population is ethnically homogeneous, has formed a society with few social grades by providing non-elite education and its people share a homogeneous set of values. Because of this homogeneity, informal rules and non-verbal communication, which are often referred to as 'rhythmic breathing', have developed at Japanese firms. The extent of job duties and the share of jobs are decided with some ambiguity. Not clearly defining the duties and powers of each individual and having them debate business decisions has enabled firms to make more rapid changes in response to changing circumstances.

In a heterogeneous society, on the other hand, statutory rules and planned communication have developed. When people with different cultural backgrounds try to achieve a common goal systematically, they clearly state all aspects of the words in detail and leave no ambiguity in order to avoid misunderstandings and conflicts. This is seen in US firms, where contracts become very important and manuals for duties and job descriptions are formulated (Ishida, 1989).

Japanese organizational structure

The organizational structure of Japanese firms has some characteristics influenced by the culture.

Extent of duties

Although the main duties and responsibilities of each individual are clarified to some extent, other peripheral duties are set with a large discretionary zone so that employees can take complementary action. For these duties, workers discuss with their colleagues and subordinates in order to share the responsibilities in accordance with their circumstances. The same is also seen in employment adjustment. Japanese firms respond to economic fluctuations on a certain scale by having their employees work overtime and establishing a flexible division of roles instead of adjusting the labour force immediately, whereas US and European firms tend to lay off their employees in an effort to eliminate excess labour force and thus reduce their burden in response to an economic recession or worsening business performance.

When the job description of each individual is clear, as in US and European organizations, organizational efficiency is secured to some extent as long as individual workers pursue their own duties, even when human relations at the workplace are bad. Japanese firms often lack this aspect. Therefore, the management always struggles to create and maintain a workplace where the organization works voluntarily with good human relations.

There is a huge gap in the distribution of goods, people and money in US and European firms between upper- and lower-ranking employees. Although the top management is assigned considerable power and mid-ranking employees are given a reasonable degree of power, lower-ranking employees have no power and simply follow their bosses' orders. In other words, the organization consists of prominent leaders and powerless masses (Ishida, 1989). On the other hand, the distribution gap within Japanese firms is relatively small. Workers are more equal and they are industrious and self-motivated.

Recruitment and internal promotion

One characteristic of the personnel structure of Japanese firms is that they are more likely to employ new graduates with no working experience. This is because they believe that innocent new graduates will more easily learn the set of values and the behavioural patterns unique to the firm and acquire their unique skills (Koike, 1985).

Employees are generally internally promoted and accumulate experience and career progression through cross-sectional job experiences and job changes within a firm. By doing so, they learn corporate culture and skills that cannot be acquired at other firms. This is why few employees of Japanese firms change their job to work at other companies.

Consistent high-standard non-elite education has long provided the market with a high-quality labour force with an equivalent value system. The lack of grades in the social structure creates a sense of equality among workers, and helps prevent excessive gaps in compensation and promotion based on performance between higher- and lower-ranking members. Promotion is gradual and based on long-term employment.

Compensation

Compensation is decided based on the length of service, ability, attitude (cooperativeness, sense of responsibility and sense of loyalty) and performance. In Japanese firms the gap of compensation is relatively small for a short period of time. This disparity gradually widens over time. The seniority system in Japan does not simply prioritize seniority but is an outcome of the length of service and abilities. It is a competitive compensation plan, designed largely to reflect individual differences over a long period.

THE INFLUENCE OF TRADITIONS ON BEHAVIOUR, SELF-PERCEPTION AND RELATIONSHIPS

It is a long time since corporate globalization became active. The international environment around Japan affects corporate management in various ways as the impact of multicultural elements increases. The products and technologies of a firm are less likely to be affected by the culture and politics of one nation from a global strategic perspective. On the other hand, as global business activities advance, customs, sets of values and codes of conduct of employees between the head office and multiple overseas offices are more likely to be affected in various ways.

Even at global firms that have promoted global strategies for localization ahead of other firms, the head office has initially taken charge of the personnel reshuffle at the international level for technical transfers, the spread of products and the unification of quality standards. For this reason, the head office decides on the top management of their overseas offices.

When the overseas office has been managed under the supervision of the head office and the management stays there only two to three years, they cannot understand the customer preferences and business practice in the overseas market, meaning it takes quite some time to operate it smoothly. In the worst case, more than a few companies have given up their overseas operation and withdrawn. In most cases, such firms did not understand the market well and precluded cultural diversity to build human relations between workers with different cultural backgrounds at the workplace.

There has been interdisciplinary research on localization to achieve effective globalization by reflecting on the cross-cultural problems that occurred previously through the localization process. The following is some research on global firm management in Japan and the behaviours and sets of values of local employees.

Cultural impact on attitudes and behaviours

According to a survey on leaders of multinational firms (Hofstede, 1991), the culture and socio-economic elements where the firms are based explain 50 per cent of the attitudes and behaviours of the leaders. This shows that these aspects have more impact than their duties, age and sex. A similar survey was also conducted with the leaders of global firms living in Japan (Nagai, 2005).

Prior to the survey, the following hypothesis was set up: 'Managers working at an overseas office are under pressure to unify systems and institutions internationally when an organization implements a globalization strategy and the behaviour of managers' leadership moves toward the same direction.' Therefore, as Figure 11.1 shows, a hypothesis was made that works on the following formula:

$$\begin{array}{cc} \text{Difference I} (A-B) & \text{Difference II} (A-C) \\ \text{(international unification)} & < \quad \text{(extension of local diversity)} \end{array}$$

However, the survey revealed an opposite result. The behavioural pattern of firms in the same area is similar, regardless of whether they are multinational or local firms. Local leaders accept the leadership behaviours of the country where the overseas office is located, despite the accepted behaviours of the global strategies. The survey concluded that local culture is deeply related to the sets of values and attitudes of individuals and their behaviours based on the same, and that they cannot be easily changed with the firm's unique corporate culture.

$$\text{Difference I} (A-B) \quad > \quad \begin{array}{c} \text{Difference II} (A-C) \\ \text{or} \\ \text{Difference III} (B-D) \end{array}$$

In the survey (Nagai, 2005), although global firm managers in Japan were evaluated as being highly cooperative within an organization, and having high internal coordination ability and responsibility, they received relatively low scores concerning their ability to make quick decisions at their own discretion and their motivation to achieve a goal, which are valued at US and European firms.

Leadership difference	Difference II (A – C)	Difference III (B – D)
Difference I (A – B)	A. Local multinational US company	B. Multinational US company
	C. Japanese company (located in Japan)	D. Local Japanese company (located in US)

Figure 11.1 Leadership difference

Cultural impact on job duties

Interviews were conducted with the local management and personnel section chief of 50 Japanese multinational firms concerning their job duties and management skills required for the management (Holt, 1993). In the comparison of Japanese and US managers, there was no clear difference in their roles and responsibilities. However, the skills necessary to perform their roles and responsibilities differed and it was concluded that this was attributable to cultural and social differences.

This means that both Japanese and US managers have the same basic roles and responsibilities as managers: to be leaders; to bring results; to train their subordinates; to build a cooperative system between sections; and to make improvements to satisfy customers. After the factor analysis, 19 skills required to be in managerial positions in Japan were selected, ordered according to the degree of importance. Beforehand, a similar survey was conducted with 2000 people in managerial positions in the overseas offices of US firms. Based on this survey result, the skills required to be in a managerial position at US firms were compared.

According to the survey result (Figure 11.2), although 60 per cent, or 15 skills, are common, Japanese and US employees at a managerial level showed differences in their belief of the level of importance. Three of the four skills Japanese managers regard as most important are thought to be behaviours influenced by the socio-cultural impact of the spirit of sharing the same destiny or behind-the-scenes manoeuvring within the group-oriented society. In the US, which is a multiethnic society and where individualism is respected, managers are expected to have major power and lead the organization with abilities including promoting innovation, giving influential speeches and managing from a global perspective, and are well versed in financial issues.

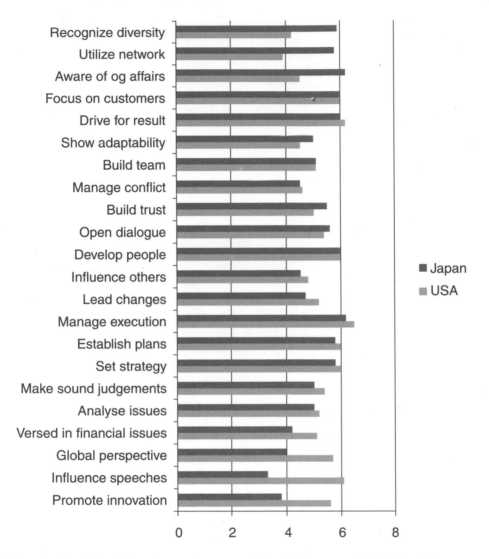

Figure 11.2 Priorities of management skills in Japan and the United States: importance ratings

DEVELOPING CULTURALLY APPROPRIATE COACHING

Who needs coaching in different cultures?

I explained that Japanese culture and society had an impact on the formulation of strategies and personnel management of global firms to some extent. I also explained that they strongly influence the sets of values and codes of conduct of the managers and employees of such firms.

In this section, I will give some examples of specific coaching given to personnel of firms facing various cross-cultural problems and needing coaching.

As Figure 11.3 shows, there are three types of people requiring coaching in this chapter. Type A includes non-Japanese workers in managerial positions dispatched to Japan from their head office overseas for a relatively short period. Type B includes top Japanese managers living and working in Japan for a multinational firm based outside the country. Type C includes Japanese people dispatched to an overseas office as part of top management from a Japanese firm. In this chapter, I will discuss Types A and B, for whom there is likely to be a high demand for coaching.

Company	Coachees	Coaching needs	Coachees	Coaching needs
Japanese	*Head Office/ Japanese managerial position*	*Less*	*Local/Japanese managerial position*	*Medium type C*
Non- Japanese multinational	Non-Japanese managerial position	Large type A	—	—
Non- Japanese multinational	Local/Japanese managerial position	Large type B	—	—
	Located in Japan		Located overseas	

Figure 11.3 Who needs coaching in different cultures?

CASE STUDY: PAUL

Paul is an American Caucasian male in his late thirties working at a Japanese corporation of a US pharmaceutical company. He began working at its Tokyo office as an executive director for developing new medicines one and a half years ago. His term in Japan was for three to four years. He had had marvellous achievements as the director of clinical development at the head office and came to Japan to 'get the new development system of the Japanese subsidiary on track.' Before coming to Japan, he had worked overseas for two years in the Netherlands as the development manager. He cannot read or write Japanese. Although he communicates in English with a few Japanese staff, his secretary serves as an interpreter to give daily business instructions and lead meetings when staff members who cannot speak English are involved.

This company established its Japanese corporation 17 years ago. There are about 1,000 employees in sections such as new drug development, marketing, packaging and distribution. There are about 300 employees in the development section for which the executive director is responsible. More than 95 per cent of employees are Japanese.

The development of new medicines in the Japanese market has required the construction of a traditional and complex relationship with the Ministry of Health, Labour and Welfare and other authorities involved in the approval of new medicines, as well as university hospitals and Japanese physicians. Therefore, the new medicine development section had been led by a Japanese director since the establishment of the Japanese subsidiary.

Competition relating to new drug development had intensified and there had been an active move to develop new large-scale drugs ahead of competitors, introduce them to the market at a global level and recover the development costs incurred over the last six to seven years. The firm's new network had enabled an efficient operation and strong ties between branch offices, centred around the head office. This is how the American executive director came to be dispatched to Japan as the manager of the development section.

The president of the Japanese company (Japanese), who is Paul's boss, had stated six months previously that Paul was not getting on well with staff in the office.

Paul felt he had failed to build good relationships with Japanese staff after an incident at a meeting. A Japanese manager responsible for statistics and analyses was opposed to a new data analysis method proposed by the head office, saying that the related Japanese authorities would not approve it. Paul was angry at the Japanese manager, fiercely banging a table at his negative attitude and shouting at him in front of other participants in the meeting.

When he was in the Netherlands, although discussions became heated, this approach triggered suggestions of productive ideas in some cases. This incident was just a heated meeting for him. Although it was the first time he had expressed his anger, the bad relationship with the surrounding Japanese staff has continued ever since.

Because Paul felt the need to deepen his personal relations with his Japanese staff, he kept his office door open so that anyone could come to his office to talk. However, the only visitors were the staff who came to his office to gain his approval or give him a daily report. No one else visited his office to enjoy conversation with him.

Paul soon began giving strong instructions to his staff. Although he was disappointed that the Japanese staff answered only when he asked questions, and always awaited instructions and took no actions voluntarily, he adopted the instructive attitude, partly because the new medicine development project was behind schedule.

For Paul, coaching offered a way to think afresh about the culture of his business unit in Japan and how he could adapt his approach to be more culturally sensitive. He hoped that figuring out the secret code behind the Japanese culture would lead to an early improvement of the problem.

Meetings at Japanese firms do not require explanations of background information. In many cases, some decisions have already been made before the meetings. Because most Japanese organizations have highly developed formal and informal information networks, it is better to think that everyone shares most of the information concerning proceedings within the firm. The dissenting opinion of the Japanese manager in charge of statistics and analyses is believed to have been shared among and agreed on by Japanese employees before the meeting. When Paul expressed his anger and confronted the person in charge, he saw this as debate. The staff, however, saw it as a challenge to the group. Attention needed to be paid to the traditional decision-making process of Japanese firms and how leaders become involved in them.

In Japan particularly, there is a strong sense of the person in charge of the work being the leader there in the organization. Even board directors and head office superiors cannot change decisions concerning the work easily.

Japanese people are often said not to express their feelings in a good or bad way. It should be recognized that leaders, in particular, expressing their anger obviously in front of many people is not generally accepted. Japanese people respect experience and age. Paul may have given the impression of being a young destroyer rather than an aggressive reformer to Japanese people.

Paul needed to understand that his behaviour could cause misunderstanding due to cultural differences. Being straightforward can give the impression of being blunt and discussing the agenda directly may give the impression of being arrogant and impudent.

Paul also needed to be more aware of cooperative interpersonal skills. Although American people get to the point directly, they talk a lot and do not always listen to other parties. The coaching helped Paul acquire the interpersonal skills needed to carefully observe the behaviours of Japanese people and sense their subtle non-verbal communication in order to communicate with them.

Lacking basic knowledge about Japanese language and culture could also cause misunderstandings. Information and books about Japanese business practices can easily be obtained through the Japan External Trade Organization and the United States Department of Commerce.

Because experience and age are respected in the business world in Japan, it is generally recognized that individuals in their early forties or younger should not assume top management posts there, even if they have excellent achievements. This should be considered when dispatching directors from the head office.

CASE STUDY: YAMAMOTO

Yamamoto is a Japanese GM (general manager) working at a Japanese firm of a major US clothing store chain. He began working at this firm two years ago, after leaving his post as chief of the clothing section of a major Japanese department store. He had substantial experience in the sale of men's and women's clothing and understood the Japanese clothing market on both the manufacturing and distribution sides very well.

This Japanese firm with US capital was established about three years ago. It has more than 20 stores in eight major cities in Japan and has achieved positive sales. It also has a sister clothing company under a different brand name, which entered the Japanese market a decade ago and has achieved great success. There were great expectations of this new firm. However, sales have not reached the figures expected.

Simon is Yamamoto's boss, an American and the president of the Japanese firm of the sister clothing company. Yamamoto communicates with Simon in English at a daily conversation level and his presentations for the US head office are given through an interpreter. His seven direct subordinates include two Americans dispatched from the United States; one is the vice-president in charge of personnel affairs and the other is in charge of the finance section.

There were some complaints about Yamamoto from his subordinates and American colleagues. They claimed that what was decided in the morning was changed in the afternoon, and his subordinates then had to change their priorities.

Although Yamamoto let his subordinates do their work, he was told that his attitude was *laissez-faire* as he watched on calmly without giving advice or instructions. He did not praise the achievements of his subordinates. Yamamoto often called out to his subordinates 'Hey, you', during meetings, which annoyed other attendees. He says that the expression is often used at conventional Japanese firms to show affection.

Some subordinates also said that he was not interested in training his subordinates as he prioritized short-term sales and profits.

Because excellent middle management plays a central role for most Japanese businesses, the top management rarely give specific instructions or stand at the forefront. In contrast, US head office staff usually feel that the strategies of Japanese top management are weak or the speed of decision-making is slow and that they do not push themselves forward to achieve targets.

Yamamoto has not achieved the expected business performance and has not developed the abilities of his subordinates, including the middle-management. As a result, his evaluation was relatively low.

There was a problem in terms of information flow. He met a limited number of his subordinates separately and obtained the necessary work-related information through the subordinates he met.

Because the organization was horizontal, there was no official exchange of information with workers in different sections. Therefore, when there was a change in a decision, informal information swirled around and priority issues were not changed speedily, which often resulted in confusion. Yamamoto was the one who was blamed for such situations.

In the clothing industry, product manufacturing (differences in taste, physical differences, materials), complex distribution routes, differences in advertising, a gap in the attitude towards customer service, handling claims and the selection of distributors all fall on the personnel in marketing and sales who are versed in the Japanese market and how to appeal to customers. Both sides need to realize that it requires an understanding of cultural differences, staff who can offer opinions about the differences to the head office, and top management with sophisticated knowledge and flexibility in order to succeed in this industry.

Explanations to the US head office to gain its support are more easily understood when they are provided in accordance with the Western style and behaviour pattern. Yamamoto needed to acquire the skills demanded by the US head office. He also needed to develop his relationships with his staff.

Although Yamamoto had worked at a Japanese firm for a long time, he had not realized information sharing would be hindered so much in his new position. Coaching helped him to develop a plan. It was decided to hold a meeting at least once a week by function and rank in order to confirm that they shared the same ideas on policy development. He also established a system to respond to abrupt changes in priority issues.

CONCLUSION

As business activities become increasingly global, the differences in basic human behaviours, such as customs, sets of values and codes of conduct between the head office and multiple overseas offices become more apparent. In the process of globalization, the local characteristics where the overseas offices are located, such as the local language, culture and politics, significantly influence the business behaviours and sets of values of local employees, as well as interpersonal relations within the organization.

Although there was little difference in the roles and responsibilities of managers between Japan and the United States, there was a difference in the skills required to pursue them, and socio-cultural elements are believed to have some impact in this area.

Specifically, the three important skills that Japanese managers are expected to have, to be aware of organizational affairs, to utilize human networks, and to recognize the value of diversity, are due to the socio-cultural influence required in the behind-the-scenes manoeuvring and common destiny of groupism. On the other hand, in a multiethnic society where individualism is respected, as in the United States, managers are expected to promote innovation, give influential speeches, manage with a global perspective and be well versed in financial affairs to lead an organization with great authority at the top, which differs from the case in Japan.

We also found that Japanese management respects the importance of raising employees' willingness to work, promoting complementary and flexible working behaviours, raising their sense of belonging to the company and creating a cooperative relationship between labour and management.

Local culture is deeply associated with the sets of values and attitudes of individuals and their behaviours and cannot be changed easily with merely unique corporate culture. Thus, it is essential that managers working at global firms have the ability to distinguish what is common and what is different between different countries, and to choose the behaviours and actions appropriate in the particular country.

References

Hall, T E (1987) *Hidden Differences: Studies in International Communication*, Bungei Shunju
Hofstede, G H (1991) *Cultures and Organizations – Software of the Mind*, McGraw-Hill UK, London
Holt, K (1993) The study of managerial competencies in Japan, *Japan Journal of Human Resource Management*
Ishida, H (1989) *Japanese Human Resource Management*, Kigyo to Jinzai, Keio University Sangyo kenkyusho
Koike, K (1985) The internal labor structure of economic system, Toyokeizai Press, Tokyo
Nagai, H (2005) *The Qualities of High Performance Global Leaders*, Hakuto-shobo

Further reading

Ikeda, R (2007) *Cross Cultural Communication*, Sanshu-sha, pp 22–24
Hayashi, Y (2002) The study of organizational commitment and factors, *Sangyo Soshiki Kenkyu* **16**(1), pp 59–70
Kamiya, E (2008) Effects of transformation leadership: Subordinate model and team performance, *Journal of Risho, graduate school study*
Matsbara, T (1994) The study of charismatic leadership: leadership behaviors and group effects, *Sangyo Soshiki Kenkyu* **8**(1), pp 29–40
Nisbett, E R (2003) *The Geography of Thought: How Asians and Westerners think differently... and why*, Diamond, pp 43–46
Taniguchi, M (2005) *Diversity Management*, Diversity Performance, Hakuto-shobo pp 41–49

Watanabe, M (1999) *Organizational Psychology Measurement* Hakuto-shobo.

Yamagishi, T (1998) *The Structure of Trust: The Evolutionary Games and Mind and Society*, University of Tokyo Press, Tokyo

Part 3

Ethnicity, age and gender difference

12

Coaching black British coachees

Tinu Cornish

INTRODUCTION

This chapter presents a brief introduction to the history of settlement in Britain of three of the largest black communities in the United Kingdom. The political heritage of black British people is also discussed. The chapter then proceeds to compare the cultural differences and similarities between the three groups and the mainstream white British community. The impact of aspects of these cultural differences on leadership and behaviour at work are explored and the implications for coaching identified. However, cultural differences are not the only source of different experiences in the workplace for black coachees. Issues and approaches for coaching a black coachee dealing with actual or perceived discrimination will also be explored. Finally, the chapter will consider the issue of career constraint.

HERITAGE TRADITIONS

Immigration from the Caribbean

Television programmes that feature the migration of black people to the United Kingdom often open with a shot of the passenger ship SS *Empire Windrush*, shortly after it landed at Tilbury Docks in England, on 21 June 1948. The camera lingers on the groups and pairs of smartly dressed black people, who were part of the first wave of Caribbean settlers to Britain, as they descend the gangplank full of excitement and hope at the start of their new life in the 'Mother Country'. Unfortunately reality soon hit. Accounts of the experience of Caribbean migrants at the time attest to the shock of rejection (signs in lodging houses saying 'no blacks, no Irish, no dogs'); and the struggle to find work whilst enduring the separation from family and communities back home.

Many Caribbean migrants arrived with the assumption that their stay would be short and lucrative, but widespread discrimination meant that Caribbeans were excluded from highly paid and skilled jobs, particularly in those sectors that were highly unionized (National Archive, 2008). Although plenty of work was available in the public sector, relatively poor pay and a high cost of living meant that Caribbean migrants were unable to amass enough savings to return home and permanent settlement became the norm. Typically children who had been left 'back home' with their grandparents were sent for to join their parent(s) in England, often joining families comprising new siblings and partners. These children's experience in the education system, of discrimination and poor quality, mirrored that of their parents at work. This consolidated a pattern of disadvantage that continues to this day, with unemployment rates for black men and women at 14 per cent and 9 per cent respectively, compared with 5 per cent and 4 per cent for white men and women respectively (Office for National Statistics, 2002).

Immigration from West Africa

Post-war migration to the United Kingdom from West Africa (particularly Nigeria and Ghana) was typified by young people coming to university for undergraduate and postgraduate studies. Many of these individuals would be the sons and daughters of relatively wealthy parents. A common perception of West Africans is still that they are 'always studying' and they will, if anything, tend to be overqualified in respect of their actual occupation (Lindley, 2007). Since the 1980s, the increasingly poor economic conditions in West Africa prompted more widespread migration to the United Kingdom, and migrants from this part of Africa now come from a wide spectrum of backgrounds. Over three-quarters of West Africans live in London. West African communities tend to be devout and Evangelical and Pentecostal churches have sprung up to cater for congregations drawn from these groups.

Immigration from East Africa

Nearly 70 per cent of Africans are Christians, while 20 per cent are Muslims. The majority of African Muslims come from East Africa, principally from Somalia, Sudan, Ethiopia and Kenya.

Of the East African migrants, the Somali community has a particularly long and unique history of settlement in England and parts of South Wales. During the 19th century, Somali men were employed as seafarers in the United Kingdom and in Aden (in Yemen). An Act of Parliament passed in 1894 restricted Somalis to jobs in the seafaring industry and a pattern of settlement linked to the port towns emerged (see www.portcities.org.uk). There was more settlement of Somalis in London after the war. During the 1970s and 1990s, Somalis fled civil war in East Africa. The Somali community fares extremely poorly on many measures of community success. For example, one estimate of the unemployment rate among Somali men in 1999 was 87 per cent (Frieda and Walters, 1999). In another example, a survey of educational attainment in a London borough's schools in 2000, only 3 per cent of 16-year-old Somali pupils obtained grade C and above in GCSE exams. The average for all pupils was 47 per cent and for other black Africans was 28 per cent (Ali and Jones, 2000). The impact of religion, language literacy and gender are thought to lie behind these statistics (Harris, 2004).

An important difference between Christian and Islamic communities is often thought to be the role of women. This may be less likely to be different in the African community. In Christian West Africa, whilst men may be seen as the head of the household, women have always been market traders and independent economically. In today's society, this translates into a commitment to career development and studying to gain higher qualifications. Women-headed households can be a feature of the Caribbean community. Economic necessity means that women in this situation are more likely to work full time, as they do not have the luxury of long career breaks or part-time work. In the Somali community, a tradition of female-headed households, while the men were away at sea, has been reinforced by the break-up of families due to war and famine and the subsequent flight from these situations. Somali women have always had the right to divorce; and in Britain the mass unemployment of men and a reliance on benefits has resulted in an increase in divorce, leading to a further increase in women-headed households (Harris, 2004).

Political heritage

As well as having a cultural identity, black people typically have a political identity. This is usually formed by an awareness and understanding of black history and the perception, experience and subsequent challenge of discrimination. (For a detailed discussion of identity see Nazroo and Karlesen, 2003). Black people can have a strong cultural identity and a weaker political identity; the opposite can also be true. For each individual the balance will depend on their personal history, how integrated their community or family is into the mainstream, their experiences and the beliefs and values of the specific individual.

Although the roots of black political history are the abolition of the slave trade, it was the breakdown of gender and race divisions during the Second World War, and the independence movements of former colonies, that created a climate ripe for the development of the civil rights movements in the 1960s. The black civil rights movement in the United States served as an inspiration for similar demands in the United Kingdom. By 1976, the Race Relations Act (and the Sex Discrimination Act) had been ratified by parliament. This act outlawed race discrimination at work, and in the provision of goods and services. The act also established the Commission for Racial Equality to monitor compliance with the act.

In the 1980s, generous funding was made available for minority support and campaigning groups. In the public sector, black staff banded together to advocate for change within their organizations. This advocacy led to the adoption of equal opportunities policies, and the implementation of fair selection procedures. Equal opportunities training became established as a standard part of the induction process for most staff in the public and not-for-profit sectors. Larger private sector organizations also adopted a similar approach.

Twenty years later, progress remains patchy. Unemployment rates for black African and black Caribbean men remain three times that of white men. Black Caribbean women fare better, with unemployment rates twice that of white women, but for black African women the rate is back to three times higher. In the public and not-for-profit sectors, in the major urban areas, black people are often well represented in the operational and supervisory roles and are successfully accessing middle management roles. However, moving into senior management remains a considerable challenge and most organizations are characterized as having a 'snowy peak'. In the private sector, if you walk around a larger company based in an urban area, you are likely to notice that the black and brown faces are concentrated in the support services – Finance, IT, HR, Customer Services and Administration; with only the odd black person in operational and managerial roles. A research project in 2005 found that only one UK-born black director was appointed in a FTSE 100 company that year (Singh, 2006).

THE INFLUENCE OF TRADITIONS ON BEHAVIOUR, SELF-PERCEPTION AND RELATIONSHIPS

Before moving on, it may be useful to differentiate and define some of the terms – 'race', 'ethnicity', 'nationality' and 'culture' – that are often used interchangeably in this area, but which, in fact, have different meanings.

▌ **Race** refers to a person's biological differences, principally the visible differences between people.
▌ **Ethnicity** refers to one's membership of an ethnic group. An ethnic group is legally defined, in the United Kingdom, as one in which members of that group must have a long-shared history and a common cultural tradition. Additionally, they are likely to (but do not always) have a common geographical origin from a small number of common ancestors and a common language, literature or religion.
▌ **Nationality** refers to one's citizenship, as shown in one's passport.
▌ **Culture** refers to the codes or conventions that are specific to peoples or societies made up of ideas, habits, beliefs, values, traditions, customs, food, dress, music, humour. It is often influenced by religion.

Black British people, therefore, share a similar racial background but come from a variety of different ethnic groups. They may share some cultural similarities but will also differ widely.

Different cultures can be compared on the basis of a variety of different cultural dimensions. Some of these dimensions have been shown to influence behaviour in the workplace (Hofstede, 1980, 1991; Triandis, 1994; Trompenaars and Hampden-Turner, 1998). Table 12.1 is adapted from one developed by Stone and Stone-Romero (2004) to compare US subcultures. It sets out the cultural differences between the three black ethnic groups discussed in this chapter and white British people. However, it should be noted that this is not based on empirical evidence.

However, citing research by Triandis (1994), Stone and Stone-Romero warn that 'individual differences in gender, socio-economic status, historical background and religion often influence the values of individuals within a given subculture. More specifically, the research revealed that, regardless of national culture... men and individuals from high socio-economic backgrounds tend to be more individualistic than women and individuals from low socio-economic backgrounds.' (Stone and Stone-Romero, 2004, pp 83–84).

Certainly it has been my experience that possible negative aspects of collectivism, such as loyalty to tribal and religious groups, are more prevalent in lower status jobs. The further up the organization one goes, the less likely it is for cultural differences to be a feature; probably because

Table 12.1 Cultural dimensions

Cultural dimension	West African Christian	Caribbean Christian	East African Muslim	White British Christian
Individualism – ties between people weak; look after self and immediate family **Collectivism** – ties within group strong; group looks after you in return for loyalty	Collectivist	Middle	Collectivist	Individual-istic
High Power Distance – accept hierarchy and status differences **Low Power Distance** – minimize hierarchy and prefer consultation and participation	High	Low	High	Low
Achievement – accomplishment is basis for identity and status **Ascription** – identity and status on the basis of rank in the community	Ascriptive	Both	Ascriptive	Achievement
Universalistic – universal codes of practice and principles apply to everyone and everyone should be treated the same **Particularistic** – importance of relationships and accommodating individual needs and specific circumstances	Particular-istic	Middle	Particular-istic	Universal-istic
Time Orientation Rigid – time is linear, punctuality and time management important **Flexible** – interpersonal relationships more important than time management; great deal of latitude about what it means to be on time **Future** – plan for the future and delay gratification, focus on one task at a time	Flexible Present	Flexible Present	Flexible Present	Ridged Future

Table 12.1 Cultural dimensions *cont.*

Cultural dimension	West African Christian	Caribbean Christian	East African Muslim	White British Christian
Present – spontaneous, relaxed, less delayed gratification, process more important than outcome				
Communication Directness **Direct** – get straight to the point, facts **Indirect** – social niceties important, can 'beat around the bush'	Direct	Direct	Indirect	Middle
Displayed Emotionality Low – calm, unemotional, neutral **High** – free expression of emotion, passion	High	High	Low	Low
Credible Sources	Family, Older people, High-status persons	Family, Experts	Older males, Family, High-status persons	Experts, Accomplished, High-status persons

people who can demonstrate the majority culture's values are more likely to be promoted. There are benefits, though, of an ascriptive value system for discriminated-against groups, in that one's self-worth is not dependent on one's status at work (Croker and Major, 1989).

It is not uncommon for black coachees to manage the dichotomy between the culture at home and at work by developing two personas, a work persona and a personal persona, particularly when the coachee feels that people at work are going to be judgemental or hostile to their lifestyle at home. The personal persona is often fiercely protected at work by the adoption of two strategies. The first consists of not sharing more than the bare minimum of personal information with work colleagues. The second involves not taking part in social activities with colleagues after work, often citing religious differences and childcare needs as the reason. Unfortunately, though, these two strategies, whilst protective for the individual, can negatively impact on their career.

For black coachees, personal information can also include roles taken within their community and religious organizations. But it is often precisely these experiences (because of barriers in the workplace) that make a major contribution to the development of the black coachee's leadership and motivational skills. If the split in the personas is too great, the coachee may not even recognize that they have these transferable skills, let alone that they should transfer them to (and promote them in) the workplace. As such, the coachee deprives themselves of their 'cultural capital'. I have found this to be particularly so when the leadership role is carried out within a religious capacity.

A British study (Campayne, Harper Jantuah and Peters, 2006) identified that successful black and ethnic minority women leaders (half black, one-third Asian, remainder mixed) characteristically demonstrated eight leadership qualities, influenced and shaped by their experience as minorities:

▌ Bicultural competence – being familiar with both British values and the norms of their ethnic group gave them the ability to manage and lead across cultures.
▌ Multiple perspectives – cultural breadth and learning from the challenges faced because of their race and gender gave them the ability to see things from multiple perspectives and often come up with novel solutions to problems.
▌ Cultural capital – experience gained outside the workplace through voluntary work with community or religious organizations stood them in good stead in terms of building up leadership and motivational skills.
▌ Transformactional leaders – both transformational, being able to challenge the status quo and implement change, and transactional, regularly delivering results without affecting the overall direction of organizational travel.
▌ Self-mastery – a sense of assuredness in their innate talents and a resilience to deal with challenges and setbacks.
▌ Presence, passion and power – able to communicate their views with conviction and enthusiasm and hold the attention of others.
▌ Value-driven leadership – being guided not so much by monetary rewards as the desire to make a positive contribution to their organizations and communities.
▌ Spiritual belief – in no small way fundamental to their success.

These qualities are very similar to those thought to be essential for Authentic Leaders (George *et al*, 2007). Authentic leaders 'demonstrate a passion for their purpose, they practice values consistently, and lead with their hearts as well as their heads. They establish long-term, meaningful relationships and have the self-discipline to get results. They know who they are.' Authentic leaders typically reported that overcoming difficult challenges in their lives was the catalyst for developing a passion to lead. It follows that reviewing a coachee's personal history and identifying the strengths they have gained from it ought to be an essential feature of any coaching done with black coachees.

The negative impact of not socializing can be threefold. Firstly, the coachee misses out on all the networking and informal information sharing and decision-making that happens on these occasions. Secondly, they also miss out on the opportunity for social de-categorization that can happen when people get to know each other better, ie one is seen as an individual, not just in terms of one's ethnic or racial identity (Crisp and Hewstone, 2006). Thirdly, an essential feature of effective leaders is their ability to forge good relationships between their staff. For a lot of staff, part of the reward of work is the social needs they have met there. It is difficult, therefore, to be effective as a manager without the capacity to foster a positive social connection with staff, peers and superiors.

Black coachees for whom this is an issue need to be encouraged to recognize that if they can't or won't 'join them' – for example, in the pub or on the golf course – they need to identify alternative ways of achieving the same ends. In addition to being creative about social activities, I have encouraged black coachees to make the sorts of icebreakers, exercises and techniques used in team building a regular part of their team meetings. This helps people to get to know each other and bond together in the absence of shared cultural norms.

CASE STUDY: CHARMAINE

Charmaine had recently been promoted from within the team and was the new head of the service. It was recognized that this appointment was quite a stretch for her and I was commissioned to support her development during her first year. One of the themes we had explored during coaching was how she could empower staff to become leaders after years of their being treated like children by the previous manager. She decided to do this by encouraging everyone to take responsibility for a particular project or initiative. One of the Muslim staff took on responsibility for organizing the Christmas get-together. She did this by booking a table at a popular Indian, Muslim restaurant. The rest of the staff were happy to eat Indian food, but they were not happy about the fact that there would be no alcohol (especially since the service paid the bill on these occasions!). Charmaine received lots of complaints from the rest of the team and real pressure was exerted to override the staff member's choice. But she knew this would be undermining and, with the support she received during our coaching sessions, she held firm. In the end the occasion went really well. The staff member had made a good choice of restaurant, and the team learned they could have fun in each other's company without alcohol.

DEVELOPING CULTURALLY APPROPRIATE COACHING

Black coachees can face a constant dilemma about whether to alter the way they behave in order to fit in, or accept that they will never fit in. Many will not want to change aspects of themselves that they see as being expressions of their culture. To take one example, a cultural dimension that can persist, regardless of hierarchy, is the tendency to have a more direct and passionate communication style. Interestingly, there also appears to be a gender bias in the perception of this communication style because it is often black women who are complained about as being 'too loud' or 'aggressive'. If this feedback is given to them, coachees will often feel offended and attacked. A typical response is to ask why they should change and not the majority culture. I often joke at this point that one solution may be to start wearing a badge saying 'proud to be loud'!

Coachees facing such dilemmas can be asked to identify what the value is of the different cultural perspectives/behaviours/attitudes of their community and the majority community (Rosinski, 2003). The next step would be for the coachee to consider whether there would be anything to be gained from borrowing the valuable aspects of the other culture's approach. To continue with the 'loudness' example, the value of a passionate communication style could be that it is likely to be interesting and inspiring and to help you get your point across. The value of a low emotion communication style could be that it may be more logical and considered and creates more space for listening. Blending both communication styles would result in the coachee being both logical and inspiring, able to get their point across well and listen to others. The next step, if this is what the coachee wants, would be for the coach and coachee to work together to develop the skills needed to help them achieve this. The goal of this approach is to support the coachee to develop their unique leadership style that reflects their cultural strengths, but also incorporates successful methods from other cultures.

One of the benefits of using a cross-cultural approach is that it enables both the coach and the coachee to see the majority group as another ethnic group. Problems coachees face in the workplace may be due to cultural differences and not discrimination, as is often thought to be the case. Taking a cross-cultural perspective can remove some of the perceived threat of these situations and make it easier to identify strategies that meet the needs of both groups. This is empowering for the coachee because more options means more hope of a successful outcome. Extensive research in the United States has shown that constantly feeling one is being discriminated against can have negative impacts on health, well-being and self-esteem (Branscombe, Schmitt and Harvey, 1999; Miller and Kaiser, 2001). A feeling of high hope, on the other hand, has opposite effects (Snyder, 2000).

CASE STUDY: CONRAD

Conrad was a highly successful senior manager in a city firm. He came to coaching because he was feeling extremely bitter about not being offered a director's post that had recently become vacant. He was reluctant to move to another company in case he found the same situation there. He was beginning to believe that the only way he was ever going to be a director was to set up his own company. When I asked him what he felt the main barrier was to his advancement, he cited the 'old boys' network amongst the senior managers. He felt that his face was never going to fit as they had all been to public schools and Oxbridge universities. His background had been very different. He felt that deep down they were all prejudiced and however well he performed they would never let a black man be one of them. This left him feeling powerless and helpless and feeling that his only option was to leave. I asked him to consider if his explanations for their behaviour might change if he thought of them as another ethnic group. Amongst other things, he realized that their forming a group was not simply about being elitist, but because they shared the same culture, background and interests. They understood each other and it was easy for them to relax together. It was therefore not surprising that they liked each other, especially since they also shared an interest in running the company. Conrad also accepted that all groups of similar people acted in the same way. Reframing his perception of this group from a bunch of elitist racists to a bunch of friends freed Conrad up emotionally and energetically to come up with a number of strategies for penetrating this clique.

Race discrimination

Discrimination on the basis of race is still a real possibility (Aston, Hill and Tackey, 2006). A second- or third-generation black British person may be virtually identical culturally to a white British person, but have a very different experience in the workplace, purely on the basis of racial differences alone. It is therefore vital when working with black British coachees for the coach to have the capacity to respond to both actual and perceived race discrimination.

Actual discrimination

Whilst overt discrimination can be, and still is, a factor, coachees are more likely to raise issues of covert discrimination during coaching sessions. A qualitative study that investigated instances of conflict experienced by black employees (Alleyne, 2004) found that 'conflict was frequently initiated by subtle comments and behaviour that targeted aspects of the individual's race or cultural identity'. Examples included not being noticed, silence instead of supportive responses, not being afforded pleasantries, and being labelled as aggressive, scary or difficult. The impact on the individual's well-being ranged from anxiety and distress to depression and various physical symptoms. Alleyne identified, though, that the *extent* of the impact was moderated by the 'feelings, reactions and stances adopted by the black worker'. The challenge for the coach in these situations is to help the coachee identify both the appropriate action to deal with the discrimination, and how to manage their own thoughts and feelings, so that the impact of the discrimination is not exacerbated by their own response. Additionally the coach needs to remember that there is a legal dimension to dealing with discrimination and both the coach and coachee may need to seek expert advice.

Perceived discrimination

A dreadful irony for black coachees is that even when there is no discrimination occurring, the fact that it could occur can cause additional pressures for them. The concept of stereotype threat is one example that can be particularly relevant. Stereotype threat is 'the fear of confirming a negative stereotype about one's own group, through one's own behaviour, in situations that are salient to that stereotype' (Steele and Aronson, 1995). Research into stereotype threat demonstrates that this anxiety can interfere with optimal performance because attention is diverted away from the task onto worries about whether one's performance is being evaluated in light of the stereotype (Steele and Aronson, 1995). These pressures can be exacerbated if the coachee is the token representative of their group. In such situations, the black coachee not only has to deal with the situation at hand, but also has to manage the uncomfortable feelings and cognitions caused by the stereotype threat. A simple technique that can help coachees to recover more quickly in these situations is one borrowed from neuro-linguistic programming (NLP). Before the difficult event, the coachee vividly imagines an occasion when they felt confident and performed well. They then anchor that experience by touching the back of their hand. During or before the difficult event, if negative feelings and thoughts start to intrude, they can touch the back of the hand to help rekindle their confidence.

Stereotype threat has also been shown to indirectly affect feedback-seeking behaviour (Robertson *et al*, 2003). There are two strategies that can be used when seeking feedback: either directly asking peers or managers for feedback; or indirectly monitoring the environment and relevant others to observe their reaction to one's behaviour. Because indirect feedback is more ambiguous, it is less effective for performance management. In their study of the impact of stereotype threat on solo black US managers, Robertson *et al* (2003) found stereotype threat related positively to indirect feedback seeking. They also found that stereotype threat led to a greater tendency in black managers in their sample to discount feedback from white supervisors because they doubted the accuracy and motivations of the feedback source. I have commonly found that the anxieties of both parties about feedback has meant that white managers can be extremely reluctant to give feedback to black staff because of a fear that they might be accused of being racist. An effective way of intervening in these situations, if the coach can work jointly with the coachee and their supervisor, is to get both parties to agree specific, behaviourally anchored performance criteria before feedback is given. This helps to develop trust and confidence in the process. Generic 360-degree instruments are unlikely to be suitable for this purpose.

Feeling unsupported in the workplace because of solo status and/or lack of confidence in their line manager creates a demand for coaches of a similar racial background. In addition, lack of effective supervision may well have deprived these coachees of the opportunity to be taught effective management and leadership methods. Coaching therefore is as likely to be about ongoing support and development as it is about short-term problem-solving. If this is the case then this should be discussed when agreeing the coaching contract.

Career development

In this final section I want to look briefly at the issue of career constraint. It is not uncommon for black coachees to have ended up in their current career by chance rather than choice. Often this is due to the combined effects of real or perceived discrimination, historical patterns of employment, poorer educational outcomes, poor careers advice, and lack of role models.

CASE STUDY: NAVALLETTE

Navallette and I had originally met at antenatal classes. After losing touch for many years, we were delighted to bump into each other again. She later phoned me to see if I would be willing to help her think through her career options, now that her children were old enough for her to return to work. She had no wish to return to her previous work in administration. Her current career goal was to become a learning mentor in a secondary school but she lacked confidence and felt she had nothing to offer. To try and get a clearer picture of what may have caused her lack of confidence I asked her to draw a life-line. When we went through her life journey it was not the death of her mother when she was 16 that made her suddenly start crying, but dropping out of university after her first year. This was a profound moment for her. It was only with the surprise of these tears that she realized how strongly this experience had affected her confidence and belief in herself. Now that she had recognized where her self-doubt came from, she was able to push past it and take the steps necessary to progress her career goals.

Coachees may come to coaching wanting to get help with promotion, but it soon becomes evident that they do not have a passion for leading in the area they are currently working in. Many will be involved in activities and projects outside work that are more illustrative of their true talents. Others, though, may not have tapped in to their true interests at all. The coach needs to use methods that will reveal core talents, strengths, interests and values, without their being filtered by limiting assumptions, expectations and beliefs. I have found that five-factor personality tests are particularly helpful, not just for the insight they give the coachee into their traits but also because it helps them to focus on the 'I' independent of social labels.

Another technique I commonly use is one borrowed from Appreciative Inquiry (Watkins and Mohr, 2001). I ask the coachee to think of a peak work experience, (however brief and however rare). I then ask them to identify, specifically, what they were doing that contributed to that key moment. I will also ask them to identify whether anything in the context also contributed to the peak moment. From there, we explore what type of career would give them the best opportunity for this peak experience to be the norm. Even where a career change is not possible, coachees may be able to think of sideways moves or ways of enriching or changing the focus of their current role, so they can do more of the work that they have a passion for. It is on this foundation that effective leadership can then be built.

SUMMARY

Coaching is often thought to be about short-term and specific performance and development issues. Mentoring is seen to be concerned with longer-term professional and personal development. One of the themes that emerges from this chapter is the likelihood that the coach will need to fulfil both roles when coaching black coachees due to an actual or perceived lack of support in the workplace. The chapter highlights the need for black coachees to become adept at developing a variety of strategies for managing their own response to events, the events themselves and the wider context within which the events take place. Fortunately, black coachees' experiences of overcoming barriers, operating cross-culturally and leadership within their own communities means they will typically have the resources to do this. The role of the coach is to help the coachee to challenge limiting beliefs, identify the strengths their background has given them and to harness these strengths to achieve their performance, career and life goals.

References

Ali, E and Jones, L (2000) *Meeting the Educational Needs of Somali Pupils in Camden Schools* [online] http://www.camden.gov.uk/ccm/content/education/services-for-children-and-parents/camden-la-support-services/file-storage/meeting-needs-of-somali-research.en;jsessionid=ajgrxAQ04dY-

Alleyne, A (2004) Black identity and workplace oppression, *Counselling and Psychotherapy Research*, 4(1), pp 4–8

Aston, J, Hill, D and Tackey, N D (2006) The experience of claimants in race discrimination Employment Tribunal cases, *Employment Relations Research Series No. 55*, Department for Trade and Industry [online] http://www.berr.gov.uk/files/file27818.pdf

Branscombe, N R, Schmitt, M T and Harvey, R D (1999) Perceiving pervasive discrimination among African Americans: Implications for group identification and well-being, *Journal of Personality and Social Psychology*, 77(1), pp 135–49

Campayne, C, Harper Jantuah, C and Peters, J (2006) *Different Women, Different Places*, Diversity Practice and Katalytik Ltd, London

Crisp, R J and Hewstone, M (2006) *Multiple Social Categorization: Processes, models and applications*, Psychology Press, Hove

Crocker, J and Major, B (1989) Social stigma and self esteem: The self protective properties of stigma, *Psychological Review*, 96, pp 608–630

Frieda, B and Walters, N (1999) *Combating social exclusion: A comparative study of Bosnian, Kurdish, Somali and Senegalese communities in the UK, Germany, Denmark and Italy*, held by the Information Centre about Asylum and Refugees in the UK ICAR, International Policy Studies Institute, King's College London

George, B *et al* (2007) Discovering your authentic leadership, *Harvard Business Review*, February, pp 129–38

Harris, H (2004) *The Somali community in the UK: What we know and how we know it*, Information Centre about Asylum and Refugees in the UK ICAR, International Policy Studies Institute, King's College London

Hofstede, G (1980) *Culture's Consequences: International differences in work related values*, Sage, Beverly Hills

Hofstede, G (1991) *Cultures and Organisations: Software of the mind*, McGraw-Hill, London

Lindley, J (2007) The over-education of UK immigrants and minority ethnic groups: Evidence from the Labour Force Survey, *Sheffield Economic Research Paper Series*, SERP Number: 2007013

Miller, C T and Kaiser, R C (2001) A theoretical perspective on coping with stigma, *Journal of Social Issues*, 57(1), pp 73–92

National Archive (2008) [accessed 8 March 2008] Moving here – 200 years of migration in England [online] www.movinghere.org.uk

Nazroo, J Y and Karlsen, S, (2003) Patterns of identity among ethnic minority people: diversity and commonality, *Ethnic and Racial Studies* **26**(5), September 2003, pp. 902–30

Office for National Statistics (2002) *Annual Labour Force Survey 2001/2002*, HMSO, London

PortCities UK [accessed 8 March 2008] [online] www.portcities.org.uk

Roberson, L *et al* (2003) Stereotype threat and feedback seeking in the workplace, *Journal of Vocational Behavior*, **62**, pp 176–88

Rosinski, P (2003), *Coaching Across Cultures: New tools for leveraging national, corporate and professional differences*, Nicholas Brealey, Boston

Singh, V (2006) *Ethnic and International Diversity in FTSE 100 Boards*, EURAM Annual Conference

Snyder, C R (2000) *Handbook of Hope: Theory measures and applications*, Guilford Press, New York

Steele, M C and Aronson, J (1995) Stereotype threat and the intellectual test performance of African Americans, *Journal of Personality and Social Psychology*, **69**(5), pp 797–811

Stone, D L and Stone-Romero, E F (2004) The influence of culture on role-taking in culturally diverse organizations, in *The Psychology and Management of Workplace Diversity*, eds M S Stockdale and F J T Crosby, pp 78–99, Blackwell Publishing, Oxford

Triandis, H C (1994) *Culture and Social Behavior*, McGraw-Hill, New York

Trompenaars, F and Hampden-Turner, C (1998) *Riding the Waves of Culture: Understanding cultural diversity in global business*, 2nd edn, McGraw-Hill, New York

Watkins, M J and Mohr, B J (2001) *Appreciative Inquiry*, Jossey-Bass/Pfeiffer, San Francisco

Further reading

Cook, M (2004) *Personnel Selection: Adding value through people*, Wiley, Chichester

Edgerton, E and Palmer, P (2005) SPACE: A psychological model, *The Coaching Psychologist*, **2**(2), November, pp 25–31

Senge, P M *et al* (1994) *The Fifth Discipline Field Book*, Nicholas Brealey Publishing, London

Stewart, J *et al* (1999) Ethnic differences in incidence of stroke: Prospective study with stroke register, *British Medical Journal*, **318**(7), pp 967–71

Utsey, O S *et al* (2006) Moderator effects of cognitive ability and social support on the relation between racism-related stress and quality of life in a community sample of black Americans, *Cultural Diversity and Ethnic Minority Psychology*, **12**(2), 334–46

13

Coaching black American coachees

Gregory Pennington

INTRODUCTION

Increasing both the quality and quantity of leaders is an essential ingredient in an organization's ability to execute its strategy and sustain high levels of performance. As the workforce becomes increasingly more diverse, organizations have the opportunity and the challenge of ensuring that they are effective in developing and fully utilizing all of their resources. Executive coaching continues to be an important resource in the development of leaders. As the pool of leaders and potential leaders becomes more diverse, it is important to assess the effectiveness and application of development tools, like executive coaching, in the full leadership pool, including black managers. This chapter explores the effectiveness of executive coaching to black Americans. It will provide some examples of coaching situations as a context for this discussion. It will also offer some reflection regarding the context of race in the United States and how it may impact black US executives. Lastly, this chapter will provide a list of key issues in coaching this population with suggestions for how to address them.

HERITAGE TRADITIONS

It is helpful to provide several coaching situations as a context for viewing how the traditions of culture impact coaching black Americans. Consider the following coaching situations, how you might initially assess the situation, and how you would approach them as an executive coach.

Keith

Keith was offended that his company, an electric utility company, had designed a mentoring programme specifically for black Americans. He had recently been denied a promotion to officer level in favour of a peer whose effectiveness as a manager he did not respect. He now reported to that person. Though he had been given feedback about why he was not promoted or selected, he did not appear to accept the feedback and was even described as 'whining' about the decision. His manager and a Human Resources representative wondered whether finding an executive coach for him would be worthwhile.

Scott

Scott, a manager in a pharmaceutical company, was described as someone who had the potential to become a director. His problem was that his communication style interfered with his effectiveness and credibility. While his work was considered at least adequate and in many cases outstanding, he seemed to always miss the mark when presenting information to peers, internal clients and senior management. His immediate manager wondered whether he was strategic enough to be promoted to director. He asked: 'Is it just a matter of communication style or is there evidence of a more fundamental limitation?'

Pat

Pat's region in a food and beverage company was viewed as underperforming. Rather than being seventh or eighth in the country, there was a strong belief by others that it should be first or second. Pat admitted to setting goals that were more realistic than challenging, and had already received and generally accepted feedback that more passion was needed in conveying a mission to the organization. There was also a suggestion that Pat was not playing 'politics' as effectively as possible.

Carl

Carl was a member of the executive team when the company began its succession planning to replace the CEO. He was considered a long shot because he was the only one of the final three candidates who had not led an operating unit. He took on that role once one of the other candidates left for another company and the remaining candidate was placed in the successor role. When that person failed and left the company, Carl assumed he would be chosen. Those closely involved in the selection, however, thought that he still needed more exposure and experience before becoming CEO and made it clear that he should attend an executive leadership programme first. Partly because he already had an MBA in Finance, Carl thought and said aloud 'What does a black man have to do to be CEO?' As his question got retold, without his knowledge, key people began to wonder whether he was the right person for the job if he was too sensitive about race.

As an experienced executive coach, how would you approach working with Keith, Scott, Pat and Carl? What difference does it make to you and your approach that Keith and Carl are described as black American men?

The race of Scott and Pat is not presented, so perhaps the approach you imagined was colour-blind. They are also black Americans in Fortune 250 US corporations. Does their racial identity alter how you assess the situation, how you approach them, or what themes you anticipate?

Key assumptions

Let us make some key assumptions. As an executive coach, you already know something about executive coaching. Generally that means you have some foundation in understanding human behaviour, leadership and business. It also means that you may start a coaching engagement by learning what you can about the business context, the job demands, and the keys to success, and by conducting some sort of assessment of the potential coachee. You provide feedback, and you develop and/or facilitate the development of an action plan to change behaviour that results in or at least is significantly correlated with measurable improvements in performance. This set of assumptions is not where we will focus.

Let us also assume that race is a factor when coaching black US executives in the United States. While it would be interesting to tweak and refine the first assumption, and practitioners by and large engage in rational debate about the nuances of executive coaching and how to weigh the relative impact of one dimension over another, discussions of race are usually met with more resistance of various kinds, and fuelled by emotion more than logic. Let us take some time to provide at least a general context for understanding how some of the dynamics of race influence leadership and its effectiveness in US corporations. Understanding the heritage and traditions of race in the United States is critical to being an effective coach to black US executives.

The history of blacks in America cannot be fully understood without recognizing that the history of race is particularly influenced by the institution of slavery in the United States. A full discussion is obviously beyond the scope of this chapter. One lingering and powerful dynamic of slavery that continues to impact black Americans in corporate America and elsewhere is the attention that was devoted to proving that slaves, Africans and their descendents are actually sub-human. Despite recent discoveries regarding the genotypic validity of race, skin colour has been a noticeable and notable difference among people. Colour has been a focal point for explaining differences in social roles, ability, values, norms and even full humanity. In two separate books, Stanton (1960) and Haller (1971) chronicle the history of scientific attitudes towards race from 1815 through to 1900. The assumption was that descendents of Africa are inferior. A substantial amount of the focus on inferiority was dedicated to proving that blacks are intellectually deficient. Even though there is ongoing scientific debate as to how measured levels of 'intelligence' relate to success, there is little debate that levels of intelligence differ among ethnic groups (Hernstein and Murray, 1994).

Fortunately, there is an equally relevant and positively oriented tradition among black Americans that represents a source of pride and strong identity. Nobles (1991) argues that understanding the social, psychological make-up of black Americans includes understanding how the influences of West African philosophies shape that community. Of particular relevance to this discussion is recognizing the notion of unity and kinship that persists in the black American community. Often referred to as 'collectivism' and more popularly captured in the phrase 'it takes a village to raise a child', the sense of identifying with the black community is arguably one of the strongest traditions to consider when coaching black American executives. What behaviours define me as black? What behaviours and accomplishments might be perceived as lifting up my race? Which ones will be perceived as 'denying my heritage'?

Does race really matter? Biologically speaking, many argue that race is meaningless (Graves, 2001). Apparently of the 30,000 to 40,000 genes that make us human, only about six determine skin colour. While one can understandably argue that this lends credence to the belief that we are all 'just' human, few social scientists will deny that race does exist. Malcolm Gladwell (2005) provides an interesting perspective on how 'thin-slicing' and our adaptive unconscious lead us to make rapid decisions based on few pieces of data supported by our experiences. We all process a significant amount of information in a relatively short amount of time. It would make sense that the most obviously noticeable data would be processed consciously or unconsciously. Though we cannot see the six genes that determine race, we can notice differences in skin colour. Though our direct experiences with people of different colours than ourselves may be limited, it is not likely that someone in the United States has not at least heard of an incident in which a person's behaviour was attributed to race. In two seconds, in a 'blink', we connect new data to old experiences and perceptions.

Nevertheless, are we, particularly in the United States, and particularly black Americans, overly concerned with race? There is evidence to support this notion. 'According to the Joint Center for Politics and Economics, 81 per cent of Black professionals think workplace discrimination is still common. This is not merely the belief that job discrimination exists, but that it is common.' (*Fortune Magazine*, 1998).

Is this merely a perception? Does it actually impact performance? There is some experimental research that supports the anecdotal experience of many black executives who believe that their performance is viewed differently from that of their white colleagues. Thomas and Gabarro (1999) paint distinctly different paths for development between minority executives and their white counterparts. In an effort to explain some influences on those differences, they cited earlier research (Greenhaus and Parasuraman, 1993) and suggested: 'Experimental research has shown that people are more likely to attribute excellent performance by a majority group member to the majority person's own efforts and abilities. In contrast, the same level of performance by a minority is more likely to be attributed to the situation or the effort of others' (Thomas and Gabarro, 1999: 118).

Even if some degree of discrimination, or at least some elevated level of consciousness, exists for some of us regarding race, does it interfere with people being successful in the business world? Clearly the success stories of black Americans like former CEOs Kenneth Chennault (American Express), Richard Parsons (Time Warner) and Stanley O'Neal (Merrill Lynch) are testimonies of accomplishment in corporate America. Slay (2003) raises several interesting questions for further research to help understand the complexities of how race impacts the social identities and effectiveness of black US leaders. Whether comfortable or uncomfortable talking about race and its impact on success, whether perceptions by others of their leadership ability are influenced by race, it seems inevitable that race gets considered.

As a coach you should assume that successful black US executives believe or aspire to believe in the fundamental meritocracy of corporate America. This belief sustains their focus on meeting and exceeding measurable standards of performance. They know that bottom-line results and the work ethic associated with them are critical success factors. Personally and professionally, it appears difficult to dilute one's focus and distract others by engaging openly in discussions of race early in their careers. Does race stop one from being successful? No. Does it influence the effort it takes to be successful, and ultimately the level or quality of success? Perhaps. Daniels (2004: 128) offers an interesting quote from Richard Parsons, CEO of Time Warner at the time: 'Many people have written in the abstract that race is the quintessential question in America. I used to reject it out of hand because I thought it was silly. But I'm beginning to think that they are right... we just can't seem to get past it.'

Livers and Carver (2002) drew upon 39 in-depth interviews with black US executives conducted by researchers at the Center for Creative Leadership, surveys of 270 black US professionals, and 20 in-depth personal interviews, and arrived at a similar set of realizations. These included noting how similar the experiences of black professionals were, regardless of things like education, organization, job level or geographic region. They were also struck with how the experiences of black professionals differed from those of their non-black colleagues.

DEVELOPING CULTURALLY APPROPRIATE COACHING

As companies strive to fully utilize and fully develop their leadership, an increased focus has been directed on executive coaching as one resource. If there are recognizable differences in the experiences of blacks and non-blacks as leaders in corporate America, would the application of executive coaching have to be different in order to be effective? What does the effective coach need to know and do with this population?

A research project undertaken by Pennington (2001) on black Americans has helped provide a perspective on this question. These senior-level black American executives represented a variety of companies. Their experiences and perceptions provided the insight needed to identify themes and patterns that would address these questions.

Ninety per cent of this group acknowledged that 'race matters'. They identified career obstacles influenced by race that needed to be addressed. They also identified similar patterns of coping and adjustment that appeared at least distinctive in black American experiences if not unique to them. The value of mentors, for instance, is not unique to the success of black American executives, but the options for finding them, the process of building relationships, and the challenges of valuing differences contribute to distinctive dimensions of mentoring when differences exist between mentor and mentee.

The executives were asked whether there was any perceived value in executive coaching and whether they currently had an executive coach. Interestingly, 90 per cent of the participants said there was value in coaching and articulated specific elements of what they would find valuable in coaching. Their comments could be grouped into two broad areas: *personal support* and *environmental navigation*. Under *personal support*, they talked about identifying and building on strengths, and addressing developmental needs. Under *environmental navigation*, they talked about the value of a coach to help identify obstacles and allies in the corporate environment. It was the coach's ability to help the executive to navigate the political waters and to identify the keys to success that was considered valuable.

Somewhat surprisingly, only 30 per cent of this group actually had formal coaches. There was some effort to distinguish between coaches, mentors and sponsors. One executive said that he did not have one particular coach, but utilized what he referred to as his own 'board of directors' who offered different types of support in different circumstances over the course of his career. Nevertheless, it was noteworthy that 90 per cent of this group of executives saw the value of coaching but only 30 per cent of them were actually using the service of one. This discrepancy raises several questions, including: How prevalent is the use of coaching; at what level of the organization are coaches being used; and is there a differential use of coaches among black US executives compared to white executives? There has already been research reported that talks about the difficulty of finding mentors for black US managers. Executive coaching may simply be an extension of this lack of resources to serve as mentors.

We also asked the executives how being a black American affected their current role and effectiveness. There were three distinct categories of responses: 'Not at all'; 'Very much so'; and 'Always, in subtle ways'. Only three of the respondents said 'Not at all'. Those three talked about their industries in terms of bottom-line deliverables and asserted that it was only about delivering results. Thirteen of the group, roughly 43 per cent, indicated that being a black American clearly impacted their current role and effectiveness. Their stories included assertions that you were expected to be better qualified as a black American. They also recounted stories that suggested they were more likely to spend time preparing themselves through interim assignments and enduring more extended timelines before increased responsibilities than their white counterparts. They also acknowledged frustration that though they were often invited to share their perspectives regarding black people, they often met resistance when they offered those perspectives uninvited. One of the executives noted that on Wall Street, it was commonly accepted that there was a 'Black tax' that you had to pay to play.

Another 14 participants, roughly 46 per cent, thought that race always influenced their roles and effectiveness, but in subtle ways. The most striking example for this group was the perception and anxiety around being smart enough to do their job. Sometimes the questions were raised as curious responses about the quality of your educational credentials, sometimes embedded in the perceived extra scrutiny about work products, and often euphemistically represented as concerns about whether the person was strategic enough. Each of these participants was willing to take personal responsibility for 'second-guessing' how others perceived their capabilities. They were also consistent in believing that it was important to assume that there would always be a percentage of people who will doubt the capability and performance of black Americans.

We asked what coaches should know or do differently when working with black US executives. All of the responses began with the importance of the coach understanding the business and the general keys to success for an executive in that particular business environment. They also noted that having a basic understanding of the differences and a willingness to engage in the discussion of their impact on being successful were valuable. One response was that the coach should help raise the 'racial IQ' of the organization. While race was not considered to be directly relevant to every aspect of performance in a corporate environment, it was apparent from the comments of these executives that recognizing the presence of race as 'background noise' at least was important when working with black US executives. In very concrete terms, they indicated that a coach should be first willing, and then able, to engage in this discussion when it was raised and when it was relevant.

Finally, we asked whether race was a factor in selecting a coach. The clear and consistent response was that it depended directly on the objectives of the engagement. A distinction was made between an overall objective of emotional support and one of career support. If the emphasis was placed on providing empathy and accelerating the possibility of understanding and relating to the emotional elements of success, it seemed more important to consider the potential benefits of racial affinity as a major factor in selecting the coach. It was also noted that people may be asked to consider the hypothetical question of 'When you have two equally qualified candidates, one white and one black, do you choose the black one?' In contrast, the more revealing question would be 'If you have two equally qualified coaching candidates, both of whom are black, how do you choose?' The effort of differentiating between two black candidates as a coach helps to isolate the underlying competencies and benefits that one assumes are related to race.

When the clear objective for coaching is weighted towards accelerating and enhancing effectiveness in job performance and career advancement, the decision-making criteria for a coach were squarely centred on the coach's ability to help understand and navigate the corporate environment, with less regard to the coach's racial identity. Understandably, many of the participants noted that ideally you could find elements of affinity and navigation in the same person, regardless of their race.

These interviews suggested five key elements to consider when coaching black US executives. They are presented in the following sections with recommendations about how to address each issue. The coaching situations introduced earlier in the chapter are used as reference points to illustrate these dynamics of race to be considered.

1. Race matters

The race card is present even if face down. You are more likely to understand its impact if you find ways to raise it as the coach. It is too costly for the executive to play it. In the coaching situations presented earlier in the chapter, both Keith and Carl are examples of the premise that race matters. In Keith's case he had openly stated that race was not to be used in determining how to approach him. 'Why do you have to have a special mentoring programme for blacks?' he asked. He had also mentioned, as do most executives, 'What difference does it make that I am black?' As an executive coach, it is critical to understand that once Keith decided that I could be trusted as an advisor to him, he willingly raised the question of how being black impacted his approach to work and the approach of others to him.

In Carl's case, of wondering 'What does a black man have to do?', he was reflecting in hindsight about having had to suppress the question of how race matters until he had exhausted all of the other potential variables involved in being promoted to CEO. For others in the company who were involved in assessing him for the CEO role, the mention of race seemed 'unusual', 'inappropriate', and possibly a reflection of Carl having been the wrong choice all along. From Carl's perspective, he was reminding himself of the lesson learned on Wall Street: that one should assume there will be an added tax because you are black.

What you can do as coach:

▮ Find a way to open this discussion. Most executives will not volunteer it to you. Having an understanding of race and how people in the organization react to race will increase the effectiveness of the executive and the coach. Find the right time to ask: Does it matter here that you are black?

▮ Understand what behaviours are interpreted differently when demonstrated by blacks compared to non-blacks. Some behaviours that are considered to be assertive by one group may be viewed as aggressive when demonstrated by another group, for instance. Ask: In what instances does being black make a difference?

▌ Be clear about the objectives of the coaching engagement. Are you helping the executive navigate the political waters as a black executive, or helping them change the culture, or helping them manage their frustration and coping skills in an environment they accept will not change? Ask: What do you want to focus on?

2. Rumours of intellectual inferiority flourish

Innate intellectual ability is still the predominant belief in companies: 'Some folks are born smart and some folks are not.' Even though the question is not usually asked specifically in terms of intellectual ability, it is often inferred at the executive level in questions about 'strategic thinking'. The history of standardized testing, with lower average scores for blacks compared to other groups, contributes to a fundamental belief that blacks are genetically inferior in terms of intellect. From an executive coaching perspective it is important to understand how blacks and non-blacks are frequently impacted by conscious and unconscious suspicions about the fundamental capabilities of black Americans to do higher-level problem solving. The question always resides as 'background noise' and interferes with the person asking appropriate questions to define what is meant by 'strategic' and to validly assess their capabilities and those of others. In the case of Scott in the coaching situation described earlier, both he and his manager went directly to wondering about more innate or entrenched issues of 'something else' rather than assuming a more simplistic need to develop better communication skills.

Sometimes the 'rumours of inferiority' (Hammond and Howard, 1988) take on the opposite manifestation of overlooking obvious deficiencies. I remember a white colleague's initial impression of a black executive we assessed, which included 'He's pretty bright and pretty articulate.' Ultimately the executive turned out to be 'pretty bright' relative to my colleague's stereotyped 'lesser expectations' for a black person. As I continued working with the executive, he eventually came to appreciate that no one had ever given him candid feedback about his true capabilities and he had spent most of his career wondering and worrying whether he was 'in over his head'. He was, and no one along the way had dared to give him that feedback.

What you can do as coach:

▌ Insist on defining behavioural characteristics and performance versus indicators (eg 'Able to synthesize a wide range of information and identify overall themes' versus 'A Harvard graduate'). Ask the executive and others: What behaviours convince you that he/she is capable or not capable of doing the job?

▌ Force others to define 'strategic thinking'. It is used as a substitute for questioning innate intellectual ability. Ask the executive: What did they mean by 'strategic thinking'? (often the executive accepts the question without appropriately challenging what is meant by it). I have also found it helpful with the executive and with their manager to ask: Who in the organization is a good example of a strategic thinker?

3. Warring souls at peace

Though one's title and socio-economic status gives one more options, it does not change one's core identity. You cannot look at a black person and *not* see the colour of their skin. They cannot deny their colour and their self-identity will always include race. A director I coached in a utility company struggled with the costs of becoming an officer because he viewed it as 'assimilation' and worried that it would be viewed by some as 'selling out' to 'become white'. Others I have worked with reflect on the casual comments of white colleagues who view them as 'not like the others'. In the earlier coaching example, Pat struggled internally with the networking expectations at the company. Pat knew it was important to interact with everyone and did reasonably well at it. The challenge was managing the constant amount of energy it took to weigh whether comments would be seen as 'too black' by one group or 'too white' by another.

What you can do as coach:

▌ Explore the person's outside-of-work activities. Compare, contrast and leverage those skills and interests. Black executives are similar to others in constantly balancing work and life. This can be more of a strain if one perceives that their 'outside' identity and activities are not valued by those in the work setting. As a coach one should always ask: What do you do outside of work? The follow-up question I ask is: How does that blend with what you do at work?
▌ Accept the person's perception of having 'to do more' because of a 'black tax'. Whether they personally believe it or not, I have never worked with a black executive who did not eventually mention the topic of race and whether it 'costs more' to be black. Coaches fail when they avoid this discussion. The simplest coaching intervention is to ask: What do you mean? If they have this perception, the coach's focus should be on understanding it and how they cope with this perception/reality.

4. More 'how to' than 'hugs'

Given an overall goal of increasing one's impact on the organization, there is more value in a coach providing directions to navigate the environment than there is in a coach who is exploring for insight. Navigation includes mapping the environment, charting the paths of least resistance and most impact, and running interference to minimize obstacles. In the coaching example with Keith, he wanted to subtract race as a variable, not because he did not think it was a factor, but because he wanted to make sure he had not overlooked any of the basic steps needed to reach the officer level. He was arguing that he already knew it would take more and he already knew he had to blend his 'black' identity with his corporate one. He wanted assurances that he was still on the right basic path.

What you can do as coach:

▮ Identify the written and unwritten rules of success in the organization. I often ask the executive: Who are people who represent profiles of success in the organization, black or white? Embedded in their stories are valuable keys to navigating the environment.
▮ Identify where and when race will be perceived as an obstacle. Successful executives are skilful at assessing the variables they can manipulate to be effective. Similar to asking an executive how they will factor in the division president's resistance, as a coach you can ask: How does race factor into being successful?

5. Race does not always matter most, but the bottom line does

Ultimately all executives understand that they must contribute to the bottom line. Ultimately, and ideally, the evidence of their contribution and success will be measurable and objective. Nevertheless, you must accept the paradox that it is critical to consider race in order to get to the point where race does not matter.

What you can do as coach:

▮ Actively listen to the person's perspective about race.
▮ Challenge yourself and your coachee to understand the feelings, thoughts and behaviours related to the discussion of race.
▮ Work together to subjectively and objectively analyse how race impacts behaviour and business results.
▮ Explicitly distinguish between those areas where race matters and where it does not.
▮ Focus on what assumptions and actions the coachee can take responsibility for in order to be as effective as possible.

SUMMARY

The view of this chapter is that race matters but does not, however, stand alone. If the coach starts there they miss the critical sequence of supporting the black executive's ongoing exploration of how to integrate perceptions of race by themselves and others into the existing roadmap for success in their company.

What is outlined above represents more of a personal framework than anything. Simply stated, the framework is: Identify where race matters, create and implement strategies that can get past potential barriers, and leverage potential advantages. One area that was not covered but could be added to the strategies suggested above is how the coach can work with other managers across the organization to raise the 'racial IQ' of the organization and its wider members.

References

Daniels, C (2004) *Black Power, Inc.: The new voice of success*, Wiley, Hoboken, NJ

Fortune Magazine (1998) What African-Americans think of corporate America, June 9, p 141

Gladwell, M (2005) *Blink*, Time Warner Book Group, New York

Graves Jr, J L (2001) *The emperor's new clothes: Biological theories of race at the millennium*, Rutgers University Press, New Brunswick, NJ

Greenhaus, J and Parasuraman, S (1993) Job performance attributions and career advancement prospects: An examination of gender and race effects, *Organizational Behavior and Human Decision Processes*, **55**(2), pp 273–97

Haller, J (1971) *Outcasts from Evolution: Scientific attitudes of racial inferiority: 1859–1900*, University of Illinois Press, Urbana

Hammond, R and Howard, J (1988) Rumors of inferiority: The hidden obstacles to black success, *The New Republic*, September 9, pp 17–21

Hernstein, R and Murray, C (1994) *The Bell Curve: Intelligence and Class Structure in American Life*, Free Press, New York

Livers, A and Carver, K (2002) *Leading in Black and White: Working across the racial divide in corporate America*, Jossey-Bass and The Center for Creative Leadership, San Francisco

Nobles, Wade W (1991) African philosophy: Foundations for black psychology, in *Black Psychology*, 3rd edn, ed RL Jones, pp 47–64, Cobb & Henry, Berkeley

Pennington, G (2001) *Coaching African American Executives*, unpublished presentation at Society of Consulting Psychology, Mid-Winter Conference

Slay, H S (2003) Spanning two worlds: Social identify and emergent African-American leaders. *Journal of Leadership and Organizational Studies*, 9, pp 56–66.

Stanton, W (1960) *The Leopard's Spots: Scientific attitudes toward race in America 1815–59*, University of Chicago Press, Chicago

Thomas, D A and Gabarro, J J (1999) *Breaking Through: The making of minority executives in corporate America*, Harvard Business School Press, Boston

Further reading

Aderfer, C P (2000) National culture and the new corporate language for race relations, in *Addressing Cultural Issues in Organizations: Beyond the corporate context*, ed R T Carter, pp 41–63, Sage, Thousand Oaks, CA

Carter, R T and Pieterse, A L (2005) Race: A social and psychological analysis of the term and its meaning, in *Handbook of Racial-Cultural Psychology and Counseling: Theory and Research*, Vol 1, ed RT Carter, pp 19–34, Wiley, Hoboken, NJ

Davis, G and Watson, G (1982) *Black Life in Corporate America – Swimming in the Mainstream*, Anchor Press/Doubleday, Garden City, NY

Goleman, D (1995) *Emotional Intelligence: Why it can matter more than IQ*, Bantam Books, New York

Jones, J M and Carter, R T (1996) Racism and racial identity: Merging realities, in *Impacts of Racism on White Americans*, 2nd edn, eds BP Bowser and RG Hunt, pp 1–24, Sage, Newbury Park, CA

Kochman, T (1981) *Black and White Styles in Conflict*, University of Chicago Press, Chicago

Lewis, R and Walker, Blair S (1997) *Why Should White Guys Have All the Fun?: How Reginald Lewis created a billion-dollar business empire*, Wiley, New York

Valerio, A M and Lee, R (2005) *Executive Coaching: A guide for the HR professional*, Wiley, New York

West, C (1993) *Race Matters*, Beacon Press, Boston

Winum, P (2005) Effectiveness of a high-potential African-American executive: The anatomy of a coaching engagement, *Consulting Psychology Journal: Practice and Research*, **57**(1), pp 71–89

14

Coaching Indian sub-continent heritage coachees

Indrani Choudhury

INTRODUCTION

The recent economic boom in India has focused global attention on the under-utilized human resources of this vastly populated developing country. Countries like Britain have a valuable resource in those citizens whose ethnic origins are in the subcontinent and who are sufficiently familiar with the culture and customs of the subcontinent to act as a resource for British firms. Unfortunately there is very little research (Kenny and Briner, 2007) into the experience of British Asians in the workplace, except in relation to discrimination, selection and assessment. Coaching is one option in the bundle of strategies for development. In this non-empirical chapter, I introduce factors that the coach needs to consider when formulating a coaching strategy with British Asians from the subcontinent. The chapter provides a baseline for the reader to develop his or her understanding in this area using the 'looking glass model'. The chapter touches on migration patterns, religion and customs and links these to the evolving psychological framework of the coachee, which is critical in identity formation.

Ethnicity is often used to denote people with common ancestry (Smith, 1986). However, the term is ambiguous and subject to multiple interpretations in application. In this chapter I am referring to current British nationals whose parents and grandparents originated from the subcontinent or from Asian communities in East Africa, Mauritius, etc. The issue is further complicated by the fact that India, Pakistan and the former East Bengal, now Bangladesh, are all relatively new nations, despite a rich common history, tradition and culture. Although in terms of ethnicity they may be similar (depending on how the term is defined), the intergenerational national identity, as non-resident Indians (NRI) workers across the globe, is becoming increasingly differentiated.

HERITAGE TRADITIONS

British Asians from the subcontinent are a unique group and though they may conceptually be viewed as one group for demographic and research purposes, the differences between them are significant. There is greater similarity between a Bangladeshi and an Indian from West Bengal in terms of language, dress and food habits than between Indians from Punjab and Bengal. Furthermore, even within a regional group the migration patterns may have been different, and have influenced their assimilation into British society. Hence there are likely to be significant differences in their experience of ethnicity and their conceptualization of the 'ethnic self' in relation to other elements that contribute to their self-identity.

British rule in India meant that a number of the major systems prevalent there even today are versions of British systems. A British system of education, introduced in India to ensure a continued supply of minor officials, is still maintained to this day, albeit in a modified version. Following independence and the horrors of partition, life in India in some areas was tough. Hence the voucher scheme introduced by the British government, to provide a workforce for its booming industries and health service, was attractive to individuals from the subcontinent who wanted a better lifestyle.

There were two main groups of immigrants: professionals such as qualified doctors, nurses and engineers who wanted to further their careers by accessing British postgraduate training, which was considered superior to that offered in newly independent India; and unqualified manual workers, farmers, etc mainly from the Punjab. Some, though skilled, could not get jobs in their professional field and instead took unskilled or semi-skilled jobs. This must have had an impact on the parents, whose dreams were shattered, and on the next generation, who must felt the burden of realizing their parents' dreams.

The immigrants around this time were often financially supported by their families back home to pay for the trip to the United Kingdom. They came on their own, and the factory workers lived in overcrowded accommodation, taking it in turns to sleep while they worked in shifts. When siblings and cousins were old enough, relatives in Britain were expected to find jobs for them and accommodate them until they were financially independent. This gave rise to clusters of Asians from a particular region living in close proximity for emotional, social and linguistic support. A number of the men had marriages arranged with women from back home, as was the tradition. While the men worked and were exposed to Western culture and language, the women stayed at home to bring up the children, isolated and unable to communicate with their English neighbours. This was an added motivation to gravitate towards those towns with inhabitants from their region back home. Certain areas of Britain became associated with certain groups from the subcontinent. For example, Southall became associated with the Sikh population and developed social and religious amenities to cater for the population. Neighbours from the region became surrogate families. The wealthier professional families did not tend to reside in these areas but dipped in and out to access the facilities.

In the late 1960s and early 1970s, East African Asians began arriving as a result of pressure from the 'Africanization' policies in Kenya, Tanzania and Uganda. In 1972, Uganda's military dictator, Idi Amin, expelled Asians. Unlike the professionals and unskilled workers of the earlier wave from India, some of the East African Asians had been wealthy entrepreneurs. They could not bring their financial resources with them. However, being entrepreneurial they started new businesses from scratch, and worked all the hours they could to establish themselves financially in the United Kingdom.

THE INFLUENCE OF TRADITIONS ON BEHAVIOUR, SELF-PERCEPTION AND RELATIONSHIPS

The spiritual core – beliefs and values

The subcontinent where most of the British Asians have their roots is multi-lingual and multi-faith. This is especially the case in India, which accommodates many different religions, though Hinduism is the primary one. Buddhism was a development from Hinduism and Buddha was himself a Hindu prince. Islam was introduced into India when Muslims invaded India in the Middle Ages. Sikhism is a relatively new religion compared to Hinduism and Islam. It adopted aspects of both the Hindu and Muslim religions and so has features common with both. The Parsees, who were originally from Persia (now known as Iran), brought Zoroastrianism when they fled from Persia. Christianity was introduced into India following the opening of the Western trade routes, initially by the Portuguese and later by the Dutch, French and English. There are also pockets of Judaism in India. Despite the numerous religions in India, the population mainly live in harmony, apart from the occasional conflict between the Hindus and Muslims. The different religious households maintain their religious traditions and rites whilst at the same time being influenced by the beliefs of the other religions, especially Hinduism. Hinduism is a very pragmatic religion and is prone to interpretation to support an individual's actions. The moral code is also flexible. Hence corruption and religion can coexist in harmony within an individual.

The Hindu belief in Karma, which is also incorporated into the Sikh religion, and the Muslim belief of 'Insha'Allah' (Allah willing), have influenced individuals' views of their agency. This creates an acceptance of outcomes that has been described by Gunaratana (2002) as one of the elements of mindfulness. The locus of control is therefore perceived as being externally predetermined and beyond human control. The belief in Karma gives a different concept of time and an emphasis on significantly delayed gratification, which goes beyond a single lifetime. Freedom from 'Maya' or attachment to earthly goods and emotional ties is essential for liberation. However, this is seldom accomplished in one lifetime. Nevertheless, a detachment from worldly possessions helps to create an internal stability that enables us to focus the mind on the meta aspects of life.

It is important to bear in mind that different families and individuals adhere to their religion to different degrees, and therefore it is difficult to generalize the extent to which these beliefs impact on their thoughts, emotions and behaviour.

Relationships

Traditionally the respect of elders underlies all religions in the subcontinent and is a central aspect of community life. The word 'Guru' is used for teachers (religious or otherwise), elders, etc. The disciple shows humility in the presence of his teacher/Guru. This, in essence, is different to a relationship of equality between coach and coachee. The traditional veneration of age as an embodiment of wisdom can sometimes make it difficult for an Asian manager to feel comfortable being coached or mentored by someone younger than them. This veneration is sometimes generalized to those above one in the hierarchy, in whatever organizational context, and can give rise to sycophantic behaviour.

In the subcontinent, whatever the religion, family and community life is very important. Hence there is a tendency when interacting with an individual to find out more about their background than is common in the West. Social networks often reflect the individuals' regional, religious and economic/professional backgrounds. The process of identifying others from a similar background is made easier by the surnames, which reflect their regional origin, their religion and their caste. Their thinking, judgements, expressions of emotion, and behaviours in the social/family context are likely to be different from those displayed in the work or professional context. They are also likely to be treated differently at work and outside work. There is negligible research (Kenny and Briner, 2007) on the emotional impact of a highly skilled professional having a high status in the work context and a less favoured position in the wider community. It could be argued that the attraction of social interaction within one's ethnic group is an emotional safety net because of the similarity of experiences within the group.

Perception of self and others

Most of the immigrants from the early 1960s and 1970s saw themselves as being fortunate to be allowed to live in Britain, so they conformed and worked hard. Racial discrimination and harassment were common, but they were accommodated and the emotions arising were suppressed and rationalized as the financial gains were considerable. Most of the subsequent racial conflict involving British Asians appears to involve those who were born and brought up in this country. In my view, the second generation saw themselves as British, equal to their indigenous counterparts. They reacted against their parents' subservient acceptance of the discrimination meted out and overtly challenged it. There is currently a trend amongst the younger generation to establish a British Asian culture, reflected in music and dress, which is a fusion of the East and West and critical to their identity.

The development of the cultural identity of this group and their acculturation into Western culture varied depending on family circumstances (social and economic context of the family, parental background and extended family culture). Information relating to a coachee's history and background does assist in understanding how they think, make judgements and respond in different contexts. However, one needs to be very sensitive in asking for this information as the coachee may conclude that their British identity is being minimized and they are being stereotyped. Unfortunately the spectre of discrimination has not been laid to rest, despite legislation.

DEVELOPING CULTURALLY APPROPRIATE COACHING

Our background and experiences shape our mindset (Gerhart, 2004). These form the underlying structure of the individual. Although protected from the public eye, this mindset influences how we interpret experiences and the nature of the information we select and process. I prefer to use the analogy of lenses, which tint our perception and give us a unique, individualized perspective. Here the background and experience is the tint. Each of us therefore has our own individual 'looking glass'.

Figure 14.1 provides a structural perspective of the 'looking glass model' with its component parts. It is not a sequential process-oriented model but a cognitive framework for collecting information, formulating hypotheses, testing them and planning interventions. As it is beyond the scope of this chapter to describe the model in great depth, I have limited the discussion to the application of the different elements in relation to coaching individuals of British Asian heritage from the subcontinent.

Different individuals may focus on the same situation but their perception is likely to differ because of the differences in the composition of their 'looking glass'. For each individual, what they perceive is the reality. By ignoring alternative perspectives, an individual is operating with only limited information, which increases the chances of error. Differences in perspective can be quite challenging even when others are similar to us in ethnicity and social background. These challenges are exacerbated when individuals come from totally different backgrounds well beyond our experiences, resulting in a different system of perception and sense-making strategies.

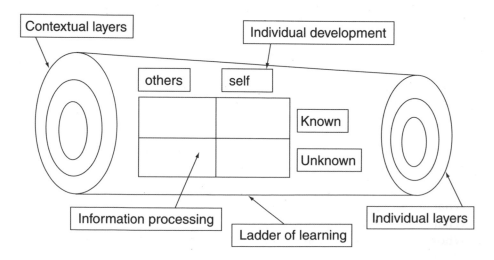

Figure 14.1 Looking glass model

It is important at this stage to share my background so that the reader can appreciate the perspective through which I view coaching coachees from the subcontinent. I have been coaching in the United Kingdom for a number of years. However, I was born and received a major portion of my education in India. Early experiences, as we know, are critical in shaping the frameworks used to make sense of the world. I perceive myself as being embedded in the Indian culture, assimilating aspects of Western culture as an overlay. In terms of national identity I am British with a strong emotional and spiritual link with India. This chapter is written from my perspective of a coach with Indian heritage. My comments on coaching coachees with Indian heritage have to be interpreted in this context.

An essential prerequisite in the coaching process is an in-depth understanding of the 'looking glass' used by the coach to make sense of his or her personal experiences (processing system) and how it could impact on their interpretation of the coachee's experiences. Attribution theory offers an explanation of how and why we perceive individuals who are different from us less favourably. A large proportion of bias continues to reside in the 'blind spot' quadrant shown in Figure 14.3 (a feedback unit) at a subconscious level, which subtly influences the quality of coaching.

In order to understand the coachee's world, the coach needs to understand the context within which the coachee operates. The context incorporates the culture, those subtle and nebulous processes that influence our thinking and behaviour in particular contexts. Figure 14.2 illustrates an aspect of the 'looking glass' for understanding the different contexts and experiences that influence the meaning-making systems of individuals.

In order to understand another individual or group, we need to understand their history, social systems and experiences, which shape their values, beliefs, psychological framework and behaviour. We also need to know the relevance given to these factors by the individual and to keep an open mind about those factors that could have a more subtle and powerful influence at a more subconscious level.

I have found some of the questions below useful in enabling me to understand what sense my client is making of a situation, where the same event could have different meaning for someone else:

Tell me what happened. Or: Describe what happened.

What does this mean to you?

What are your feelings about this?

What would you prefer to do to resolve this dilemma?

Whose opinion do you value most at home/work/socially?

What advice would X [the individual valued] give if you went to this person with the problem?

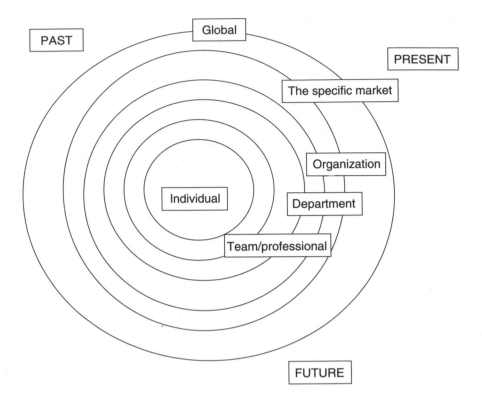

Figure 14.2 Levels of contextual analysis

The cultural layers

The demands of adaptation required for the work and social culture are not unique to British Asians. An individual operates within different cultures at different times (Fukuyama, 1995; Carmel, 1999; Rosen, Marshall and Philips, 2000). In fact, Martin (1992) comments that people may think of themselves as belonging to one culture and in the next moment identify themselves with another. Kondo (1990) and Hobsbawm and Ranger (1992) state that people are moving in and out of multiple identities at any one time, and Bhabha (1995) was of the view that fixed identity was a legacy of a 'colonial mindset' that offered a simplistic view of identity construction.

The paradigms for understanding cultural differences developed by Hofstede (1980), Hampden-Turner and Trompenaars (1993) and Hall (1976) have dominated cross-cultural research. The evidence base for most of this research was the business context. Furthermore, as Hicks and Peterson (1999) point out 'although cultural hypotheses help coaches anticipate differences, a person's perspective cannot be predicted from what might be distinctive about their culture and could lead to misconceptions because... each person is a unique configuration of a variety of influences, including personal experiences, genetics, and sub-cultural forces that transcend national cultures... to create the person's view of the world, way of thinking, and behaviour.'

Graham (2006) states 'people who will succeed in the 21st century are those who transcend race and build relationships, who continue to grow and develop as individuals and who bring value to themselves and those they represent.' The multifaceted aspects of individuals' psychological make-up have to be understood by the coach so that he or she can facilitate the coachee to understand how this impacts on his or her response in different contexts. This will allow the coachee to understand their reactions better and bring more of this knowledge from the 'unknown' to the 'known' area.

Personal development

Figure 14.3 highlights the public and private aspects of an individual, which influence the processing of incoming and outgoing information. The purpose of coaching is to acknowledge one's own blind spots and facilitate the coachee to explore their blind spots in a safe and secure context that then provides a wider perspective of situations encountered. In coaching coachees of Asian origin, there can sometimes be a marked difference between areas of mental and emotional make-up harnessed at home and at work. Although there is little research on the emotional impact of this discrepancy combined with the different cultural demands from the different cultural layers, my experience is that the discrepancies can lead to dissonance and stress. The case studies involving Amit and Tara illustrate the issues raised by below-the-surface thoughts.

The complexity of the individual's make-up is ignored when humans formulate an opinion, albeit a very superficial one, about each other within the first few seconds. The purpose of coaching is to extend knowledge about oneself and the coachee.

Figure 14.4 expands on this theme by using the concept of layers to accommodate the different dimensions of the individual. The layers are permeable and influence each other consciously or subconsciously.

As a business-coaching psychologist, I am interested in the middle layer, which I have expanded in Figure 14.5.

It is the bridge between the inner and outer layers. This central layer, which incorporates our thoughts and emotions, influences our outer layer and how we present ourselves to others and is in turn influenced by the inner layer. This critical central layer tries to align the inner and outer layers.

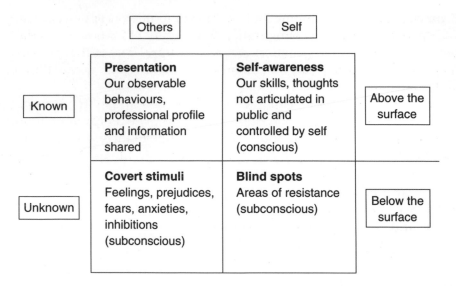

(Based on the Joseph Luft and Harry Ingham Johari window, developed and adapted by Indrani Choudhury, 2008)

Figure 14.3 Johari window of self-awareness

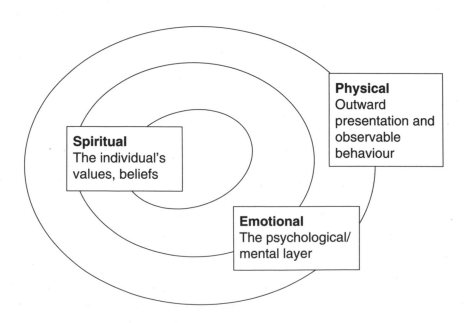

Figure 14.4 The individual's layers

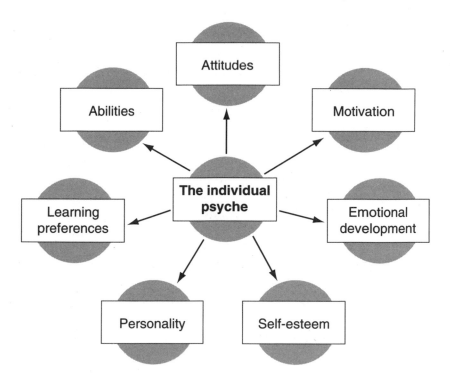

Figure 14.5 The individual psyche

Considerable non-alignment can result in dissonance (see Ismail's case study) and in extreme cases to near disintegration of the individual (see Tara's case study). Our intellectual and emotional development follows a certain pathway, though at different individual rates. Thus in order to understand an individual's psyche (central layer), we need to understand the stage of development the individual is currently operating at. *Any coaching needs to adapt the interaction to where the client is at present.* In my opinion the development process in the adult is not as dependent on new neurological pathways as in infancy and adolescence, but on the adult assimilating information from experiences, utilizing the cognitive skills already in the repertoire, and transforming the knowledge to the next stage of complexity with opportunities for wider application in novel settings.

In terms of development, I find Kegan and Lahey's (1984) Theory of Development useful. Kegan describes it as movement from subject to object. In Kegan's schema, things that are subject are experienced as unquestioned and simply part of the self. This is similar to the inner and middle layers in Figure 14.3. These are the lenses through which we see. Things that are objects can be questioned, acted upon and shaped. Kegan also describes different stages and orders along the development journey, which are reminiscent of those in the Bhagwad Gita[1], the religious text of Hindus (Swami Nikilananda, 1944). The Gita states that at the early stages of development one is focused on the self and ego, and gradually through transformational learning one realizes that the earlier focus on the ego was due to ignorance and provides a simplistic world view. The transformational learning encourages detachment from the self, and one is then able to stand back and look critically at events in a wider context. From the perspective of a Hindu, this development process can take more than one lifetime.

In terms of facilitating the development process, I find Bloom *et al*'s (1956; 1964) Taxonomy very useful in identifying which stage of the hierarchy an individual is operating at in relation to a particular domain of activity. As with other developmental processes, an individual may be operating at a certain level in one activity, but when thrown into a new context reverts to his or her previous default level unless the new level is well established.

Figure 14.6 details the different levels in the hierarchy. The earlier stages refer to informational learning and the later stages need to be engaged in transformational learning. In my view, the taxonomy needs to be extended to incorporate reflection as a separate rung on the ladder of learning (Bloom's intention may have been to incorporate it under evaluation). It is this process that harnesses our meta-cognitive strategies and focuses on conscious control of our learning. We learn from others without requiring to be taught by others. This is what I perceive as lifelong learning as mentioned

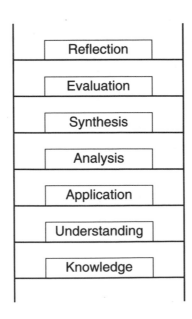

Figure 14.6 The ladder/taxonomy of learning

in the Bhagwad Gita. Briefly, I see the coaching process as a means of providing the coachees with opportunities to review their performance through different lenses, to consider and reflect on what they can assimilate within their existing constructs so that they can be proactive in their self-development.

Essential prerequisites

It is essential to understand our own cultural heritage and world view before we set about understanding and assisting other people (Ibrahim, 1985; Lauver, 1986). This understanding includes an awareness of one's own philosophies of life and capabilities, recognition of different structures of reasoning, and an understanding of their effects on one's communication and helping style (Ibrahim, 1985). Lack of such understanding may hinder effective intervention. Subtle ethnocentric bias could lead the coach to make inaccurate inferences about a client's motivation and other personal attributes.

In my opinion, when coaching individuals whose culture and background is different to the coach's own, the coach needs to be very alert and functioning at an optimal level throughout the session in order to notice even minimal differences. Tadmor and Tetlock (2006) suggest that a person will switch from automatic to conscious attention in new situations that contain much ambiguity when previous models of behaviour seem inadequate. One therefore has to make more effort not only to notice the differences but also to articulate questions that do not make the coachee defensive. Questions beginning with 'Why', unless carefully crafted, could give the coachee the impression that they need to rationalize their behaviour to fit the coach's frame of reference. I find questions beginning with 'What' followed by 'How' (if necessary) are preferable.

Suggestions for facilitating the process of coaching:

▌ Listen to the words and tone of voice used by the coachee.
▌ Continuously focus on the coachee's body language.
▌ Check interpretation and understanding of what has been said. Use headlines.
▌ Start from the coachee's current position and perspective.
▌ Use the coachee's language to shape thinking.
▌ Use reframing techniques to formulate a range of hypotheses and broaden the coachee's perspective.
▌ Coachee leads in formulating action.

CASE STUDY: AMIT

Amit was a senior manager in a large department. During the first session, his tense body language and curt responses gave the impression that he did not want to be at these sessions with me. When this issue was raised with him, he assured me that the sessions were useful. His body language was giving me a different message. His posture was tense, his tone flat and his eyes had a distant look rather than being focused on his current surroundings. I asked him: 'What do I need to do so that you feel really enthused by this session?' When I described what I was seeing and the conclusions I was drawing from it, he relaxed slightly and then began to express his anxieties. It appeared he felt he had been bullied by his manager and felt humiliated. He had applied for promotion under a new manager and had not been successful. The only feedback he had got was that he needed to be better at relating to colleagues as they found him unapproachable.

Although this mirrored my initial observations, I wanted him to explore situations and behaviours that could be giving those messages, and also to try and identify his thoughts in those situations. He then spontaneously informed me that he had similar problems at home. Although I was reluctant to go into marital issues as part of his performance coaching, he was keen to discuss them. It appeared that he and his wife (who was English) were always arguing. I asked him to describe the last argument. He mentioned that it was over dinner. His wife had cooked a meal and then just before he started eating he asked for some chilli sauce and his wife got annoyed. He explained that he liked his food spicy and always used a lot of chilli sauce on his food. I asked what his wife had cooked and how much time it had taken, etc. According to his response, his wife had spent the afternoon preparing this meal – a dish he liked. She had set the table nicely and then his request for the chilli sauce had resulted in the argument. I asked him if he had tasted the food before adding the sauce and he replied 'No'. I then asked him to imagine himself in his wife's place. Consider what he would need to do to cook this meal. What his wife could be doing that she might also enjoy if she were not cooking for him. As he was now in 'wife role', what reactions would he have liked to see as the family tasted the dish? He realized suddenly that he had asked for chilli sauce without tasting the meal. He acknowledged that his reaction would be more severe than his wife's if she had added anything to a dish cooked by him without even tasting it. We then discussed how the same incident can look from different perspectives. He explained that his wife's negative attitude towards his chilli sauce made him feel that she was being critical of his cultural background. He now realized that it had been a 'normal reaction' to her cooking not being appreciated.

He then informed me that when he was young his family had been ostracized as his father was an alcoholic and the family was very poor. They were rejected by the English families on their street. While he was reflecting on these earlier experiences, he suddenly said 'I assumed everyone was critical of me because of my background. I therefore decided to protect myself before the attack.' We discussed how the 'chilli sauce' lens could also be used in the work setting. When asked to describe a recent incident at work, he was able to describe the incident and his associated emotions. It was only as he looked through his colleagues' lenses that he appreciated the consequences of his actions and their reaction to him. He realized he had to leave his 'chilli sauce' lens aside and try and appreciate the situation from the perspective of others before reacting. This realization had a profound impact on him. He later informed me that his relationship with his wife and children had improved considerably and his manager confirmed that the change in his attitude had made him a valued member of the team.

My rationale for including this case study is that it illustrates:

▮ the need for the coachee to articulate his perceptions and explore the landscape with his 'looking glass';
▮ the non-alignment between the different layers and the nature of dissonance it caused;
▮ the need to consciously acknowledge that the 'looking glass' used by others may display a different kaleidoscope (the pieces may be the same but the overall pattern is totally different);
▮ the processing units are different as we prioritize some experiences by bringing them to the surface and push others into the depths of our unconscious. These early experiences, even if placed at the subconscious level, can influence our behaviour quite subtly. We all carry these early painful experiences as baggage with us all our lives. When an individual becomes conscious of the content of the baggage, then this awareness gives them the choice of how they manage it.

CASE STUDY: ISMAIL

Ismail was a senior manager with responsibility for six teams of professionals. He sought coaching to improve his performance as he had not been promoted. He informed me that he had more professional qualifications than any other member within the department. However, another member of the department had been promoted. His appraisals had not thrown up any issues and his manager had told him he was performing well. He felt so aggrieved that he was considering going to India but his children would find it difficult to settle there.

During the coaching process it transpired that it was unclear whether there was a shared understanding between Ismail and the directors regarding the requirements for this promotion. It was a task for Ismail to identify the appropriate people he could have a conversation with in order to have a clearer picture of the requirements. He acknowledged that the professional qualifications gave him technical skills in a particular area and that there were no comments to suggest that he was not considered technically competent. His task was to find out about the other qualities. The subsequent sessions involved reflective discussion on evaluating his outputs in the different competency areas from different perspectives. He then agreed he needed to identify his strengths and areas for development. He sought the support of his manager so that the manager could assist him with the evaluation of his outcomes and in identifying opportunities to gain experience in his areas for development.

My rationale for using this case study is that it illustrates:

▮ The illusions that can be created by depending on one perspective and its impact on other elements (central individual layer – self-esteem). In this case the coachee's 'looking glass' was offering a narrow, telescopic perspective that focused on the individual contextual layer – discrimination because of ethnic origin.

▮ the non-alignment between the individual, team/professional layer and the organizational layer;

▮ the impact of an inadequate organizational layer (lack of robust performance management system) on the individual (reinforcing discrimination of ethnic minorities);

▮ the interaction between the different elements – the cultural layers and the individual layers;

▮ the need to shift from the subject to the object in terms of development. The shift from one paradigm (discrimination) to another paradigm (requirements of the organization).

CASE STUDY: TARA

Tara was a very able professional woman who came to Britain when she was four with her professional parents as a self-referral. She was respected for her technical skills but colleagues were apprehensive of her high standards and expectations. The issues she identified were her inability to cope with unfairness and the difficulty she had in refraining from challenging colleagues when their behaviour did not meet the high standards she set or their values were dissimilar to her own. She had a strong sense of justice and equality and engaged in voluntary work to promote this within the community.

She did not always consider the impact her communication had on others. Her behaviour meant that she was becoming increasingly isolated. Her career progression had suffered and she was also feeling depressed.

She initially presented as a confident, assertive woman who readily expressed her views. She dressed smartly and had assimilated the dress culture of the West. Being a Catholic, she belonged to a congregation of mainly white professional families. Her skin colour was the only physical indication of her ethnicity. Unlike traditional Hindu families, her nuclear family did not have strong ties with the extended family in her country of birth.

During the coaching session she informed me that her parents had separated when she was a teenager and although she had been a 'daddy's girl' her relationship with her father deteriorated when she realized that the break-up was due to marital violence. During the coaching session she mentioned that she felt negative towards her mother for not standing up to her father as this could have prevented the situation reaching a stage that necessitated her father's departure.

Tara seemed confused and angry about the causes of her limited career progression. Feedback about her work from her manager and clients was positive. She felt she was being discriminated against or that she was not capable of achieving her goals/potential. Her self-esteem was very low and she felt she 'was not good enough'. As a practical exercise we looked at her achievements and the skills they required. We put this on a timeline where we had already plotted significant life events, which had required her involvement. This highlighted her achievements against the odds. Tara acknowledged that '[she] had not done badly'. When I said that she had done well, tears welled up in her eyes as no one had ever said this to her before. We then reviewed conflict situations that she had recently encountered. She found it difficult to spontaneously consider other perspectives. It was one of the few occasions when I had to encourage her to adopt physical poses to express emotions different individuals may have experienced in conflict situations.

The reason I have touched on some of the issues above is to illustrate how the different layers had been influenced by events and the impact of this on her behaviour and emotions.

My observations and assessment of Tara's responses suggested that she could be at Kegan's third order of mind, although I could not be totally certain as this would require further assessment. Tara had difficulty when the different layers were not aligned or demarcated. She tended to see things as 'black or white' and had difficulty coming to terms with the fact that there may not be a right answer and she needed to make the best choice given the information available.

In terms of the taxonomy of learning she was reflective, though only from a limited perspective. Although very articulate, she did not always successfully articulate and conceptualize her values so that they could form the basis of discussion for reconciling differing perspectives. Though reflective, her focus was subjective. She had difficulty viewing situations objectively and then reflecting on the information acquired, hence the range of coaching questions focused on alternative perspectives. Articulation of her responses helped to bring these alternative views into her conscious awareness. Sometimes circular questioning was useful, eg 'If your grandfather [whom she admired and respected] was here what would his reaction have been?' Such questions enabled me to see the different meaning-making systems used by individuals from similar backgrounds to hers.

Tara decided that the management role within an organization did not utilize her skills and during our coaching sessions decided to retrain as a barrister.

This case illustrates:

▮ the critical importance of understanding the different layers in the individual element and their implications for processing information;
▮ awareness of the extent and influence of different compartments in the information processing unit – self-awareness blind spots;
▮ the impact of the coachee's focus on one contextual layer at the expense of the others. in this case the individual layer at the expense of the team and other layers;
▮ the importance of appreciating the current state of the sub-elements (self-esteem, motivation, attitudes – see Figure 14.5) in the central layer of the individual rather than using an outdated corrupt version (no one had acknowledged this coachee's achievements against the odds).

CONCLUSIONS

In this chapter, I have tried to facilitate an appreciation of the history and heritage of the British Asians from the subcontinent. The chapter is merely an introduction to arouse the curiosity of coaches working with this group. The 'looking glass' model introduced in this chapter is one paradigm. I have found that it provides a flexible structure to analyse the complexity of individuals' experiences and synthesize the myriad of patterns into a coherent shared perspective. As the British Asians assimilate aspects of British culture and relegate aspects of their Asian heritage, the 'looking glass' will have to be adjusted so that it is always fit for purpose. Coaching individuals from a different background is a challenge and it provides both coach and coachee with a wealth of information for development and learning.

References

Bhabha, H K (1995) *The Location of Culture*, Routledge, London

Bloom, B S *et al* (1956) *Taxonomy of Educational Objectives. Handbook I: The cognitive domain*, Mckay, New York

Bloom, B S, Krathwhol, D R and Masia, A (1964) *Taxonomy of Educational Objectives: The classification of educational goals. Handbook II: The affective domain*, Allyn & Bacon, Boston, MA

Carmel, E (1999) *Global Software Teams: Collaborating across borders and time zones*, Prentice Hall

Fukuyama, F (1995) *Trust: The Social virtues and the creation of prosperity*, Hamish Hamilton, London

Gerhardt, S (2004) *Why Love Matters: How affection shapes a baby's brain*, Bruner and Routledge

Gunaratana, B H (2002) *Mindfulness in Plain English*, Wisdom Publications, US

Hall, E T (1976) *Beyond Culture*, Doubleday, Garden City, NY

Hampden-Turner, C and Trompenaars, A (1993) *The Seven Cultures of Capitalism*, Doubleday, New York

Handy, C (2002) What's Business For? *Harvard Business Review*, **20**(12)

Hicks, M D and Peterson, D B (1999) Leaders coaching across borders, in *Advances in Global Leadership*, eds W H Mobley, M J Gressner and V J Arnold, JAI Press, Stamford, CT

Hobsbawm, E and Ranger, T (1992) *The Invention of Tradition*, Cambridge University Press, Cambridge

Hofstede, G (1980) *Culture's Consequences: International differences in work related values*, Sage Publications, Thousand Oaks, CA

Ibrahim, F A (1985) Effective cross-cultural counselling and psychotherapy, *The Counselling Psychologist*, **13**, pp 625–38

Kegan, R and Lahey, L (1984) Adult leadership and adult development, in *Leadership*, ed B Kellerman, Prentice Hall, Englewood Cliffs, NJ

Kenny, E J and Briner, R B (2007) Ethnicity and behaviour in organisations: A review of British research, *Journal of Occupational and Organisational Psychology*, **80**, pp 437–57

Kondo, D K (1990) *Crafting Selves: Power gender and discourses of identity in a Japanese workplace*, University of Chicago Press, Chicago

Lauver, P J (1986) Extending counselling cross-culturally: Invisible barriers, paper presented at the annual meeting of the California Association for Counselling and Development, San Francisco, CA, ED 274937

Luft, J and Ingham, H (1955) The Johari window, a graphic model of interpersonal awareness, *Proceedings of the Western Training Laboratory in Group Development*, UCLA, Los Angeles

Martin, J (1992) *The Culture of Organisations: Three perspectives*, Oxford University Press, New York

Rosen, R, Marshall, P and Philips C (2000) *Global Literacies: Lessons on business leadership and national cultures*, Simon & Schuster, New York

Smith M G (1986) Pluralism, race and ethnicity in selected African countries, in *Theories of Race and Ethnic Relations*, ed J Rex and D Mason, Cambridge University Press, Cambridge

Swami Nikhilananda (1944) *The Bhagavad Gita*, translated from Sanskrit, Ramakrishna-Vivekananda Center, New York

Tadmor, C T and Tetlock, P E (2006) Bi-culturalism: A model of the effects of second culture on acculturation and integrative complexity. *Journal of Cross Cultural psychology*, **37**(2), pp 173–90.

Further reading

Benz, K and Maurya, S (2007) Five keys to successful business coaching In India, *Business Coaching Worldwide*, **3**(2)

Bergen, J G and Fitzgerald, C (2002) Leadership and complexity of mind, in *Executive Coaching Practices and Perspectives*, eds C Fitzgerald and JG Berger

Dafoulas, G and Macculay, L (2001) Investigating cultural differences in virtual software teams, *The Electronic Journal on Information Systems in Developing Countries*, **7**(4), pp 1–14 [online] http://www.ejisdc.org

Hampden-Turner, C and Trompenaars, F (2000) *Building Cross Cultural Competence: How to create wealth from conflicting values*, Yale University Press, New Haven

Hofstede, G (1994) *Culture and Organisations: Software of the mind*, HarperCollins, London

Kegan, R (1982) *The Evolving Self: Problem and process in human development*, Harvard University Press, Cambridge, MA

Kegan, R (1994) *In Over Our Heads: The mental demands of modern life*, Harvard University Press, Cambridge, MA

Lahey, L E *et al* (1983) *A Guide to the Subject Object Interview: Its administration and analysis*, Harvard Graduate School of Education, Cambridge, MA

Meyer, J P *et al* (2007) Employee commitment and support for an organisational change: Test of the three component models in two cultures, *Journal of Occupational and Organisational Psychology*, **80**, pp 185–211

Ogbonna and Harris (2006) The dynamics of employee relationships in an ethnically diverse workforce, *Human Relations*, **59**, pp 379–407

Otazo, K (1998) The inside story in advances in global leadership, in *Advances in Global Leadership*, ed W H Mobley, M J Gressner and V J Arnold, JAI Press, Greenwich, CT

Prasad, A and Prasad, P (2000) Stretching the iron cage: the Constitution and implications of routine workplace resistance, *Organisation Science*, **11**(4), pp 387–403

Rosinski, P (2003) Coaching across cultures, *International Journal of Coaching in Organisations*, **1**(4), pp 4–16

Stedman, G (2006) *Diversity: Leaders Not Labels*, Free Press

Watson, W E, Kumar, K and Michaelson, K K (1993) Cultural diversity's impact on interaction, process and performance: Comparing homogeneous and diverse task groups, *Academy of Management Journal*, **36**, pp 590–602

NOTES

1 These religious verses have been translated from Sanskrit by numerous authors, each providing a slightly different interpretation. The Gita read alongside other religious texts and Hindu philosophy facilitates understanding and an opportunity to apply the thinking to one's life.

15

Coaching with men: alpha males

Eddie Erlandson

INTRODUCTION

Helping male leaders make major changes in their work styles can be as challenging as getting them to take a pay cut. Our research shows that roughly 75 per cent of senior executive positions in major corporations in the United States and Europe are held by determined, confident alpha males striving to be nothing but the best in their field.

In my work with alpha male leaders, either as clients or as managers of clients, I've learned that they all share one challenge: they must decide they want to change. And, given their success, these leaders can be dubious about doing things differently. I make it a priority to use techniques that help coachees make a sincere commitment to change their leadership styles.

In this chapter, I will focus exclusively on one type of male: the alpha male – the dominant, confident, results-driven leader whose very strengths can also present risks. I will discuss the tools I find most useful when working with this type of coachee: an in-depth, interview-based 360-degree assessment; a constructive and detailed feedback session; and a meeting with the coachee, his manager and his team in which the coachee shares what he's learned.

THE ISSUE OF GENDER IN COACHING

My work with both men and women executives – alphas or not – has revealed the potential for significant differences in coaching them. It's important to remember that, while clear differences have emerged from research, we highlight average differences between men and women. Generally speaking, men are drawn to competition and attaining positions of dominance, while women assign greater value to collaborative relationships and networking. Female leaders have an equal desire to be 'top dog' but more typically go about their pursuit by being more consultative and inclusive and less dominating than men.

Most important is how male and female leaders respond to a need for coaching and feedback. Although men and women are equally open to making changes in their leadership, they tend to manifest their openness as well as their resistance differently. Women tend to be more receptive to advice, directly soliciting it from their coach; in fact, seeking counsel is how many women bond with others and they often actively seek out mentors. Men, on the other hand, may require some help in being receptive to feedback.

Instead of simply accepting feedback, men often explain that they've already tried the suggested ideas and why those approaches didn't work. They also like to talk about prior successes, at times bragging about themselves and how well things have gone since the last session. Male leaders may provide you with details that justify their behaviour, and many are inclined to blame someone or something else for what has happened. Given this resistance, coaches will be hard pressed to succeed by providing unsolicited advice that points out what men need to do differently. What works best with male executives is to explore whether they're interested in getting coached and giving them a choice about whether to proceed. This is just what happened when a male client recently called me for input on a significant presentation he was writing for a CEO I coach. Each time I offered an idea, he explained why his approach was better. After a couple of rounds I finally asked him to clarify what he wanted from me, and then I just listened. Everything shifted in that moment; all of a sudden he became quite receptive to alternative ideas.

Defensiveness in women leaders typically shows up differently. Women may tend to exhibit passive defensiveness by agreeing with coaches when they really don't agree; they may commit to action and then not follow through. They tend to take feedback personally and complain to others after sessions, instead of being direct with the coach.

Once coaching begins, men and women give attention to different priorities. Men generally focus on business results and not as much on how to get a fellow executive to buy in to an initiative or how to coach subordinates to improve their performance. Because men lock onto quantifiable results, coaches must point out the measurable business consequences of their leadership shortfalls. Male leaders are not generally moved by the fact that their behaviour upsets people, but if their actions impede performance, it hits home. Women key into different information. Female leaders generally don't like to hear that they aren't working well with people or that people don't like working with them. After all, their ability to form strong relationships is one of their advantages – it impacts their ability to influence, engender loyalty, and motivate and mobilize others.

These differences can be further understood in terms of Baron-Cohen's (2003) work on distinguishing systemizing and empathizing traits. Women tend to be empathizers who care about the feelings of others. They are less likely to fight, and they get what they want through collaboration and reciprocity. Men, on the other hand, are generally systemizers. They excel in logical and quantitative analysis. They're less concerned about the feelings of others; instead, they are more transactional with people, who they see as a part of the system.

Alpha males and alpha females tend to reflect these fundamental gender differences as well. A great many alpha males see coaching as a soft, touchy-feely fad with little substance, and they're about as eager to be coached as they are to share their feelings. Even if they respect coaching, they don't think *they* need it. Since the problems in their organizations are someone else's fault, they are more inclined to bring in a coach to work with someone on their team. By the time they're offered coaching, they already have some awareness that their style causes some problems. But they consider this a minor side-effect of the medicine they dispense to cure business ailments. Since they've been successful, they tell us not to rock the boat. They are afraid that taking the edge off their style will destroy their secret ingredient of success. Ironically, of course, the alpha males who are most hostile to the idea of coaching are the very ones who stand to benefit most from a good coach.

THE EVIDENCE OF DIFFERENCE

Because of the popular image of the alpha male, with his powerful physical presence and tough-guy demeanour, we seldom hear the term *alpha female*.

But a great many women in leadership positions do possess the fundamental traits that define alphas. I am focusing on alpha males for two primary reasons.

First, there are more of them, and I coach more men than I coach women. In general, men are more likely than women to have alpha characteristics, and the business world contains many more alpha males than alpha females, especially in the top executive ranks. As a consultant, I've noted this disparity in every company I've worked with, and my observations have been confirmed by research data. US-based studies on the infamous glass ceiling offer further evidence of the male–female ratio at the highest corporate levels. A US survey by the Catalyst organization (Prime, 2005), for instance, found that while women hold 50.3 per cent of all management and professional positions, only 7.9 per cent of the top earners are women in the *Fortune 500*, and only 1.4 per cent of CEOs are women.

The second reason for focusing on alpha males is that a great deal of wreckage is caused by boys behaving badly. In our research (Ludeman and Erlandson, 2006) men scored much higher than women on measures of the alpha risk factors I describe later in the chapter. What does this mean? In short, alpha females get angry, but they're seldom as belligerent as alpha males. They like to win, and they set aggressive goals for themselves and their teams, but they're not as intimidating or as authoritarian as their male counterparts. And while they can be fiercely competitive, they're less likely than alpha males to use ruthless tactics or to see peers and colleagues as rivals who have to be destroyed. This is why you don't see *New Yorker* or *Spectator* cartoons about domineering alpha females.

What is an alpha?

I have coached hundreds of executives, including Boston Red Sox CEO Larry Lucchino; Vice Admiral Keith Lippert, director of the Defense Logistics Agency; and vice-presidents and senior executives at companies like Adecco, Coca Cola, Dell, eBay, Eaton, Gap, KLA-Tencor and Microsoft. Even though alpha males differ in style, they share some key characteristics.

The *Oxford English Dictionary* defines an alpha as a person tending to assume a dominant role in social or professional situations, or a person thought to possess the qualities and confidence for leadership. These modern-day Beowolfs take the form of confident managers, savvy CEOs and world leaders of the pack. As I use the term in my work, *alpha* signifies a powerful, authoritative personality type with a specific set of traits. Alpha leaders are aggressive, results-driven achievers who insist on top performance from themselves and others. Courageous and self-confident, they are turned on by bold, innovative ideas and ambitious goals, and they pursue their objectives with tenacity and an urgent sense of mission. Their intense competitive drive keeps them focused on the gold – silver or bronze simply won't do – and they're always keeping score. Often charismatic figures who command attention, they exert influence even when they're one of many leaders in a large organization or still working their way up the corporate ladder.

Some alpha males are larger-than-life legends who run large companies; others lead in relative obscurity at the top of little-known firms or even small departments. The healthy ones – well-balanced human beings in full command of their alpha strengths – are natural leaders trusted by colleagues, respected by competitors, revered by employees, and adored by Wall Street. But other alpha males are risks to their organization and some-times themselves. These leaders get depicted in Dilbert cartoons, not management textbooks. Inspiring resentment instead of respect, and fear instead of trust, they create corporate soap operas that make life miserable for co-workers, create expensive problems for their companies, and derail fast-track careers – including their own. Why? Because their greatest strengths turn into tragic flaws. Evidence of this alpha ambiguity can be seen on the covers of *Fortune* and *Forbes*, on the front pages of newspapers, on CNN and ESPN: alpha males leading the way to amazing accomplishments, earth-shaking breakthroughs and skyrocketing profits – and abusing power, bankrupting companies and wearing handcuffs.

Strengths become risks for alpha males when they over-use them. Farson (1996: 137) noted that 'strengths can become weaknesses when we rely too much on them, carry them to exaggerated lengths, or apply them where they don't belong'. People with the virtue of persistence sometimes turn stubborn, for example, and brilliant analysts can think themselves into a corner. The stronger the positive qualities, the more likely they are to erupt as negatives. This is what happens to many alpha males, and because they have inordinate influence, their pendulum swings can be ruinous. To one degree or another, they fluctuate between healthy and unhealthy alpha tendencies: their magnetic leadership commands respect, but their aggressive tactics create resistance, resentment and revenge; they are cele-brated for their achievements but loathed for the carnage they leave in their wake; people stand in awe of their competence and can-do energy, but they often hate working with them. Hogan, Brady and Fico (2008) note that helping to prevent strengths from becoming deficits is one of the key purposes of executive coaching. Coaches should help coachees recognize when they are at their best, according to Hogan *et al*, but also when their strengths go too far in the direction of their problems. The rewards and risks of alpha traits are summarized in Table 15.1.

Table 15.1 The Alpha Syndrome: when strengths become liabilities

Alpha attribute	Value to organization	Risk to organization
Dominant, confident, takes charge	Decisive, courageous leader; gets people to take action and move forward	Doesn't develop strong leaders; intimidating; creates fear; stifles disagreement
Charismatic, magnetic leader who leads the way	Brings out the best in others; gets people to do more than they thought was possible	Manipulates to get his way; uses charm to lure people down *his* path
Aggressive, competitive	Determined to win; turns others into winners	Competes with peers; alienates colleagues; reluctant to give others credit
High achiever with a strong sense of mission	Action-oriented; produces results; energizes teams to reach impossible goals	Takes high levels of performance for granted; expects the impossible and fails to acknowledge what's required to achieve it
Bold, creative, innovative thinker	Dreams up ingenious ideas; solves intractable problems; sees further than others	Arrogant, stubborn, overly opinionated; imposes own views; closed to others' thinking
Persistent, tenacious, determined, steadfast	Has courage of convictions; always moves forward; willing to take unpopular stand to get results	Drives self and others to exhaustion; urgent, impatient; thinks rules don't apply to him
Strong appetite for newness and change	Values speed, drives people and organizations towards needed change and rapid growth	Overzealous; undervalues organizational alignment; launches into action before gathering support from others
Farsighted, sees what's possible	Recognizes gap between today's reality and tomorrow's potential	So focused on future that present and near term are neglected; loses sight of business viability
Sees what's missing	Proactively spots problems; adjusts, corrects, prevents things from getting worse	Can be critical, demeaning; fails to appreciate others' contributions; people feel demoralized

Table 15.1 summarizes the alpha male syndrome: the very strengths that make alphas so effective become their downfall when they're overused, excessive or misplaced.

Research today: data on alphas

Based on our extensive experience working with alphas in their natural environments, we have developed a detailed questionnaire that measures the extent to which an individual has alpha characteristics. The Alpha Assessment (Ludeman and Erlandson, 2006b) was developed over a series of three validation phases on a population of 1607. The subjects all worked full time in the business world, many in high-ranking leadership positions: 1484 were drawn from the readership of *Harvard Business Review*, and 123 more came from personal business contacts. Of these 1607 subjects, 63.79 per cent were male and the average age was 41.2 years. Ethnically and racially diverse (65.2 per cent white, 3.2 per cent African American, 20.8 per cent Asian, 4.5 per cent Latino and 6.3 per cent 'other'), they hailed from an astonishing 106 nations and spanned hundreds of different industries, among them agriculture, telecommunications, high technology, real estate, education, oil, automotive, finance and banking. More than three-quarters (77.5 per cent) said they supervised other people. At the time of writing of this chapter, over 10,000 individuals have taken the Alpha Assessment.

In addition to helping us refine the assessment tool itself, the validation phase yielded some fascinating data about alphas. When factor analyses were applied to the risk factors identified on assessments from about 1500 managers and executives, three distinct themes stood out: anger, impatience and competitiveness. These themes represent a compelling summary of alphas that create trouble: they see everyone as a rival, every situation as a contest for supremacy. They are demanding and impatient for results, often veritable powder kegs.

Here is a comment about an executive from a series of 360 interviews I conducted at the request of the company CEO: 'We never know which Mike is going to show up in the morning, the effervescent guy with the big smile who can't wait to take on the world, or the maniac who's going to explode the first time someone rubs him the wrong way.' Like other volatile alpha males, Mike's sunny side was dazzling and infectious, but his dark side made Darth Vader look like Peter Pan. When 'the happy warrior' showed up, everyone was ready to follow him to the barricades. When 'the ogre' emerged from his cave, they wanted to hide under their desks. In general, employees are willing to cope with an occasional outburst, especially if it's predictable. But arbitrary, frequent and abusive tantrums cross the line into destructive intimidation.

The four types of alphas

All alpha males are aggressive, competitive and driven to achieve. They think big, aim high and attack their goals with courage, confidence and tenacity. But each of the four types expresses these common qualities in different ways. Understanding their nuances gives coaches deeper insight into alpha males, helping them to pinpoint strengths the coachee can build upon and risks they need to address. With this more granulated view, coaches and coachees can work together to identify a specific course of action, just as a doctor can devise a better treatment plan knowing a patient's specific malady.

Here is a brief summary of each type's primary behaviour traits:

▌ **Commanders**: Intense, magnetic leaders who set the tone, mobilize the troops and energize action with authoritative strength and passionate motivation, without necessarily digging into the details.
▌ **Visionaries**: Curious, expansive, intuitive, proactive and future-oriented, they see possibilities and opportunities that others sometimes dismiss as impractical or unlikely, and inspire others with their vision.
▌ **Strategists**: Methodical, systematic, often brilliant thinkers who are oriented towards data and facts; they have excellent analytic judgement and a sharp eye for patterns and problems.
▌ **Executors**: Tireless, goal-oriented doers who push plans forward with an eye for detail, relentless discipline and keen oversight, surmounting all obstacles and holding everyone accountable for their commitments.

Coaches should note that the alpha leader types are not mutually exclusive. While virtually every alpha has one dominant type, alphas will typically have one or two secondary patterns as well. For example, a visionary alpha might also have strong strategist tendencies, while another visionary might have executor traits as a secondary characteristic. Although each type is statistically unique, there is an approximate 20 per cent correlation between them.

In my experience, the most effective alpha leaders are those who blend the functional elements of more than one type – or are smart enough to surround themselves with associates who add the strengths of other types to the mix. You can see where all four styles have value, and that, depending on the circumstances, different combinations and proportions would be ideal. Unfortunately, not all alpha males learn the priceless lesson of working with complementary types.

Let's now turn to alpha risks. As with the general alpha male traits, each type has specific strengths that can turn into weaknesses – the very issues you'd address as coach:

- **Commanders:** Commanders' noble intention is to make things happen, and they push people hard to accomplish their goals. Their primary risk is driving *so* hard they run over others like bulldozers. Their leadership challenge is to learn how to align people around a common direction and to inspire and orchestrate productive action rather than mandate it.
- **Visionaries:** Visionaries' noble intention is to move an organization forward into an uncertain and unknown future. Fuelled by a fertile imagination, they lead with passion and enthusiasm. Their primary risk is becoming so overzealous that they ignore reality, bite off more than they can chew, and lead their team over a cliff. Their leadership challenge is to become practical prophets by adding the skills of listening, planning and executing to their intuitive gifts.
- **Strategists:** Strategists' noble intention is to select the optimal direction and get the best result. They approach the task armed with data and exceptional powers of reasoning and analysis. Their primary risk is becoming overconfident know-it-alls in love with their own brilliance. Their leadership challenge is to invite others to contribute their unique intelligence and creativity.
- **Executors:** Executors' noble intention is to get things done the right way. Masters of project management, they dig into the details with relentless determination. Their primary risk is becoming control freaks whose micromanaging creates roadblocks and paralysis. Their leadership challenge is to create ownership, commitment and genuine accountability.

WORKING WITH GENDER DIFFERENCES IN COACHING

As I discussed earlier in the chapter, coaching men is typically different from coaching women. And, while coaching alphas – men or women – can be similar by virtue of their 'alpha-ness', on the whole, coaching alpha male executives has its own unique challenges and rewards.

Committing to change

The first step in working with these hard-hitting, results-oriented over-achievers is to help them become coachable. Ideally, this occurs while showing them the benefits of modifying their style to become more open and transparent. Even when alpha males see the impact of their behaviour and acknowledge the need to change, they often remain ambivalent about actually doing it. They try to shift the focus to changes they wish others would make: if only others would change, they wouldn't need to! However,

Table 15.2 Summary of strengths and risks of each alpha type

Alpha type	Value to organization	Risk to organization
Commander	Decisive, strong, authoritative; exudes confidence; often charismatic; has a big appetite for achievement and thirst for victory; brings out the best in others	Solo player; domineering and intimidating; argues to win points; generates fear and self-protective culture; competes with peers; envious; loose with the rules
Visionary	High standards and expansive goals; inspires with view of future; makes creative leaps; strong convictions, unwavering faith and tenacious will; trusts instincts	Over-confident about ideas; excessive bravado; defensive when challenged; closed to input; ignores reality, losing support of pragmatists; spins the truth
Strategist	Quick, probing mind; objective, analytic, data-driven, methodical; sees underlying patterns, leaps beyond the obvious and integrates disparate ideas	Opinionated know-it-all; smug, arrogant, pretentious; has to be right; can't admit mistakes; cold and unemotional; lacks team spirit; disconnects from others
Executor	Disciplined; tireless pursuit of results; uncanny eye for spotting problems; gives excellent feedback and wake-up calls; moves people to goal-oriented action; helps others grow	Sets unreasonable expectations; micromanages; prone to workaholism and burning out employees; impatient; overly critical; focuses on shortcomings; expresses displeasure, not appreciation

as with all coachees, since they can't force others to change, they can exert control only by zeroing in on their own behaviour.

In examining their resistance, most alphas admit they're afraid that changing will limit their power to drive high-level performance. To them, acting nice would be both inauthentic and ineffective, and they refer to stories about sweet, kind executives who are well-liked, but not productive. I assure them that it's simply not in their nature to become too soft. Again and again, I return to the crucial alpha concern: results. I show that verbally abusing people in meetings triggers performance anxiety, or that getting overly attached to their opinions wastes time. Leaders want results, so I talk with them about how their behaviours may limit their results. Humour is a great way to puncture a coachee's fear. One especially tough coachee with the steely bearing of a Marine said bluntly, 'You want to turn me into a wimp!' I replied, 'You become a wimp? I'm not *that* good.'

Some alphas are afraid they won't be able to make the necessary changes put forth to them. They think they're being called upon to change the basic structure of their personalities. I explain that traits such as poor listening and impatience are not wired into the genetic code; they're merely habits they've picked up that can be modified or eliminated. Another common point of resistance is that some alphas want to know exactly *how* they'll make the necessary changes before they commit to the task. Explicitly or implicitly, their attitude is 'Tell me what you want me to do and I'll decide whether to say yes.' Knowing how to accomplish a goal before committing resources to it can be a wise attitude in some business scenarios. But in some cases it puts the cart before the horse. Quite often, it's only when coachees have made a firm and sincere commitment that solutions begin to fall into place; only after they take some uncertain steps towards their destination does the best pathway become visible.

To help them cross the threshold into commitment, I ask them to clarify their intentions with three simple questions:

1. Are you willing to make the needed changes?
2. Are you willing to do whatever it takes to do so?
3. Are you willing to allow me to assist you?

Alphas who respond with a clear 'Yes' move to the next phase with conviction and enthusiasm. From others I get a vague half-yes, usually conveyed in non-verbal cues. For example, the coachee might declare 'I wouldn't be here if I wasn't committed.' Well, they certainly would if their manager enrolled them in coaching. Another clue to resistance is the impatient head-nod that says 'Just get on with it; I'd rather be someplace else.' And you'd be surprised how many people utter 'Yes' while actually shaking their head from side to side, in an apparent 'No'. With these coachees I probe further until they come to see the roots of their mixed feelings.

Perhaps most important is the connection between coach and coachee. One reason coaches fail to connect with alphas is that they allow them to begin the process without a firm commitment to change. I've learned from experience that some coachees will pay lip service to coaching objectives, and even seem excited in the moment, only to lose interest when they return to work. I insist on a clear yes or no to the above three questions before ending my initial session. I make it known that I do not work with people who are not committed to change.

What is a 360-degree assessment?

The 360-degree assessment process I use when coaching alphas is an in-depth, categorized report comprised of comments from a coachee's manager, peers, direct reports and clients. Because alpha males respond best to concrete data, I find that detailed interviews packed with compelling verbatim statements carry much more weight than the usual 360s, which contain only high-level write-in comments added to online survey ratings. I interview as many of each person's colleagues as possible, including direct reports, peers and other executives with whom they collaborate – or *should* collaborate. The goal is to determine what behaviour works and what doesn't, and to back those findings with solid evidence.

The verbatim comments are organized into major themes and then scored, using colour coding to depict strengths and weaknesses. This makes the content analysis easy to read at a glance. Dark green represents an area of great strength; light green indicates an area that has shown improvement since the previous assessment; white is neutral advice about something the respondent thinks the alpha should do; yellow is a warning sign that certain behaviour might need attention; orange is a definite development area; and red is a deficiency that people feel is undermining productivity and efficiency. Nothing says 'You need to change' as convincingly as long lines of red and orange. Alphas expect to see lots of cool greens and mellow yellows; but it's often fiery reds and oranges that get their attention.

For maximum impact, I spend a concentrated six hours reviewing the 360 results with each coachee. Most alphas have been dishing out simple feedback most of their careers. This process turns the tables on them, and often it's their first wake-up call. Following the graphic overview, which appeals to the typical alpha's love of metrics, I review the verbatim comments of their co-workers. Since alphas tend to respond well to straight talk and hard-hitting language, I preserve the emotional candour of the interview data during the editing process, also ensuring anonymity. This information usually packs the wallop of a sneak attack. They invariably say something like 'Wow, these people I deeply respect think I am stubborn and don't want to listen? They're afraid to disagree with me because I'll call them stupid?' One of my first alpha coachees summed it up memorably: 'It's like being told I have interpersonal BO!'

At this point most alphas are ready to examine the implications of the report. I ask questions such as:

▌ If you don't change, what are the likely consequences?
▌ Which behaviours would you benefit most from modifying?
▌ How might you do things differently?
▌ If you change in those ways, how will your team members react?

Focusing on specific areas of competency satisfies the alpha penchant for detail and mobilizes their action orientation. It leads directly to goals that they can envision achieving.

I then soften the blow by balancing the critical feedback with the strengths their colleagues singled out. I also point out that some of the behaviour that now cries out for change served them well in the past, but might cause problems at the senior level, where inspiration, collaboration and team-building skills are required for better results. This removes the right/wrong judgement and frames their behavioural objectives as career development issues.

Capitalizing on the alpha drive for achievement and their sense of adventure, I suggest they experiment with their own behaviour. Some jump right into it; others need to be reassured that changing won't dull their competitive edge. This might require translating some of the 360-degree comments. For example, suppose someone has said the coachee is a micro-manager who ought to delegate more. Alphas might see this as a call to abdicate control. I point out that their ability to dig into details and execute the fine points of a strategic process are reasons for their success, but that the challenge is to apply this skill in the right ways, at the right times. A micro-manager, for instance, needs to be reflective and detail-oriented in the initial stages of a project in order to provide clear instructions and set proper agree-ments, rather than digging in and pointing out what's wrong after someone has done the work. Thus, I assure them that changing won't stop them from digging into the details and driving their troops to extraordinary accom-plishments. They'll simply do these things more effectively and with fewer unwanted side-effects. Alphas are not always convinced, but they're usually intrigued enough to give it a shot, especially if I engage their competitive instincts by challenging them to shift those red and orange bars into the green zone.

Nothing ensures follow-through for an alpha better than voluntarily sharing 360-degree results with everyone who participated in the process. This step can be extremely vulnerable for alpha males, who are not usually inclined to admit their shortcomings. The atmosphere can get so tense that ordinarily talkative people lose their tongues, especially in corporate cultures where self-revealing candour is as foreign as Aramaic. It's essential that the team leaders acknowledge the challenge of self-disclosure and do everything possible to make the person who's sharing his 360 feel at ease.

I begin these meetings by having the alpha thank everyone for the time they spent on his report and let them know he appreciates their honesty. He then summarizes the content of the 360 – both the strengths reported and the areas that need improvement – and describes how he felt when he read them. Admitting he was dismayed to discover that his style was confusing to teammates, or that he feels bad for having hurt people's feelings, can transform the audience from guarded to receptive. Even more powerful is when the alpha admits he's not sure how to fix the problem and asks for help. Such humble candour lets everyone know that it's safe to be honest. I then open the floor to dialogue.

Following this vital phase, we encourage the focal person to reflect on what he's heard and to describe how he intends to address the most important items. Having committed to a specific developmental plan, he concludes by requesting ongoing feedback and support.

With few exceptions, these 360-degree meetings catalyse a change in group dynamics. Participants feel the impact immediately and are stimulated by the possibility of future transformation. The alpha males on centre stage emerge knowing that their teammates want to help them become better, stronger leaders, not cut them down to size. They also discover that being straightforward about their challenges is a powerful influencing skill. By baring their necks and finding a friendly hand instead of a sharp blade, they come away with the opposite of what they feared: more respect rather than less. The rest of the team invariably feels relieved and hopeful, and this, in itself, is a powerful predictor of positive growth.

In addition to whole-team meetings, I encourage coachees to meet one on one with their most important peers and their direct reports, to let them know how they plan to modify the behaviours that were singled out for development. By stating their intentions they marshal support and derail cynicism – an especially important factor when the alpha's previous behaviour has not inspired confidence in his ability to change.

Mirror, mirror on the wall

One tool I use in a 360-degree feedback session is the awareness trajectory (Figure 15.1) to demonstrate the central role of awareness in success. I begin by having clients enumerate their intentions in several categories, such as business outcomes, leadership results and key relationships. I then compare their intentions to their actual impact, to make them more aware of the gap between their expectations and their results. We all know that factors such as knowledge, skill and experience are vital for effective leadership, and high-ranking alpha males have all of those in spades. The wild card is their self-awareness (vertical axis) and their awareness of how they influence others, including peers, their teams, customers and other key players (horizontal axis). As each type of awareness increases, so does the level of impact.

By becoming more aware of the impact of their behaviour, coachees can enhance their ability to communicate, collaborate and create, leading directly to greater influence and sustainable business results. In turn, this

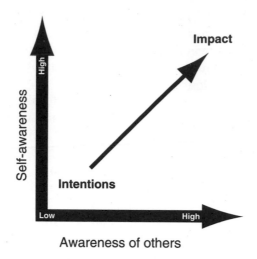

Figure 15.1 The awareness trajectory

improvement enables them to refine their intentions, bringing more authentic motivation to the surface. By asking questions such as 'What are my core beliefs?' and 'What are my deepest values?' coachees can more easily spot the gap between what they say and how they behave at work. Alphas, like most leaders, are high in integrity, and once they see this gap, they are more motivated to tackle the problems, especially when the coach points out that this sort of gap is typically interpreted by people as showing low integrity or a reason to mistrust them.

Clearing the air

When I coach teams of executives, I follow the 360 process with a 'Clearing the Air' exercise (Table 15.3), in which team members speak candidly about their past challenges in working with each other. This powerful process roots out the interpersonal sludge that stifles working relationships, and also brings to light cliques and alliances that further hinder performance. It's particularly important when communication and collaboration have suffered because of mistrust, misunderstandings or personal animosities. The process reduces tension and converts self-protection and fear into productive energy.

At the same time as they express their frustrations and concerns, people step up and claim responsibility for how their own behaviour laid the groundwork for the problems. If you think that clearing the air is too touchy-feely for a team filled with high-powered alpha males, think again. It's been responsible for a great many breakthroughs at the highest levels.

Table 15.3 Clearing the air

Instructions to participants	Participants take these steps
1. Complete these sentences, privately, to gain a fuller understanding of the situation	▌ What happened was: .... ▌ The way I contributed to the situation was: .... ▌ What I didn't do but could have done was: .... ▌ I felt: .... ▌ I'm concerned that you thought: .... ▌ I hope that you don't feel: ....
2. Hold yourself accountable by taking these steps	▌ Take full responsibility for finding a resolution. ▌ Set your intention to communicate constructively, not to win an argument. ▌ Assume that the other person has an equally positive intention to resolve the conflict. ▌ Give up all your assumptions about how the other person will respond to you. ▌ Adopt an attitude of curiosity about the other person's perspective. ▌ Identify overlapping purposes that you and the other person might share.
3. Engage in genuine dialogue with the other person	▌ Avoid interpreting the other person's behaviour. ▌ Avoid blame. Speak from your own experience, using 'I' statements rather than accusatory 'you' statements. ▌ Stay aware of how your body feels (rising tension, tone of voice, etc) and whether you find yourself getting 'worked up'. ▌ Use engaged listening. Notice whether you're preparing your next remarks while the other person is talking, and bring yourself back to listening. ▌ Keep in mind your most noble intention.

CASE STUDY: BECOMING FEEDBACK-AGILE

I witness numerous, crucial 'aha' moments in coaching, where the commitment to change happens in an instant. I sensed I was having one of those moments with Dennis, a highly successful sales and marketing executive, while reviewing his 360 feedback.

After reviewing the report, one comment triggered significant defensiveness. Dennis's face reddened, he stiffened in his chair and looked at me, as if I personally had made the comment. He launched into a passionate explanation and justification that ended with him defiantly saying 'This is absolutely wrong!' Most likely at that moment he was internally narrowing down the search for the comment culprit.

I asked him 'Does this comment seem familiar to you? And, does your response seem similar to your typical reaction to feedback?'

The silence hung heavy. We had been at this juncture before, but this time his response was different: 'I hate to admit it, but there's more truth here than I want to acknowledge. I guess I've tried to deny it, and again and again I resist hearing the truth. Maybe I can try another way.'

In this moment, Dennis made an executive move that would positively impact his leadership. He became coachable and feedback-agile. He decided to break down the defensive and prideful wall halting his growth as a leader. With my strategic insistence that he look inside and explore what was blocking his effectiveness, Dennis became open to feedback. He moved into action and as a result began to show visible signs of change to his team.

CASE STUDY: THE STRATEGIST VS THE COMMANDER

I coached a pair of contentious alphas at a company that was already causing stockholders to lose sleep. One was a young, cocky commander with a short but impressive track record that propelled him to the senior VP level before he was 30. The other was the CEO, an alpha strategist who was one of the commander's principal champions on his way up.

Their relationship began to sour once the young commander settled into his corner office. Charismatic, good-looking and charming, he attracted a cadre of loyal followers who were also young, ambitious and highly talented. His ability to motivate these energetic workers, stimulate their creativity and bring them together in a strong team environment was so impressive that analysts thought the company was poised to soar ahead of its competitors and stay there for decades. But the commander began to believe in his own mythology. Whereas before he'd been smart enough to remain humble, he now dropped all such pretence. The problem was, he still reported to the strategist, and the differences in their styles began to grate on both of them and on close colleagues.

The strategist was a nuts-and-bolts observer who could discern meaningful patterns in a pile of data that would make the commander's eyes glaze over. The CEO had come to see his former protégé as clueless about the realities of life at the top. He also saw him as ungrateful.

The commander saw the CEO as over the hill and out of touch. Less and less willing to be restrained by the strategist's insistence on methodical, tightly controlled procedures, he craved autonomy and wasn't willing to wait for it. He'd grab an inch of freedom, and the strategist would counter with a new form of control, until finally the young commander said he'd rather quit than continue reporting to his former mentor. The strategist, in turn, suggested that the company buy out the commander's contract.

Not wanting to lose either of them, the chairman intervened and soothed the strategist's ruffled feathers with some additional authority and the requisite perks, and told the commander to report directly to him. But the company was unsteady. Teams at every level were hampered by the tension, uncertainty and communication breakdowns at the top. Like iron filings drawn to two different magnets, co-workers took sides, causing widespread polarization.

It quickly became clear to me that the strategist and the commander could be an unbeatable combination if they learned to use their differences to create harmonious chords instead of dissonance. By learning about their alpha types, they came to realize that the clashes between them stemmed from their different styles, not irreversible personality conflicts. They also saw that, as alpha males, they are naturally competitive, but they were fighting each other at the expense of their common goals.

CASE STUDY: CURIOUS GEORGE

George Allen, the former deputy commander of the Defence Supply Center in Philadelphia, PA, the largest business unit of the Defence Logistics Agency (DLA), is an example of one alpha male that did not immediately see the need for a 360-degree assessment, but proved to be one of my biggest success stories.

When Vice Admiral Keith Lippert asked my partner, Kate Ludeman, to conduct in-depth 360s for his entire executive team at DLA, George was not interested. As a successful executive who was close to retirement, he thought coaching would be a total waste of time – especially six months after 9/11, when DLA was under enormous pressure to get critical military supplies swiftly and efficiently to US troops. What could a consultant who'd never run a business that size tell him about how to do his job? He marched into the room, ignored Kate's outstretched hand, and barked 'Let's not waste my time and yours. I've been like this for 30 years, and it's highly unlikely I'll change.'

Instead of trying to convince him to sit down and talk, which was what George expected, Kate said, 'Fine, you're busy and so am I. So, if you don't want to make any changes, I'm sure we can both use the four hours to do other work.' She started to close the big binder that lay open on the table. 'Wait!' George commanded. 'What's that?' He pointed to the multicoloured bar graph. Kate explained that it depicted his strengths and weaknesses in different competency areas, as reported by his colleagues.

This was a critical moment in the coaching relationship: George became curious. Scanning the graphics, he saw many of his strengths confirmed; clearly, he was held in high esteem as a leader. But he also saw that co-workers found his manner obnoxious and his attitude about his team parochial and closed-minded. What alarmed him most was the bright red bar labelled 'Ability to influence others, especially HQ'. He was stunned to discover that he was seen as weak in an area he considered vital to his job: getting headquarters to see the importance of the Philadelphia business, and therefore the need to supply the resources George requested. Shocked to learn that his alpha tendencies were hampering his ability to support his team's best interests, he sat down and read the entire report.

In true alpha fashion, George saw the problem, accepted the challenge, and approached the task of changing his ways with the same determined effort that he brought to every other objective. By learning new ways to build coalitions and to influence people without bullying them, he found he actually had a greater impact.

Coaching and working with alpha males

As much as I'm asked about coaching alpha males and how I am able to help coachees using the above-described tools and techniques, I'm asked for advice on how other leaders can best work alongside these exciting and demanding powerhouses. The following characteristics are important to adopt when coaching or working with alpha males:

▌ Use strong, direct and tenacious language.
▌ Listen intently so you can be quick thinking and smart with responses.
▌ Have a confident, bold and courageous attitude.
▌ Give feedback that is analytical and logical.
▌ Reduce complex changes to simple steps with diagrams and graphs.
▌ Be emotionally intelligent and empathetic when sharing development areas.
▌ Do not be defensive, but get curious about statements or situations that are not helping the process.

I also tell coaches and the alpha's co-workers to make sure they demonstrate personal accountability and self-confidence. When coaches and work colleagues respond to disagreement by getting flustered, intimidated, overly emotional or defensive, alphas are less likely to see them as a match or a true partner. Most alpha leaders will accept mistakes, but not denial or a lack of awareness about mistakes. Be honest and candid, while at the same time confident and self-assured.

Common interests such as sports come in handy, as does a shared sense of humour, but the best sign of genuine rapport between a coach and an alpha is the ability to tell each other the straight, unvarnished truth without fear of being judged. If coaches and coachees have a basic trust and connection, they can build a foundation for real and lasting change. Without such a relationship, the benefits of the feedback are limited.

The most important quality coaches and co-workers of alpha males must have is a dynamic balance of grit and concern. Coaches especially need the courage to speak their minds and be strong enough to stand up to alphas when necessary. At the same time, alphas need to know the people around them care. Develop the skills and the fortitude to be someone who is tough enough to tell it like it is, but also to show your compassionate heart.

SUMMARY

Research suggests that women and men display leadership traits differently in most cases. Our work with executives has also revealed that different approaches are often needed in coaching alphas versus non-alphas, as well as alpha women and alpha men.

Of any executives, coaching alpha males is, at times, the most challenging as well as the most rewarding. Alpha male leaders can be domineering, over-confident, smug and impatient, with unreasonable expectations, but they also have high standards for themselves, and are extremely bright, persistent and disciplined. Success is always their goal, and when they commit to change – as with other challenges – virtually nothing will stop them.

As I continue to coach alphas and executives of all types, I find the techniques I highlighted in this chapter to be the most valuable tools to use when helping coachees capitalize on their strengths and reign in their risks. The in-depth, interview-based 360-degree assessment provides honest and candid feedback in a data-friendly way to maximize the best qualities of alpha coachees. The development plan coachees prepare and share with their team helps them clear the air, break through walls and defensive patterns created by fear, and set the groundwork for a candid, open dialogue that often leads to far greater trust and connection. These techniques, along with a sincere commitment to change, allow even the most challenging alphas to become more effective at home and at work.

References

Baron-Cohen, S (2003) *The Essential Difference,* Basic Books, New York

Farson, R (1996) *Management of the Absurd,* Simon & Shuster, New York

Hogan, R, Brady, R and Fico, J (2008) Identifying potential derailing behaviours: Hogan Development Instrument, in *Psychometrics in coaching,* ed J Passmore, pp 171–88, Kogan Page, London

Ludeman, K and Erlandson, E (2006a) *Alpha Male Syndrome,* Harvard Business School Press, Boston

Ludeman, K and Erlandson, E (2006b) Alpha Assessment [online] www.alphaassessment.com

Prime, J (2005) Women 'Take Care,' Men 'Take Charge': Stereotyping of US Business Leaders Exposed, *Catalyst report*

Further reading

Goldberg, E (2001) *The Executive Brain: Frontal lobes and the civilized mind,* Oxford University Press, New York

Guyon, J (2005) The art of the decision, *Fortune,* November 14

Hargrove, R (2002) *Masterful Coaching,* Wiley, San Francisco

Kotter, J and Cohen, D S (2002) *The Heart of Change: Real-life stories of how people change their organizations,* Harvard Business School Press, Boston

Kramer, R M (2003) The Harder They Fall, *Harvard Business Review,* October

Ludeman, K and Erlandson, E (2004) Coaching the alpha male, *Harvard Business Review,* May

McCall, M W and Hollenbeck, G P (2002) *Developing Global Executives: The lessons of international experience,* Harvard Business School Press, Boston

Moir, A and Jessel, D (1992) *Brain Sex: The real difference between men and women,* Delta, New York

Passmore, J (2008) *Psychometrics in Coaching,* Kogan Page, London

16

Coaching with women

Kate Ludeman

INTRODUCTION

Encountering the same challenges as their male counterparts, women executives face another dimension adding complexity to their role: gender. For some women, this means that to succeed in business they must become the archetypal male leader: analytical, competitive, direct and confrontational. For others, it means relying on soft skills and engendering loyalty.

In this chapter, I will highlight the micro-inequities women face in today's working environment and how they, as well as how other gender difference research findings, shape our approach with women leaders. I'll provide an overview of gender differences, followed by a focus on three specific differences. The second half of the chapter will include a set of tools coaches can apply to address challenges presented by these differences, along with case study examples from my practice. These tools include accountability tools, auto-pilot styles, thinking trap solutions and the Alpha Assessment.

THE ISSUE OF GENDER IN COACHING

Studies confirm that certain characteristics are more likely to come intuitively to men, such as analytical systems thinking and competitiveness. Women tend to place more value on relationships, teamwork and consensus-building. Given these differences, coaches must work with the individual and how they are. Instead of trying to become more like men, which is often what organizations expect, women are most successful being themselves and strengthening any underdeveloped skills necessary to meet their goals.

After years of success coaching women, my 'aha' came in 2003 when I discovered research about micro-inequities and gender stereotyping from Catalyst (Prime, 2005), a leading non-profit research organization in New York. As a minority, women often encounter subtle inequities that may or may not be reinforced by their behaviour but that can alter how they are seen by colleagues. Women must take responsibility for working with these indirect behaviours to become stronger leaders, whether or not the inequities seem accurate or simply the result of a stereotype.

My research on gender differences in leaders identified natural strengths and risks in leaders (Ludeman and Erlandson, 2006). Over 10,000 people have completed the assessment tool, which has allowed us to explore gender differences in leaders. Our coaching experience, our own research data and a large body of scientific research all suggest that women in general display their leadership traits somewhat differently than men. We've found that more men than women are high in the alpha characteristics that are discussed in more detail in Chapter 15. Like their male counterparts, female alphas are ambitious and drawn to positions of authority, but as a rule they are less inclined to dominate. Better attuned to the emotional climate, they are more likely than alpha males to look for ways to collaborate and find win-win solutions to conflicts. They can be just as opinionated and strong-minded, but they'll search for consensus and buy-in rather than impose their will. Alpha women want to lead, but they don't necessarily need to rule.

Of course, not all men and not all women are alphas. The distinction between being an alpha and being a beta is actually greater for women, because there's an expectation that a leader will have alpha leadership traits. Thus, if these traits don't come to a woman naturally, they need to develop them. But research shows that people are less tolerant of the dysfunctional alpha traits in women than in men. Therefore, in developing alpha skills, it's important for women to focus on the positive behaviours.

Our research on alphas as well as our ongoing research on gender differences has given us a foundation to better understand the differences we have observed in working with both men and women in senior leadership positions (summarized in Table 16.1).

Table 16.1 Leadership approaches of women compared to men

Women:

▌ are more willing to admit they need help and to seek out a resource. They are often quicker to see the benefits of coaching and may even consider it fun;

▌ are comfortable with control and being in charge; want to make key decisions, but place less emphasis on dominating;

▌ like to win but more inclined to collaborate and partner to solve a problem. They compete more easily with people at a distance, for example, with outside companies or competitors; tend to be less competitive with peers than men are;

▌ are more appreciative in general than men, possibly due to the fact that women are expected to care and show that they value people's contributions;

▌ place more value on relationships and pay more attention to how people feel. As a result, they often withhold feedback at an early stage rather than risk upsetting someone;

▌ are not as comfortable giving orders. They prefer to ask for input and make suggestions. They can lull team members into believing all is well when it is not, and team can then feel blindsided when they find out their performance isn't meeting expectations;

▌ are less likely to express anger overtly. Instead, will drop hints and clues about feeling angry. They may also use anger to set boundaries or limits, which may otherwise be a challenge;

▌ are somewhat less likely than men to be strong in reflective, analytical skills, yet stronger in intuitive skills. They are able to 'feel their way' through problems.

Analyses of numerous other studies show that even when women and men have similar leadership competencies, they emphasize different aspects of their leadership. In their US-based study, Catalyst (Prime, 2005) found that senior managers perceive sharp differences in women's and men's leadership. In an extensive research study reported in 2005, Catalyst asked senior managers to independently rate women and men on 10 essential leadership behaviours. The gender differences that managers perceived followed a distinct pattern (Prime, 2005):

▌ more women than men were effective at 'take care' behaviours such as supporting and rewarding;

▌ more men than women were effective at 'take charge' behaviours such as delegating and influencing upward.

Female managers tend to be perceived as more consultative and inclusive, whereas male managers are more directive and task-oriented (Prime, 2005). There are also indications that men are biologically more dependent on the adrenalin of rapid-fire, high-risk situations, whereas women thrive on the calming influence of endorphin-producing activities, such as conversation and relationship building (National Institute of Mental Health, 2003).

THE EVIDENCE OF DIFFERENCE

There are clear differences that have emerged from our own research and that of other writers. It is important to highlight that what we are noting are average differences between men and women, rather than making statements that all men or all women have these particular characteristics. It is also worth noting, given the diversity of writers and cultures reflected in this book, that much of this research is drawn from work in the Western world, particularly the United States, United Kingdom and Europe. Whether such differences would be reflected to a similar or different extent in other cultures where gender is viewed differently, such as the Middle East, remains as yet only speculation.

To highlight gender differences that have emerged in our work, I have focused on three specific areas: systematic thinking, competition and research on micro-inequities.

(i) Systematic and analytical thinking

Baron-Cohen's (2003) research has found that men tend to excel at systemizing, while women are statistically more likely to excel at empathizing. Systemizing involves discerning the rules that govern how things work, allowing the systemizer to excel in combat, competitive strategizing and political manoeuvring. Baron-Cohen defines empathy as being able to put one's self in the shoes of others and respond in a concerned way that resonates with their thoughts and feelings. Because empathizers care about the feelings of others, women prefer to get what they want through collaboration and reciprocity.

Catalyst's findings support the notion that men tend to be stronger analysers and strategists than women naturally are. Quantitative analysis is systemizer territory; intimate communication is the terrain of empathizers. Catalyst found that men estimated that 80 per cent of male leaders are effective at problem-solving – a critical leadership behaviour – but that only 67 per cent of women leaders are effective problem-solvers (Prime, 2005).

Our original research on 7,000 clients and readers of the *Harvard Business Review* also supports these findings (Prime, 2005). Our research uncovered four alpha leadership styles: commander, visionary, strategist and executor. Men and women are equally likely to be commanders, visionaries and executors, but women are less likely to be strategists – leaders who can analyse complex situations, discern critical variables and work out the steps that follow logically from each possible occurrence with lightning speed. Our finding of fewer strategist women is consistent with women having weaker systemizing skills. Men tend to be linear, sequential thinkers who easily separate emotion from thought, while women think in a more integrated fashion, perhaps because different thought processes are more dispersed in the female brain and more localized in the male brain (Goldberg, 2001).

Women can even the playing field by giving special attention to developing their systemizing skills. Meg Whitman, CEO of eBay and a former client, did just that earlier in her career. Meg is a gifted executive with all the traditional strengths of a female leader, but she's also exceptionally strong at strategic thinking and rapid analytical processing of information. She was one of the first female partners at Bain, a leading global business consulting firm, where she was trained in a particular model of analytical, strategic thinking. This concentrated training became invaluable to Meg. She is now listed by *Fortune Magazine* as one of the USA's 'most powerful women'.

While women in general aren't as strong analytically as men, it's important to remember that some women are stronger than some men. On the whole, women may need to work a bit harder and be more committed to develop their talents in this area. Left to 'naturally' develop as leaders, they may tend to gravitate to other, less analytical areas.

Coaches can assist women by first helping them face the fact of this gender difference and their own potential shortfalls. In my experience, this is one of the areas where women tend to be the most defensive. They often talk like they think, and feel, that people should be more open to their particular way of communicating, holding this point of view as a diversity issue. What some female coachees don't realize is that when they speak in a non-linear way, they lose the people in their audience who are not able to process information the same way they do. To maximize their influence, they need not only to improve their analytical processing skills, but also to speak succinctly and sequentially.

(ii) Conflict and competitiveness

Men and women leaders also show a difference in comfort levels with conflict and competitiveness. Men often thrive on conflict, while female leaders are less comfortable with it. Studies indicate that men are drawn to situations involving competition and risk-taking, while women place higher value on cooperative relationships and working with people they like (Varian, 2006).

When a male leader doesn't like something, he states it loudly and clearly. A female leader can be less willing to force an issue publicly if she doesn't anticipate quick agreement. Being more interested in collaborating and finding win-win solutions, she'll happily debate an idea until someone's emotions are triggered, at which point she'll back down rather than press towards resolution. This is what one of my clients refers to as a 'false opposite', where women will justify not debating an issue or highlighting an apparent difference as an effort to get resolution. By talking about not wanting to be someone who creates churn or who likes to argue for the sake of arguing, the female leader may attempt to stay safe in a soft communication style. This indirect style of communication is often misinterpreted by male peers as being political, leaving female leaders feeling misunderstood and not fully appreciated for what they are trying to accomplish. This style is a defensive posture and one way women can stay stuck in their own patterns.

A study for the National Bureau of Economic Research (Niederle and Vesterlund, 2005) also found that women are reluctant to compete, while men can be overly eager to compete. In a contrived game situation, researchers found that the men were far more confident in their ability to win. What explains the discrepancy? While none of the players actually knew whether they'd won an earlier tournament, 75 per cent of the men thought they had, as compared to only 43 per cent of the women. This bolsters our observation that men are more likely than their female counterparts to see themselves as exceptionally competent – so much so that they relish visible, high-risk competitions in which they expect to stand out. Women, on the other hand, tend to lack confidence and underestimate their capabilities and thus are more likely to shy away from competition or contrary stands, even when they stand a good chance of prevailing.

Coaches must show female clients the difference between healthy and unhealthy competition. In healthy competition, leaders follow the rules of the game; they're up front about wanting to win while also doing what's right for the company. They know there will be a winner and a loser, and they're OK with that. But women leaders tend to soft-pedal their desire to come out on top, in part for fear of appearing inauthentic and political, as mentioned earlier. This makes it difficult for them to express their desire to win. Contrary to the popular negative connotation of competition, healthy competition can help women move up the career ladder, create credibility for themselves in a male-dominated workplace and maximize teambuilding and teamwork (Varian, 2006).

(iii) Micro-inequities

The term 'micro-inequities' (Rowe, 1973) explains many of the subtle differences in how men and women are treated in the workplace. These subtle cues can be conscious or unconscious behaviours like someone rolling their eyes, interrupting a speaker, crossing their arms during a conversation, sharing information with one person but not another, or publicly congratulating only one of the two people who just got promoted. Micro-inequities are not as much one-time events as they are cumulative, repeated behaviours, which communicate that certain people are valued more than others (Sarfaty, 2006). Because they are members of a minority, women experience micro-inequities more often than men, which heightens their sensitivity to these subtle slights. This sensitivity can inadvertently lead them to question their capability and even believe they are weak leaders because they are not being noticed or heard. Unfortunately, this heightened awareness means that women can overreact to a micro-inequity, reinforcing the view that women are 'overly sensitive' and take things personally.

Some psychologists believe that because of these widely shared conscious and unconscious associations about women, men and leadership, women experience a double bind that prevents them from being seen as compassionate but authoritative leaders. People more readily associate men with leadership traits like assertiveness, whereas women are associated with being caring, soft-spoken, friendly and sympathetic (Carli and Eagly, 2007). In other words, the traits necessary for strong, effective leadership are seen as not only male but the antithesis of female, probably because the long history we've had of male domination in leadership positions has made it difficult for people to distinguish between leadership and male associations (Carli and Eagly, 2007). The connection is automatic for people, even if inaccurate.

Hence, the bind: if women leaders are communal and empathetic, they are criticized for not being assertive and direct (like men); but if women leaders are assertive, direct and ambitious, they are 'rough around the edges' and not collaborative or empathetic enough. Women speaking up to defend their turf are vilified as control freaks; men acting in the same way are considered passionate (Carli and Eagly, 2007). When women do exercise typically male characteristics of ambition, assertiveness and control, they are seen as overly aggressive or insensitive.

WORKING WITH GENDER DIFFERENCES IN COACHING

Given the significant differences in how men and women approach competitiveness, analytical thinking and micro-inequities, coaches must utilize different tools and techniques when coaching female leaders. What follows is a description of the tools I've found most useful in addressing each of these gender differences.

Addressing micro-inequities

Clearly, micro-inequities present a challenge in coaching women. As coaches, we must both acknowledge them as real and also show women how to have an impact in spite of them. The only way to create change, given that micro-inequities exist, is for the female coachee to take ownership of that change. She can do this by embracing the reality that as much as she may want others to change, she has no control over whether that will happen. What she can do is be proactive and take responsibility for overcoming the inequity, regardless of its origin.

First, the coachee must relinquish control over changing others. Table 16.2 provides some perspective about what a leader can and cannot control in her work. This simple chart makes clear where we can create change – only with ourselves – even if the source of the problem seems external to us.

Table 16.2 The control files

Things I can't control	Things I can control
Whether I am recognized for my contributions	My commitment to develop strong influencing skills, contribute and perform at my best
Whether my male colleagues are given 'passes', when female leaders must work harder for the same success	How well I develop and apply the leadership competencies I know are the key to success in my organization
Whether someone respects me	How I perform; whether I deliver on my agreements
Other people's behaviours that seem unfair or unjust	How I respond to unfair behaviours, focusing on my own effectiveness and influence
Emotions I feel in the moment	How I act (or withhold action) on my emotions

In coaching women, I sometimes hit the barrier of unfairness, especially with micro-inequities, where coachees don't believe they should take responsibility for someone else's behaviour. But nothing unravels or prevents influence more than when a person feels inside that someone else should fix the problem. By identifying the problem as belonging to someone else, a woman puts herself in a victim position where she feels the effect of whatever stereotyping or micro-inequities or other challenges exist. If a woman leader, for example, feels as though she has been unjustly treated, ignored or not included in a key communication, she must acknowledge her experience of the occurrence *and* be sure she doesn't get stuck in feeling victimized. Most importantly, she must not act out her feelings by being passively resistant towards those who may have been involved in the stereotyping behaviours.

The fine line coaches must walk with coachees in these instances is this: coaches must acknowledge the coachee's experience as real, knowing that the incident or pattern may in fact be the result of an unconscious bias or behaviour. However, the coachee's experience may also be the result of her own shortcoming, lack of confidence or willingness to play the role of victim, which can provide a temporary false sense of power via righteous indignation. Either way, coachees have a choice in how they interpret and respond to these types of events. Coaches must help women experiencing micro-inequities to avoid feeling victimized by another's behaviour. Regardless of how unfair the actual experience was, she is the one who must overcome the perception (or the reality) of her shortcoming. And in the business of leadership, perception is reality if a leader wants to grow and become more successful.

Is such behaviour learnable? Absolutely. People can be taught to be accountable by looking inside themselves, wondering about their contribution to a problem and inquiring as to how they could make a situation different. The challenge is learning to explore situations from a learning mindset, where your coachee doesn't look 'out there' to explain problems or provide solutions. Instead, she takes 100 per cent responsibility for the problem and for turning it around, no matter what kind of responsibility she may believe others have. She says 'Yes' to whatever reality happens to be at that moment, and her slogan becomes 'Claim, don't blame'.

Blame is the opposite of accountability and venting about what's wrong and unfair tends to create adrenalin and drama. It adds an emotional charge to problems like micro-inequities. But blaming never makes things right, no matter how hard we try, because it puts the focus on other people who we have no power to change. Further, believing problems come from 'out there' guarantees that problems don't get corrected. So long as women leaders don't address their part of an issue, the situation or problem will return again and again, as faithful as crabgrass in the spring. Instead, coaches must help coachees to work with the reality at hand and leverage their learning, upgrade their skills, ask questions and pursue their worthy intentions.

I encourage my clients to shift from blaming to claiming and step into a higher level of accountability. The most powerful step in taking responsibility is assuming that whatever gets created out there is the direct result of something I have done or failed to do and is not somebody else's fault. In fact, it's been set up to teach me an important lesson – and if I don't get it now, then I can count on an escalation path that's designed to get my attention.

Table 16.3 lists some 'wonder questions' to help your coachees sort out the causes and conditions of results they want to own, when they don't yet see how to make the shift into accountability:

Table 16.3 Shifting into accountability

If you find yourself...	Shift by asking:
feeling angry, resentful or fearful	How can I choose ease and confidence instead? How best can I support the results I want?
repeatedly having your buttons pushed, or having a familiar feeling when a problem arises	How do I keep making choices that sustain this pattern?
feeling bottled up and stressed, with flat energy	What emotions haven't I let myself feel?
repeatedly having bad luck or negative results you don't want	Do I have an unconscious intention for things to turn out this way?
wishing someone else would change, do something or stop doing something so that you get the credit you deserve	How can I take responsibility for making this change myself?

CASE STUDY

I personally experienced an accountability dilemma in 1984 when I became vice-president of human resources for KLA-Tencor, a semiconductor inspection equipment manufacturer in Silicon Valley. Today I realize that the situation was a reflection of both some skills I needed to develop and micro-inequities that existed in a company that had never before had a woman executive. In meetings, even when I spoke up with conviction, expertise and passion, I felt ineffective and somewhat invisible. Invariably I would make a point and be ignored, only to later hear one of my male co-workers make the same point and receive accolades for his insight. I was new on a team that had had many years working together, and I wanted to be seen as credible. I began to wonder if I was being ignored because I was a woman.

This, however, kept me trapped in what I consider 'out there' thinking; in other words, to address this problem, other people would need to change. So instead of placing the blame on circumstances 'out there', I turned my attention to myself and what I could change. Whether or not the issue related to a gender inequity, I needed to make a change, right there, with that team of people in order to have the influence I wanted. My breakthrough started with my willingness to *own the problem* and look at what *I* could do differently, instead of wishing things 'out there' were different.

As soon as I took this important step, I immediately thought I could benefit from observing an unusually skilful male peer who successfully influenced our CEO and his peers, as well as his own organization. I noticed that he used many non-verbal behaviours to signal that he was about to make a point, such as leaning into the conversation. He also linked his comment to what someone else had just said, building on their ideas, instead of communicating it as a stand-alone idea. It's not that he was more dominant or assertive, but rather that he used a different method to enter the conversation and get the group to pay attention. My credibility accumulated as I began integrating some of his style into my own.

The most challenging and stimulating explorations of my life – and the ones with the greatest payoffs – have been learning what it means to commit to full accountability in every situation.

Identifying auto-pilot styles

One common derailer for leaders is reverting to a safe and familiar auto-pilot style in times of ambiguity, stress or change. Getting triggered into an auto-pilot style is often what happens when women leaders feel uncomfortable with competition, opposition or conflict. For instance, in the presence of conflict, a leader may become a collaborator or mediator because she wants to be liked and doesn't want someone angry at her. But in some instances, such a move may not be appropriate and could hinder her leadership. In order to become strong leaders, women with these style patterns must zero in on unseating their limiting styles.

These styles are formed in childhood and early adulthood, based on behaviours learned from our parents, teachers, managers and other role-models. Like directors assembling a cast of actors, we audition certain styles and 'hire' those that bring us safety, love, recognition, and all the other things people crave. The adopted styles get embedded in the unconscious mind, and we carry them with us into the theatre of adulthood, where they wait in the wings for their cues to come on stage. The more unconscious the style is, the earlier it was probably formed, and the more likely it is that we'll think 'That's just the way I am.' By the time we enter the workforce, we have developed layer upon layer of auto-pilot styles, and slip unconsciously from one role to another, until we recognize the pattern and consciously choose to make a change.

I have found that understanding auto-pilot styles has a liberating effect on coachees, because it helps them see their behaviours as a collection of habits that were formed early in their lives rather than as an unchangeable genetic trait or a reflex hardwired into their brains. An effective coach can easily spot these problematic styles by asking a few simple questions. To assist you in helping your clients identify and name their problematic styles, review Table 16.4, a list of the most common names that our clients have given to their more problematic auto-pilot styles.

Table 16.4 Auto-pilot styles

▌ Accommodator	▌ Drill down	▌ Mother hen
▌ Action Jackson	▌ Eager beaver	▌ Overwhelmed
▌ Biting critic	▌ Energizer bunny	▌ People pleaser
▌ Cheerleader	▌ Hard-head	▌ Perfectionist pied piper
▌ Complainer	▌ Harried Harriet	▌ Pollyanna good news
▌ Conflict avoider	▌ Hunker down	▌ Procrastinator
▌ Contrarian	▌ Juggler	▌ Rebel
▌ Control freak	▌ Know it all	▌ Timekeeper
▌ Cynic	▌ Martyr	▌ Uninvited fixer
▌ Debater	▌ Micro-manager	▌ Wet blanket
▌ Do it all	▌ Missionary zealot	▌ Wheeler-dealer
▌ Dreamer	▌ Misunderstood genius	▌ Worrier

These auto-pilot styles are simply nicknames that suggest a particular kind of behaviour, not hard-and-fast categories. Feel free to use them or to have your clients make up names that best capture the masks they use to handle challenging situations. In the example below, I'll show you how coaches can use this construct to help coachees make significant changes in their style.

CASE STUDY

In 2002, I was the keynote speaker for a group of about 80 executives at the Defence Logistics Agency (DLA), a large organization in the Department of Defence, which is about the size of a Fortune 200 company and which provides all supplies for US armed forces. I was coaching the top 20 executives and I was invited to remain for the day to observe their interactions during their quarterly expanded leadership team meeting. At one point I observed Linda Furiga, the chief financial officer (now retired), speak up about a profoundly important trust issue. Unfortunately the conversation continued, and no one apparently heard or responded to her comment. About 15 minutes later, the male general manager for a large distribution centre made an identical point, and suddenly everyone was listening, including the three-star admiral who was then director of the DLA.

I later learned that Linda often felt frustrated that her quiet demeanour and soft voice meant that she wasn't heard and that her ideas didn't produce the impact she wanted. What was even more interesting was learning, as I interviewed people, that sometimes colleagues would recall the substance of what Linda said, but assign credit to someone else who spoke with greater force and volume. Painfully aware of the situation, Linda was not surprised to see the following 360 evaluation comments:

■ 'She needs to assert herself in meetings and to stand up for what she believes is right.'
■ 'She's articulate, but she's not convincing because she's too soft in style. She needs to be far more forceful in her public demeanour.'
■ 'Her tone of voice conveys a sense of timidity when she should be exuding confidence.'

Linda knew her soft-spoken style was a significant risk. As the executive in charge of over $30 billion in revenue and budget, she had to persuade the Department of Defence and the US Congress to make available the funds DLA needed to carry out its mission. She knew she had to be seen as a strong leader, but she had no idea how to change the situation.

When I coached Linda, I asked her to identify the primary auto-pilot style that was problematic for her in group meetings. She immediately selected Peacemaker, where she was so focused on keeping the peace that she did not stand her ground or deliver needed feedback. This style had originally developed in childhood, when she acted as a go-between messenger with her two parents, a role with little reward or appreciation. Today she was continuing this role on auto-pilot, with a somewhat similar lack of acknowledgement.

To help her explore this style, I asked her to respond to the following questions from the perspective of Peacemaker. In other words, I interviewed the Peacemaker aspect of her that had become problematic in her executive role. I did this by addressing her as Peacemaker, using the questions below:

1. Peacemaker, what are your behaviours and feelings when you're in this style?
2. Peacemaker, how does this style create problems with other people?
3. Peacemaker, what styles does your problematic style invite in others?
4. Peacemaker, what is the positive underlying intention of this style? What are you trying to accomplish when you shift into this style?

After Linda explored these questions, we worked together to develop a plan to help her shift into a more effective influencing style. We videotaped her giving a presentation as Peacemaker so she could recognize when she automatically slipped into this old style. We then created a new, healthier and more impactful style that would support her in fully owning the power that came with her CFO role. When she gave the presentation this way, the difference was dramatic: her volume went up, she spoke forcefully throughout, and she maintained a powerful presence.

Before long, she had a crucial test of her new skills. Delivering a presentation to a roomful of high-ranking government and military officials, she conveyed a powerful, convincing and inspiring presence. As the change carried over into everyday interactions, Linda started to receive the recognition she'd always deserved. She was awarded the prestigious Presidential Achievement Award in 2005. Nothing had changed except that she had learned to hold her own with dominating leaders, and she took a page from their book by tapping into her own dormant leadership traits. In short order, she spearheaded a successful campaign to obtain the resources the agency needed to meet post-9/11 demands. Based on her briefs with the Office of the Secretary of Defence (OSD), she got the DLA an additional $6 billion in vital funding.

Systematic and analytical thinking

As I previously mentioned, women tend to be empathizers rather than systemizers who prefer to get what they want through collaboration and reciprocity rather than fighting. But women who aspire to high levels of executive leadership need to be strong in the typically male zone of being analytical.

Many coaches ignore this difference between men and women, partly because a person's approach to problems may appear to be one of the most difficult skills to help change as a coach. My own thinking has been heavily influenced by Perkins, who wrote *Outsmarting IQ* (1995). Perkins's research uncovered four intelligence traps:

▌ **Hasty thinking**: We react impulsively, mindlessly, without thinking about what we're doing. As a result, we close too quickly and settle for conventional answers, preventing proper analysis.
▌ **Narrow thinking**: We lock our minds in small, circumscribed boxes based on past conditioning. Beliefs and biases keep us from questioning our own assumptions.
▌ **Fuzzy thinking**: We become unclear and imprecise, making inaccurate distinctions such as over-generalizing or focusing on surface similarities instead of underlying differences.
▌ **Sprawling thinking**: We wander all over the place, running from one connection to the next... and the next...

CASE STUDY

A couple of years ago, I coached an award-winning leader who is the North America COO of a global giant headquartered in the United Kingdom. This female executive, who I'll call Carol, demonstrated many of the differences between alpha male and alpha female leaders. She is driven to succeed, likes being in command, is well-liked, is an excellent coach, and is both direct and extremely appreciative. All in all, she is similar to most male executives I've worked with. But, unlike the healthiest of alpha males, she had only average systemizing skills.

Naturally warm and effusive, Carol is a talented and passionate executive who easily establishes rapport and builds good working relationships. She feels that her 'softer edges' are exactly what make her an effective leader. But many men perceive her as 'fluffy' and not analytical enough, especially when it comes to crunch-time problem-solving.

At the time I was working with Carol, the CEO of the company's North America Group, a male, fought hard to place Carol in her current position, and wanted to groom her as his successor. 'She's as fine an executive as I've ever worked with', he told us. 'But her warm, open approach fuels people's gender biases. She doesn't get the credit she deserves because her more feminine style makes it easy to discount her.'

In truth, there was nothing fluffy about Carol. Underneath, she's as tough as nails and smart as a whip. But she has to work harder than men to demonstrate that she's got the left brain they have. 'My challenge is to stay tough-minded about results, effectively problem solve and still keep my affinity for people,' she says. She learned to do things like begin presentations with hard facts rather than a more personal approach, and to confront issues directly while still showing concern for people's feelings.

When Carol decided to focus on her systemizing skills, she identified herself as a sprawling thinker. As such, she'd get one idea, and as she was thinking through it, another one would pop into her mind. She would then go off in this new direction. In spending too much time exploring various options, she would become overwhelmed and thus paralysed in how to begin addressing the problem. With issues of people leadership, this type of thinking helped her understand the complexity of people, but when solving business problems or articulating her ideas in meetings, this approach made her come across as disorganized and unclear.

Sprawling thinking occurs in part because people lose track of where they are in complex matters through cognitive overload. To begin tightening her focus, Carol started taking one idea at a time and exploring it, instead of skipping from approach to approach.

One of the most valuable actions Carol took was partnering up with a male leader who was a strong analytical thinker. This allowed her to begin mimicking her colleague's logical analysis of challenging situations. She learned some of the mental models he used to tackle problems and sequential questions he explored in the face of large challenges. She also began using communication tools to help her handle her cognitive overload – things like whiteboards, notes on paper, her laptop. By thinking 'on paper', Carol was able to manage more information than she'd previously been able to.

To effectively address limiting thinking styles, as Carol did, coachees must first identify the kind of thinking they tend to respond to challenges with. Then you can help them to develop the new responses described in Table 16.5.

Women have strong analytical skills that may just be buried underneath one or two thinking traps. If we as coaches can help leaders avoid a reactive or habitual mental approach, they can usually access their analytical mind. This also helps them communicate more systematically, which makes it easier for people to follow the logic of their thinking.

SUMMARY

Coaching female leaders is a challenging yet rewarding experience. In addition to the challenges males face, women encounter micro-inequities and the double bind of needing to exhibit assertive leadership qualities yet often getting penalized for doing so. Helping female leaders see that micro-

Table 16.5 How to break free from thinking traps

If you're hasty:
▌ learn to tolerate ambiguity and uncertainty;
▌ avoid premature closure, especially with important issues;
▌ actively solicit ideas and opinions from others;
▌ stay open to new input as long as possible.

If you're narrow:
▌ solicit ideas from people who think outside the box;
▌ expand the range of information you draw upon;
▌ partner with a sprawling thinker and help each other find balance.

If you're fuzzy:
▌ dialogue with a crisp, clear thinker;
▌ practise explaining your thoughts to people who know nothing about the subject;
▌ before settling on a conclusion, ask 'Is there more to this?' many times.

If you're a sprawler:
▌ partner with a systematic, structured thinker;
▌ simplify and organize your space; cluttered surroundings clutter the mind;
▌ if you can't organize your thoughts, learn to organize how you communicate them;
▌ jot down your three main points in numeric order before sharing your ideas in meetings.

inequities are simply small trails to navigate, rather than steep mountains to climb, makes it possible for them to treat these subtle slights as a surmountable leadership challenge. By becoming accountable, and using the auto-pilot style coaching tool, the systematic and analytical thinking exercise and the Alpha Assessment, coaches will learn that with every challenge women face comes a steady determination to excel and improve.

References

Baron-Cohen, S (2003) *The Essential Difference*, Basic Books pp 38–42, New York.

Carli, L L and Eagly, A H (2007) Women and the labyrinth of leadership, *Harvard Business Review*, September

Goldberg, E (2001) *The Executive Brain: Frontal lobes and the civilized mind*, Oxford University Press, New York, p 95

Ludeman, K and Erlandson, E (2006) Alpha Assessment [online] www.alpha assessment.com

National Institute of Mental Health (2003) *Gender Differences in Behavioural Responses to Stress: 'Fight or flight' vs 'tend and befriend'* [online] http://www.MedicalMoment.org

Niederle, M and Vesterlund, L (2005) Do women shy away from competition? Do men compete too much? *National Bureau of Economic Research Working Paper No. 11474,* July

Perkins, D (1995) *Outsmarting IQ: The emerging science of learnable intelligence,* Free Press, New York, pp 152–4

Prime, J (2005) Women 'Take Care,' Men 'Take Charge': Stereotyping of US Business Leaders Exposed, *Catalyst report*

Rowe, M (1973) Barriers to equality: The power of subtle discrimination to maintain unequal opportunity, *Employee Responsibilities and Rights Journal,* **3**(2), pp 153–63

Sarfaty, C (2006) Rooting out subtle office insults, *New Jersey Biz,* 3 July

Varian, H R (2006) The difference between men and women, revisited: It's about competition, *New York Times,* Economic Section, 9 March

Further reading

Ludeman, K and Erlandson, E (2004) Coaching the alpha male, *Harvard Business Review,* May

Ludeman, K and Erlandson, E (2006) *Alpha Male Syndrome,* Harvard Business School Press, Boston

17

Coaching people through life transitions

Bob Garvey

INTRODUCTION

This chapter is, in the main, about coaching across generations, but it is inevitable that mentoring and other developmental literature should inform its content. There are many ways to think about age transitions and this chapter looks at the connections between some of these views and coaching interventions.

In the first part of this chapter, four main theories of age transition are presented. There then follows three case examples from practice, which illustrate the notion of coaching across the generations and age transition. The chapter concludes with a discussion of the theory in practice and offers a final summary of the key points.

The concept of age transition is a diversity issue. With the recent changes in UK law on age discrimination, for example, it is clearly necessary for coaches working in and with organizations to take the developmental challenges presented by ageing seriously. As the ideas presented in this chapter indicate, as people age there can be individual developmental and psychological challenges that can result in shifts in behaviour, attitude and motivations. Understanding these issues can enable a different and developmental approach to age transition and minimize the tendency to stereotype and position people in an unhelpful narrative (Gabriel, 2000; 2004), where they may be seen as 'obstructive' or 'difficult' or reluctant to change and adapt in the change dynamic of modern organizations. This notion is summed up well by the following quotation from Edwards and Usher (2000: 41):

> Through narratives, selves and worlds are simultaneously and interactively made. The narrator is positioned in relation to events and other selves, and an identity conferred through this. Positioning oneself and being positioned in certain discourses, telling stories and being 'told' by stories, becomes therefore the basis for personal identity. Narratives are unique to individuals, in the sense that each tells their own story, yet at the same time culturally located and therefore trans-individual – we are told by stories…

The seemingly conflicting issues of early retirement and the retention of experienced staff is also a consideration for organizations. Sometimes, as illustrated by the case examples later in the chapter, when people experience an age transition they may seek new challenges or feel that their experience is devalued. They may seek to leave the organization or experience motivational changes that result in a 'keep your head down' mentality. Experienced staff and those with a long service record are often sources of knowledge for organizations and these sources are not always developed or utilized. As people leave, whatever the reason, they take with them this knowledge and often its disappearance is not apparent for some time or until it is needed. If the knowledge is not available, wrong decisions can be made that could have been avoided. Careful coaching interventions may help to address these issues.

THEORIES OF GENERATIONAL CHALLENGES

The evidence from many years of research (Jung, 1958; Levinson, 1978; Erikson, 1995; Sheehy, 1997) demonstrates that as we move through life there are new challenges and opportunities to learn through and from other generations. Levinson's work is often cited as the foundation of modern mentoring. His work, which noted that the challenges of age transition are often resolved more quickly within mentoring relationships than when individuals are left to their own devices, seemed to set the tone for mentoring in the United States in the late 1970s and beyond. Since then, mentoring has been associated with working across generations for accelerated development and the coaching literature has recently embraced this issue.

In recent times there has been a clear convergence of the theory and practice of mentoring and coaching. For example, research conducted by the European Mentoring and Coaching Council (Willis, 2005) demonstrates that, in terms of skills and processes employed, mentoring and coaching are broadly the same activity. The specific use of either term seems to depend on the purpose of the dyadic relationship and the social context in which it takes place.

The following sections offer a brief overview of the main theories that underpin coaching practice in the context of age transition.

Jung

Jung (1958) refers to the notion of 'individuation'. Jung believed that a person is, potentially at least, inwardly 'whole' but over time and as a result of life's events he or she can lose touch with important parts of their 'whole selves'. He believed that through listening to and noticing the meanings and messages in both our dreams and our imagination, we can learn to remake or reintegrate our different elements and become 'whole' again. The individuation process serves to help each of us both recognize our uniqueness and tap into our true selves in order to become whole and fully harmonized as an individual. Jung saw individuation as the ultimate goal in life.

Individuation is an age-related concept, where the individual starts to reassess his or her life, and the aspects of life that may have previously been neglected or underdeveloped are re-examined. Jung suggested that the process involves a psychological separation from one's cultural foundations in order to, rather paradoxically, move forward into a stronger association with it and a deeper understanding of it.

Jung was clear that individuation is something that begins in the second half of life. Individuals reach a 'watershed' in their lives and find themselves facing the unknown. This can sometimes be a turning point that takes the form of a crisis, for example, a financial challenge, a new job, a health problem, a broken relationship, or a change of residence or profession. These life events often disrupt the balance and flow and the individual will start to question themselves and ask 'What am I doing all this for?' or 'Where is all this leading me?' This experience can sometimes express itself as self-doubt, loss of confidence or self-esteem, a loss of meaning or of religious values and a questioning of everything previously valued. Sometimes it presents itself as a deep longing or a need to change direction and, at times, it can manifest itself in powerful dreams and fantasies. In popular parlance this could be called a 'mid-life crisis'!

Erikson

Erikson's (1995) developmental framework (first put forward in the 1950s) offers a collection of ideas that could also relate to both coaching and mentoring. His model is presented as a series of opposite statements and it is the tensions between these that create age-related developmental challenges.

Erikson's developmental dimensions

▌ Stage 1: Basic trust v Basic mistrust
▌ Stage 2: Autonomy v Shame and doubt
▌ Stage 3: Initiative v Guilt
▌ Stage 4: Industry v Inferiority
▌ Stage 5: Identity v Role confusion
▌ Stage 6: Intimacy v Isolation
▌ Stage 7: Generative v Stagnation
▌ Stage 8: Ego integrity v Despair

The concept of 'Generativity' is strongly associated with some of the mentoring literature (see Levinson, 1978) and this notion goes some way towards explaining the motivation to mentor. According to Erikson, 'Generativity' can be linked to the strong human desire to procreate but it is also about bringing on, influencing and supporting the next generation. In Erikson's model, 'Generativity' is paired with 'Stagnation' and this seems to suggest that if a person is not generative they stagnate. In addition, the concept of 'Generativity' has age connotations associated with McClelland's (1985) motivational theory. This theory points out that often, when someone is driven by the achievement motive and they do indeed achieve, their motivation can change to become one of a desire to influence others. This desire to influence can often be observed in senior managers in organizations where they talk about 'giving something back to the organization' and could be viewed as a major motivation of leaders. Additionally, this helping or influencing motivation is present in many coaches and mentors.

Although 'Generativity' and 'Stagnation' are the main concerns of this chapter in the context of coaching across generations, it is worth also considering Erikson's other dimensions in relation to coaching. One such dimension is 'Ego integrity'. According to Erikson, this is a key stage of adult development. 'Ego integrity' is the ability of an individual to take life as it comes and to adapt to the rough and the smooth whilst still maintaining a sense of self-worth. 'Ego integrity' is something that is acquired by the individual following '... image bearers in religion and in politics, in the economic order and technology, in aristocratic living and in the arts and sciences. Ego integrity, therefore, implies an emotional integration which permits participation by followership as well as acceptance of the responsibility of leadership.'

This concept relates to the notion of role-modelling often found in the mentoring literature (Alred, Garvey and Smith, 2006) and is an important idea in the context of coaching for leadership. In this leadership context, the various past leadership influences on the coachee may need to be discussed for him or her to construct an image of the leader he or she wishes to be. Experience suggests that some in the workplace find the notion of role-modelling a difficult responsibility to hold. However, the role-model themselves has little choice in the matter! It is perhaps a misplaced idea to set out to be someone's role-model because this is not the potential role-model's choice. The choice rests with the person doing the role-modelling, or coachee!

Additionally, the concept of 'Ego integrity' links to the previously presented concept of individuation. Underdeveloped 'Ego integrity', or perhaps an excess of its opposite, 'Despair', may be the consequence of Jung's notion of the fragmented inner self created by life events. These issues are often presented during coaching sessions. The coachee, facilitated by the coach, is offered the potential for 'Ego integrity' to be rebuilt and, as a consequence, the coachee may build in his or her mind a model of appropriate leadership.

Levinson

According to Levinson (1978), male development may be mapped according to five development periods spread across early adulthood and middle adulthood and separated by two transition periods, 'mid-life transition' and 'early adult transition'.

Levinson's research was driven by the question 'What happens to men psychologically as they grow older?' This framework of development offers some interesting insights into cultural norming and raises the question of how far are people products of the societies they inhabit and how far are they products of their genetic makeup? In Western cultures at least, the Levinson model rings many bells. For example, it is culturally normal for people to consider the personal meaning of becoming aged 20, 30, 40, 50 and the decades beyond. It is also interesting to note that in Levinson, age transitions are approximately 5–7 years long. This idea is linked to the notion that we 'grow into' our age. Like Jung, Levinson suggests that it is during the age transition that men address the polarities of their lives and seek equilibrium. His research also clearly showed that those with mentors to assist in the transition were able to reduce the 5–7 year transition to three years.

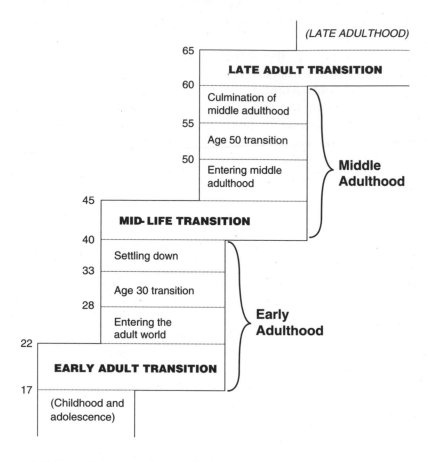

Figure 17.1 Developmental periods in early and middle adulthood

Levinson believed that 'The primary tasks of every transition period are to question and reappraise the existing structure, to explore the various possibilities for change in self and world, and to move toward a commitment to crucial choices that form a basis for a new life structure in the ensuing stable period.'

Sheehy

Sheehy (1974, 1997) describes similar age-related phases of development and suggests that women use mentors less commonly than men to assist with their age-related transitions. Her books *Passages* (1974) and *New Passages* (1997) are described as 'a road map for life'. Sheehy is clear that as the phases are linked to age, it is inevitable that everybody experiences them, but the learning that is associated with these transitions can be of variable quality and impact. Sheehy's development phases, like Levinson's, are age-related and her typography is in four parts with fairly broad bandings. Sheehy's framework is not quite so age specific as Levinson's, as she presents much broader age bandings. Sheehy has regularly updated her work in the light of the rapid social change in developed societies over the last few years. In doing this, like Levinson, she is recognizing the relationship identified early in this chapter between the basic human genetic makeup and the societies in which we participate. In short, Sheehy's model of development represents an integration of the human 'hardwired system' and the societies we create.

Sheehy's first age band is 'provisional adulthood' and falls between the ages of 18 and 30 (see www.gailsheehy.com). It is here that people experience the desire and the conflict of breaking away from their parents. The person experiences tensions between pushing hard to establish him- or herself as an independent being but also feels the pull back to the comfort of the family home. There is a conflict in this 'passage' between the excitement of believing we know what we want and the panic of uncertainty. This also links to Erikson's notion of identity formation as mentioned above.

The 'first adulthood' is experienced in the 30–45 age bracket. Here, Sheehy's research highlights the inability of some to acknowledge their age and their attempts to deny adulthood. In this 'passage' the approaching 40-year-old starts to become aware that their bodies are aging and that younger people relate to them differently. The 'passage' towards 40 creates questions about our mortality and we may ask questions like 'Who is the "real" me?' Men in this 'passage' may respond by having a final career surge in an attempt to drive themselves to the top. Others may simply opt to settle down, whereas others may still not consider these issues. This 'passage' may bring an early mid-life crisis.

The 'second adulthood' starts at around 40–70! Sheehy talks about the Flaming Fifties. It is in this period that we may start to feel discounted or that our views are ignored. Western social norms of beauty are often associated with youth and in this 'passage' we may start to feel uncomfortable as we may 'feel' younger than our birth certificate suggests!

It is in this 'passage' that a woman starts to experience menopause and these physical changes bring psychological ones as well. Women may start to become 'more focused, aggressive, managerial and political'. In contrast, some men may become 'interest(ed) in nurturing and being nurtured, in expressing themselves artistically and appreciating their surroundings' (see www.gailsheehy.com).

Sheehy also notes that for women in this 'passage', a new confidence and sense of independent self, not linked to pleasing another, starts to emerge.

For a man in 'second adulthood', he may expect to get close to the top of his career ladder as a just acknowledgement of his substantial contribution to his organization. He may not even consider reinventing himself unless a crisis hits him.

For men, Sheehy suggests that there is also a menopause during which a man may experience physical, psychological and hormonal changes which can affect virility, vitality and general well-being. Sometimes, for both men and women, a serious life event such as the death of a parent, divorce, job changes, the death of a peer or children leaving home may trigger a 'meaning crisis'.

The 'third adulthood' is old age. In this 'passage', the person may have acquired a personal sense of freedom and independence. The older person will have experienced the great loss of the death of a friend or partner but would have mourned and moved on. People in this 'passage' become concerned about 'leaving something behind'.

In summary, the issue of age-related development may be broadly viewed as transitions or passages. These four writers agree that ageing brings developmental and psychological challenges that may be resolved through supportive conversation.

IDENTIFYING RESOLUTION

The following case studies offer practical insights into how the supportive conversation may assist the resolution of these generational challenges in coaching relationships. The case studies involve three people. In the first relationship, the coach met fortnightly with the coachee for three months. In the second, they met once a month for about a year. In the third, they met once a week for six weeks.

In all cases, the meetings lasted for between two and three hours. Joe, the first case example, works in large private sector organization and Shirley, the second, works in a large public sector organization. Fred also works in a large private sector business. Joe and Fred both work for the same organization but in different divisions and they didn't know each other. Joe and Fred had separately attended a recent development centre run by their employer. The development centre identified that they both had difficulties with report writing. The coach was approached to work as an 'expert coach' to help address the writing issue. Each executive was dealt with on a one-to-one basis.

These stories are taken from notes of the conversations. The participants' names and their organizations are not identified to maintain confidentiality. Each case is first presented and then discussed with reference to the previously presented life-stage frameworks.

CASE STUDY: JOE

Joe is 48 years old. He worked with his 'old' company for many years and climbed the corporate ladder to be head of a division. He spent most of his working life in sales and had a strong network of people both internally and externally. Joe is very sociable with very well developed interpersonal abilities. His 'old' company recently 'merged', or as Joe described it, it was 'hijacked by the bigger outfit'. Joe had, in his own words 'survived the mugging' and 'had come out of it quite well'. However, his network had changed and he 'no longer felt in charge and safe in his ability.' His new network was made up of people younger than him.

Joe was having difficulties with report writing. His bosses weren't happy with his reports and he felt 'under the microscope, in a different world.' Joe felt angry: 'I can write, I've been writing stuff for years but this lot have changed the rules. Now it's not "write as you speak", it's "put a case", "make an argument", "persuade and influence, not present and tell".' Despite this, Joe was keen to learn and understand: 'After all, if that's what they want, I'd better learn it or get another job and at my age that's not so easy.'

Joe wanted to talk about other things than report writing. He asked the coach about his personal life, about his family and how he financed them, about his health and future plans. Joe was good at getting him to talk – it was one of his main skills in life. However, after finding out about the coach's personal life, Joe started to talk about his family, his large house, private education for his three children and the cost of it. He wondered if the coach thought it was worth it. He was contemplating selling off part of his garden to finance a new lifestyle for himself, 'to get out of the rat race and relax a bit, have a life.' The coach explored his options and choices.

Joe used recurring metaphors to describe his feelings and these were variations on 'stuck on the treadmill', 'hamster in a wheel', 'slave to the corporation' and 'poor little rich man'. The coach discussed these feelings and explored their meaning for Joe. Joe concluded that the merger had contributed to him 'losing my self-belief' and that the new environment was 'challenging my competence and making me feel exposed'.

Of course, Joe knew how to write and adapt to people but he had temporarily forgotten this fact. Joe understood that he needed to establish a new network, adapt his language and apply previously held knowledge in a new context. Joe was going to 'sell' himself into the new organization.

A week before the last contracted meeting, Joe e-mailed the coach to thank him and to cancel the last meeting. Here is an extract from the e-mail: 'No problem now, getting there, thanks for the reminders of my abilities and the reorientation!'

CASE STUDY: SHIRLEY

Shirley is 42 years old. She works in a public sector organization and has a strong 'public service' conviction. In the early meetings, Shirley was very quietly spoken. She lacked confidence and despite holding a relatively senior middle management position, she was quite passive in her attitude. She said that she 'felt there was more to life than this…' and that she 'was missing something'. She liked her job but wasn't feeling fulfilled or challenged. Her organization was going through considerable change and everyone's job was under threat. One of the consequences of this seemed to be a change in senior management attitudes and behaviours. According to Shirley, they seemed to think that they 'were all positioning themselves to be retained rather than focusing on managing the place' and they 'were in the "right" by virtue of their position rather than anything else'. She believed that they 'weren't interested in understanding what she did, only interested if she could do it more cheaply or more efficiently and tick the boxes'. She did not feel valued by the organization and was feeling restless.

Shirley was interested in starting her own business as a way of addressing her concerns. However, while she clearly had the knowledge and experience of her job, she lacked confidence and any commercial awareness. She met the coach several times, approximately once a month, and between meetings she applied her learning by taking a specific action or actions that had been discussed in the previous conversation. She had reflected on the conversation and incorporated it as part of her overall plan to find 'something more'.

Shirley started taking steps towards a new future for herself. She managed to take the lead with two major projects within her organization, enabling her to focus on the things that mattered to her. She made contacts with a number of consultancy businesses to learn from them, and she established her own business and recently did her first piece of independent work. Additionally, she enrolled on a Master's programme to develop her knowledge and thinking skills. It seems as though the quest for something more is being achieved through two main activities derived from the coaching conversation – developing her private business ideas and developing her profile within her employing organization. Her confidence has grown and her knowledge has increased. Shirley has become quietly confident that she is glimpsing 'something better' and is taking steps towards it.

CASE STUDY: FRED

Fred is 36 years old. He is a high flyer. He is an insurance expert and has developed his expertise in three different companies. Fred, in his own words, is regarded as an 'industry expert'. He had recently joined his current organization having left a senior post in a large, recently privatized utility. He was recruited on the basis of his specialist knowledge and Fred now holds the most senior position in the Insurance Department in his new organization.

During a recent development centre exercise, organized by his new employer for new senior managers, it was identified that Fred had a difficulty with report writing. The feedback from his manager, one level off Board level, on Fred's writing skills was rather damning.

It became very clear during the first meeting that report writing skills were a long way from Fred's own agenda! He tried hard to talk about reports and offered examples of his work to discuss but he really wanted to talk about how he felt as a new recruit in this organization.

Fred felt that his 'cultural orientation is strained' in the new business. He had observed that 'the language is different, politics are different, there are different skill requirements on me. These are in terms of changing from just giving the Board information upon which to make a decision, to me having to be persuasive and influence them.' Fred developed this theme – 'I mean, I'm not a salesman, I'm an insurance expert – that's very different.'

In the first three meetings, Fred often used variations on the same metaphor. He said 'They pay me shed loads of money, but I'm not worth it.' Or 'I'm not up to this job and they pay me bucket loads.' Or 'I don't think I'm competent, and they give me wagon loads of money.'

In these early discussions, Fred talked of resigning and leaving. He talked about the alternatives. He played in a jazz band, and he was keen to explore the possibility of doing this for a living.

By meeting four, the coach had only gone through the motions of discussing report writing; Fred just wasn't that interested. He completed the tasks he was asked to do but only in a mechanical, 'outcome' driven sort of way. During the fourth meeting, Fred said 'All my life I have been climbing the corporate ladder and now I realize that I have been leaning the ladder on the wrong wall!' The coach questioned and discussed this observation at length with Fred. He started to talk about his family obligations, the mortgage, the school fees, holidays, and his lifestyle that had become accustomed to 'shed loads of money'.

As the meetings continued, Fred wanted to talk more about report writing and in particular the challenge of communication. The coach returned to the issue raised in the early meetings of 'cultural orientation'. Fred started to realize that one of the main reasons for his reports being criticized so strongly was that he was using a different language to the readers of his reports. He realized that if he was to succeed in his written reports, he needed to use the language of the new organization and he needed to influence and persuade rather than just give information. He also realized that, if he wanted to remain with this organization, he needed to develop a new network of relationships and allies. Currently, Fred felt isolated, like the 'new boy at school'.

> Fred's attitude started to shift; he became more engaged in the communi-
> cation process and less concerned with his feelings of inadequacy and guilt at
> the amount he was paid. During the penultimate meeting, he said 'I am worth
> the money, I'm good at what I do, I just forgot that for a while as I tried to fit into
> a new organization.'
>
> During the last meeting, Fred said 'I think I've cracked it now, I can still play
> in my jazz band and do this job, it's not either or, it's both. I've got things in
> perspective – I just needed to learn the ropes, that's all.'

DISCUSSION

These people have extracted meaning from the coaching conversations. Of
course, 'meaning is ambiguous because it arises out of a process of interaction between people... Meaning is fluid and contextual, not fixed and
universal' (Riessman, 1993: 15).

The meaning that was constructed between the coach and coachees was
their meaning made in real time. It took time to construct the meaning, but in
finding it, the coachees were able to understand their respective situations
and make significant changes. Consequently, all three of these stories are
about change and transition and can be related to the theoretical ideas
outlined earlier in the chapter.

In Jung's (1958) terms, all three people, although at different age transitions, were, either by choice or through imposition, separated or attempting
to separate from one culture to join another. They were attempting to define
themselves as new people in a new context.

This manifested in Joe as a loss of self-belief, which may have developed
in him due to a reassessment of who he was, or in Jung's terms as the challenge of the reconciliation of the young and the old. There is a small clue in
Joe's story when he said that getting another job 'at my age' was not easy. Joe
was feeling his age and was concerned about the new, younger network of
people he was in – he no longer 'felt in charge'. Joe was also perhaps
mourning the loss of his old firm and finding it difficult to adjust to the new
one. He felt that his old company had 'been hijacked' by the new one, so
perhaps there was some bitterness and anger there as well.

In Shirley, individuation manifested in wanting something more, and
perhaps in Jung's terms, yearning for something she had lost or not done in
her youth. In Fred it presented as a feeling of not belonging and as an
enactment of a previous dream to become a full-time jazz musician.

In Erikson's (1995) terms, the 'ego integrity' of all three was being altered
by having to adapt either to new 'image bearers' whose lead was different to

previous experiences, or to leaders whose behaviour had changed due to imposed change. Additionally, Shirley's deep-felt emotion that 'there must be something more' to life is a feature of generativity as described by Erikson. In Erikson's terms, there was potential for these people to be slipping into either 'despair' or 'stagnation'. This is illustrated by the loss of self-esteem and concerns about the future presented by all three people, and 'stagnation' is presented as a fear of being devalued in Joe and as an opportunity to 'find something more' for Shirley.

In relation to Levinson's model, it is interesting to observe that both Joe and Fred were not only changing jobs but that this transition of job role coincided with Levinson's age transition chart. Fred being 36 years old fits within the settling down age 40 transition, and Joe at the age of 48 is entering the middle adulthood transition.

Levinson's research suggests that for both these men the transitional states were significant and that the job role changes and resultant problems of motivation were related to the psychology of the age transition. Consequently, Fred was in a life reappraisal phase. Here the neglected aspects of his life may have been calling out to him in the form of a previously held and unresolved dream – playing in a jazz band. Levinson suggests that this is the age transition when men address the polarities of their lives and seek equilibrium.

Joe, on the other hand, was facing a different age-related developmental challenge. He was checking out the coach's life experience (the coach being a similar age to Joe) and weighing this up against his own. He was wondering if he should 'get out of the rat race'. Levinson observed that men in their late 40s are in a phase of either consolidation of their lifetime gains or simply marking time before retirement. Joe did not seem to be marking time; he was attempting to consolidate and was seeking new challenges as he tried 'to create a new Young/Old integration appropriate to [his] time of life' (Levinson, 1978: 212). Joe did not want to be discarded, he wanted to participate and contribute his experience, but initially wasn't sure how he could.

For Joe and Fred, the coaching conversations seemed to assist them to reappraise and reconcile.

As Levinson's original research was focused on men, it is difficult to relate this to Shirley, but all three cases do relate well to Sheehy's framework. Joe (48) was entering his 'second adulthood' and perhaps experiencing a crisis of meaning. This interpretation could be made from his questions about lifestyle. Shirley (42) was leaving 'first adulthood' and entering 'second adulthood' with a touch of 'early mid-life crisis' thrown in. She was looking ahead to the next phase of her life to find 'something more'. Fred (36) was taking stock, approaching the middle 'passage' and having a late career surge. He was also challenged by the 'Intimacy/Isolation' dynamic in his new role and was concerned with the 'Who is the real me?' question – a highly paid executive or a jazzman? All three therefore found the opportunity to discuss their transitions helpful and the discussions helped to reconcile the emotional disturbances they were all feeling.

FURTHER QUESTIONS AND ISSUES FOR COACHING PRACTICE

This work raises questions about the coach's background knowledge and how this impacts on the developmental discussion. What if the core knowledge of the coach had been in a different area? Would this have affected the outcome? The interpretation of the stories was derived from the coach's knowledge of communication, age transition theories and organizational behaviour, but does that matter? Perhaps not if the coachees' stories are the focus of the exploration – more research is needed in this area.

Another area of consideration is the process model used by the coach. In these cases a process model derived from the mentoring literature, the three stage process (Megginson *et al*, 2005; Alred, Garvey and Smith, 2006), was used. This is in itself derived from Egan's (1994) 'Skilled Helper' framework. The process model offers a 'map' for exploration (stage 1) that leads to new understanding (stage 2) and develops action (stage 3). The coach needs to be flexible and adaptable in the application of the three-stage process, because being a 'map' it provides a choice of direction and a choice of destinations; it offers a way of planning the route but also of finding where you are when you are lost. As a 'map' it is also possible to take alternative routes. In the cases presented in this chapter, the three-stage process offers an open agenda and framework to work through. The skills employed vary according to where the coachee is in any particular part of a stage.

These ideas are summarized in Table 17.1.

The process rarely moves in a straight line from stage one to stage three. More often, in use the conversation moves about between all the stages.

There can be a temptation, under the pressure of the improved performance agenda inherent in coaching and time constraints, to get to the action plan as quickly as possible, but often the quality and the commitment to the action is dependent on the quality of stages one and two.

Summarizing regularly can help to establish the boundaries between each stage and move the conversation either on or back into the previous stage (Megginson *et al*, 2005).

Table 17.1 Three-stage process: strategies and methods

Stage	Strategies	Method/skills
One	▌ Take the lead to open the discussion ▌ Pay attention to the relationship and develop it ▌ Clarify aims and objectives and discuss ground rules ▌ Support and counsel	▌ Open questions ▌ Extensive listening ▌ Exploring and identifying an agenda ▌ Counselling skills
Two	▌ Supporting and encouraging the coachee ▌ Offering feedback ▌ Demonstrating skills	▌ Listening and challenging ▌ Using both open and closed questions ▌ Helping to establish priorities ▌ Summarizing ▌ Helping identify learning and development needs ▌ Giving information ▌ Sharing experience, storytelling and disclosure
Three	▌ Examining options and consequences ▌ Attending to the relationship ▌ Negotiating and developing an action plan	▌ Encouraging new ideas and creativity ▌ Helping and supporting in decisions and problem-solving ▌ Agreeing action plans ▌ Agreeing monitoring and reviewing arrangements

In all cases, the coachees were emotionally vulnerable and so needed space to think within a supportive and empathetic environment. The three-stage process helps to provide this.

A further issue is the use of narrative analysis as a technique within coaching. As Garvey (2005) states: 'narrative offers an alternative lens through which we may observe and interpret human social activity. This lens offers an aesthetic perspective rather than a scientific one on human activities.'

In these cases the coach employed some narrative analysis. The metaphors used by the coachees were explored and discussed and the characters that the coachees had adopted in their story were also explored. In all

cases there was a fundamental storyline of success and the coachees characterized themselves with a sense of high self-esteem. However, the age transitions and changes in the work situation had altered the coachees' perception
of their individual characters and resulted in changes of attitudes and motivations. Through exploring the stories and the characters adopted, the
coachees were able to reassess their roles and return to a previously held,
more positive perspective on themselves. Coaching can often be about
stories and their meaning.

SUMMARY

The four concepts of age-related transition presented here are in essence
very similar to each other. It is clear that age transitions may bring with them
emotional responses of, for example:

∎ loss of self-esteem and confidence;
∎ insecurity and self-doubt;
∎ concerns about the future and a meaning crisis;
∎ a reappraisal of life so far and a reinvention;
∎ the hope for 'something more';
∎ a changing sense of 'self';
∎ reinvigoration and hope.

These feelings are applicable to both men and women.

The coaching conversation can help to resolve, reconcile and establish a
new path through the coach assisting the coachee to explore his or her story.

References

Alred, G, Garvey, B and Smith, R (2006) *The Mentoring Pocket Book*, Management
Pocket Books, Arlesford, Hampshire
Edwards, R and Usher, R (2000) Research on work, research at work: Postmodern
perspectives, in *Research and Knowledge at Work*, ed J Garrick and C Rhodes,
pp 32–50, Routledge, London
Egan, G (1994) *The Skilled Helper: A problem management approach to helping*, Brooks &
Cole, Pacific Grove, CA
Erikson, E (1995) *Childhood and Society*, Vintage, London
Gabriel, Y (2000) *Storytelling in Organizations: Facts, fictions and fantasies*, Oxford
University Press, Oxford
Gabriel, Y (2004) *Myths, Stories and Organizations: Premodern narratives for our times*,
Oxford University Press, Oxford
GailSheehy.com [accessed 17 January 2007] [online] www.gailsheehy.com

Garvey, B (2005) When mentoring goes wrong, in *Mentoring competencies*, ed D Clutterbuck and G Lane, Gower, Aldershot

Jung, C (1958) *Psyche and Symbol*, Doubleday, New York

Levinson, D (1978) *The Seasons of a Man's Life*, Alfred Knopf, New York

McClelland, D C (1985) *Human Motivation*, Scott, Foresman and Company, Glenview, IL

Megginson, D *et al*, eds (2005) *Mentoring in Action*, Kogan Page, London

Riessman, C K (1993) *Narrative Analysis*, Vol. 30, Sage, Newbury Park, CA

Sheehy, G (1974) *Passages: Predictable crises of adult life*, E. P. Dutton, New York

Sheehy, G (1997) *New Passages: Mapping your life across time*, Random House, London

Willis, P (2005) *European Mentoring and Coaching Council: Standards Research* [online] www.emccouncil.org

Further reading

Daloz, L (1999) *Mentor: Guiding the journey of adult learners*, Jossey-Bass, San Francisco

Lieblich, A, Tuval-Mashiach, R and Zilber, T (1998) *Narrative Research: Reading, analysis and interpretation*, Sage, Thousand Oaks, CA

The Association for Coaching

AC MEMBERSHIP BENEFITS

The Association for Coaching (AC) is one of the leading independent and non-profit-making professional coaching bodies aimed at promoting best practice and raising the standards of coaching. Founded in the United Kingdom in 2002, with representation in over 32 countries, the AC has become known for its leadership within the profession and responsiveness to both market and members' needs.

Becoming a member gives you the opportunity to be involved in an established yet dynamic membership organization dedicated to excellence and coaching best practice.

Membership includes three categories:

1. Individual (aspiring / professional coaches);
2. Organizational (training / coach service providers);
3. Corporate (organizations involved in building internal coaching capability or cultures).

Areas of coaching include: *Executive, Business, Personal, Speciality* and *Team Coaching.*

Our vision

To be the leading membership association for professional coaches and organizations involved in coaching to enable individuals and businesses to develop, expand and achieve their goals.

Our core objectives

▌ To actively advance education and best practice in coaching.
▌ To develop and implement targeted marketing initiatives to encourage growth of the profession.
▌ To promote and support development of accountability and credibility across the industry.
▌ To encourage and provide opportunities for an open exchange of views, experiences and consultations.
▌ To build a network of strategic alliances and relationships to maximize the Association's potential.

There are many benefits coaches and organizations can access by joining the AC:

▌ *Journal*: receive *Coaching: An International Journal of Theory, Research & Practice*, and twice a year by post, the AC's international coaching journal.
▌ *Gain new customers and referrals:** through a dedicated webpage profile on the AC online membership directory.
▌ *Regular seminars and events*: monthly workshops and forums across the United Kingdom on current relevant topics. This allows an opportunity to network, compare notes and gain knowledge from industry experts and colleagues. Members are entitled to discounts on attendance fees.
▌ *Accreditation:*** eligible to apply for AC individual coach accreditation after being approved as a full AC Member for at least three months.
▌ *International AC Conference*: attend the AC's annual conference at discounted rates, with international speakers drawn from top coaching experts.
▌ *Press/VIP contacts*: raise the profile of coaching through PR activities, through the influential honorary board and contacts across the AC.
▌ *Member newsletters*: increase knowledge through sharing best practice and learning in the quarterly *AC Bulletin* and *AC Update*.

▌ *Co-Coaching*: practise your coaching skills and learn through experience and observation at any of our many regional co-coaching forum groups.

▌ *AC forums*: an opportunity to participate in AC's online forums – networking and discussion groups for members to share their views and receive advice and support from others.

▌ *Industry/market research*: gain first-hand knowledge into latest industry trends via the AC's market research reports.

▌ *Dedicated AC website*: gain access to up-to-date AC activities, members' events, reference materials and members-only section.

▌ *AC logo/letters:** add value to your service offering and build credibility through use of AC logo/letters in marketing materials.

▌ *Ongoing professional development*: acquire CPD certificates through attendance at development forums, workshops and events.

▌ *Improve coaching skills*: through special invitations to professional coaching courses and participation in workshops.

▌ *Networking opportunities*: enjoy networking opportunities to draw on the advice and experience of leading-edge organizations that are also passionate about ethics, best practice and standards in the coaching profession.

▌ *Strategic partnerships*: receive member discounts, discounted training offers, and product and service deals through strategic partnerships.

* Associate level and above only.
** Member level only.

Each approved individual member will receive a member's certificate with embossed seal.

For further information on the AC or joining, please visit the membership section of the website or e-mail members@associationforcoaching.com.

'promoting excellence and ethics in coaching'

www.associationforcoaching.com

Index

NB: page numbers in *italic* indicate figures or tables.